Churchill's Arctic Convoys

Churchill's Arctic Convoys

Strength Triumphs Over Adversity

William Smith

Pen & Sword
MARITIME

First published in Great Britain in 2022 by
Pen & Sword Maritime
An imprint of
Pen & Sword Books Ltd
Yorkshire – Philadelphia

ISBN 978 1 39907 229 8

Typeset by Mac Style
Printed in the UK by CPI Group (UK) Ltd, Croydon, CR0 4YY.

Pen & Sword Books Limited incorporates the imprints of Atlas,
Archaeology, Aviation, Discovery, Family History, Fiction, History,
Maritime, Military, Military Classics, Politics, Select, Transport,
True Crime, Air World, Frontline Publishing, Leo Cooper, Remember
When, Seaforth Publishing, The Praetorian Press, Wharncliffe
Local History, Wharncliffe Transport, Wharncliffe True Crime
and White Owl.

For a complete list of Pen & Sword titles please contact

PEN & SWORD BOOKS LIMITED
47 Church Street, Barnsley, South Yorkshire, S70 2AS, England
E-mail: enquiries@pen-and-sword.co.uk
Website: www.pen-and-sword.co.uk

Or

PEN AND SWORD BOOKS
1950 Lawrence Rd, Havertown, PA 19083, USA
E-mail: Uspen-and-sword@casematepublishers.com
Website: www.penandswordbooks.com

Contents

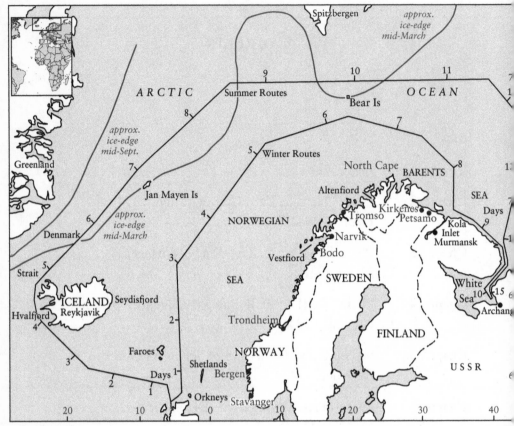

Map 1. Arctic Convoy Routes.

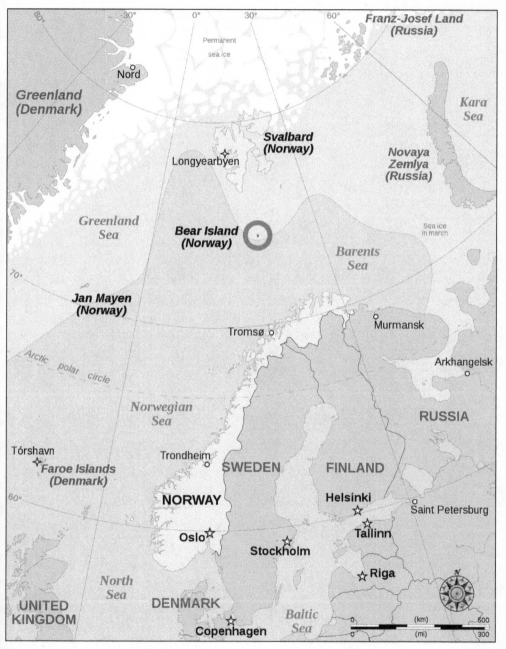

Map 2. Location of Bear Island.

Chapter 1

Introduction

Germany invades Russia – Operation Barbarossa

At 4 o'clock on the morning of 22 June 1941, Hitler launched Operation Barbarossa, the German attack on and invasion of Russia. Prime Minister Winston Churchill was told of the invasion at 08.00 that morning and that evening he made a broadcast to the nation. At the conclusion of his speech, he declared it would be Britain's policy to aid the Russians in their fight against Germany.

Following a discussion between the Secretary of State for Foreign Affairs and the Soviet Ambassador concerning the supply of war materials, Churchill telegraphed Stalin on 25 June:

> War Cabinet has decided (although it would seriously deplete British fighter resources) to send Russia as soon as possible two hundred Tomahawk fighter aeroplanes.

Churchill also promised several million pairs of ankle boots, large quantities of rubber, tin, wool and woollen clothes, jute, lead and shellac (these shipped in August with the first convoy, Dervish). He added, 'All your other requirements for raw materials are receiving careful consideration. Where supplies are impossible or limited here, we are discussing matters with the USA. Details would of course be communicated through the usual official channels.'

In a further telegram on 31 July, Churchill advised Stalin that following his personal intervention, arrangements were 'now complete for the despatch of ten thousand tons of rubber from this country to one of his northern ports'. He added, 'The British ships carrying this rubber and certain other supplies will be loaded within a week, or at most ten days, and sail to one of your northern ports as soon as the Admiralty can arrange a convoy.'

As Churchill later wrote in *The Second World War* (vol. 3, p. 461):

All of this placed a new burden on the Royal Navy. The need to aid Russia focussed attention on the sea routes to Archangel and Murmansk. On August 12th the 1st 'PQ' convoy of six ships for Russia sailed from Liverpool via Iceland to Archangel. The plan thereafter was to run convoys to North Russia regularly once or twice a month. Initially they were not attacked by the Germans. When Archangel was ice bound the convoys sailed to Murmansk.

Prime Minister Churchill met President Roosevelt at Placentia Bay (Newfoundland) between 9 and 12 August 1941 to discuss the implications of the Soviet Union's entry into the war against Germany for United States and British foreign policy and the war effort. During the conference, Harry Hopkins, the president's emissary recently returned from Moscow, briefed them on Russian requirements and discussed the supply of arms and materiel to the Soviet Union. Following this Churchill and Roosevelt pledged the supply of aid to Russia, and on 15 August sent a joint letter to Stalin. They proposed a conference in Moscow to discuss long-term arrangements as to how future Russian requirements might be met and promised in the meantime to continue sending supplies and materiel as quickly as possible.

Transporting these supplies by sea to North Russia in convoys of merchant ships, escorted by Royal Navy warships, would prove to be one of the most challenging and dangerous commitments undertaken by both the merchant navy and (particularly) the Royal Navy during the Second World War, as the route took the convoys close to the coast of German-occupied Norway and within range of surface ship, U-boat and aircraft attack. By far the shortest and quickest route from the American east coast and from Great Britain to Russia ran across the North Atlantic, via Iceland, around the North Cape of Norway, and across the Barents Sea to Murmansk, or on through the White Sea to Archangel. It took an average of ten days for a convoy to sail from Iceland to Murmansk and fourteen to Archangel. Murmansk was ice-free all year around, whilst Archangel was iced in for part of the year. The advantages of the northern route in terms of short transit distances and closeness to the Russian front-line were offset by the extreme weather conditions and by the proximity of the convoy routes to the German surface ship, U-boat, and air bases along the Norwegian coast, established after the German invasion and occupation of Norway in 1940, making it potentially the most dangerous of all the supply routes to Russia.

Before the Moscow Conference was held, in late September 1941,[1] Churchill had telegraphed Stalin on 4 September promising to try to let him know beforehand the numbers of tanks, aircraft and other supplies the US and UK could send each month. The conference concluded on 2 October with the signing of a Protocol providing for material aid to Russia over the period up to 30 June 1942, listing those items it had been agreed would be supplied. (The Protocol would subsequently be renewed each year until 1944.) Although Churchill then (in his message of 6 October) promised Stalin, 'We intend to run a continuous cycle of convoys leaving every ten days' this appears to have been one of his more grandiloquent gestures, failing to anticipate the practical difficulties and dangers associated with such a venture. In the event, despite post-war assertions recorded in Hansard that 'the work' was 'never interrupted',[2] the convoy programme did not run continuously, or at regular intervals during the war – the frequency and size of each convoy was determined by wider political and military constraints, including competing strategic military objectives and strength of the German opposition faced at the time. So the convoys were sent in a number of distinct phases or cycles, mirroring the effects of these constraints. The following chapters describe each of these phases as the patterns of activity developed and external factors determined their duration.

Chapter 2

Phase One: The Early Convoys, August 1941 to February 1942

DERVISH to PQ.11

Dervish (12–30 August)

The first convoy of seven merchant ships, code-named 'Dervish', sailed from Liverpool on 12 August 1941, escorted for the first leg of the voyage by the anti-aircraft ship *Pozarica* and trawlers *Celia*, *Hamlet*, *Macbeth*, *St. Cathan*, and *Le Tigre*. It called at Scapa Flow on 15 August and sailed from there at 18.00 the next day for Hvalfjord, Iceland, escorted by destroyers *Electra*, *Impulsive*, *Active*, and light cruiser *Aurora* (until 18 August), and arriving there on 20 August.

Dervish then departed Reykjavik for Archangel on the following day, escorted by the *Electra* (Senior Officer of the Escort or SOE), *Active*, and *Impulsive*, minesweepers *Halcyon*, *Harrier*, *Salamander*, and trawlers *Hamlet*, *Macbeth*, and *Ophelia*. The convoy was protected from possible enemy attacks from 26 August onwards by a cover force comprising aircraft carrier *Victorious*, heavy cruisers *Devonshire* and *Suffolk*, supported by destroyers *Eclipse*, *Escapade*, and *Inglefield* (26 to 30 August), who met the convoy west of Bear Island (Bjørnøya) on 30 August. The cover force then departed for Spitzbergen, to refuel before deploying on Operation EF (RN Fleet Air Arm attack on installations in the German naval base at Kirkenes and the Finnish port of Petsamo).

Dervish arrived at and anchored outside Archangel on 30 August. On the morning of 1 September, the merchant ships docked at Bakaritsa, a port five miles upstream from Archangel. The convoy was not detected, largely due to a lack of Luftwaffe reconnaissance aircraft in the area.

QP.1 (28 September–9 October 1941)

QP.1, consisting of eleven merchant ships, sailed from Archangel at 12.00 on 28 September, escorted by the cruisers *London* and *Shropshire*, destroyers

Active and *Electra*, and armed trawlers *Hamlet*, *Macbeth*, and *Ophelia*. *Halcyon* and *Salamander* provided the eastern local escort until 13.00 on 30 September. The convoy arrived safely, without incident, at Scapa Flow on 9 October.

PQ.1 (29 September–11 October 1941)

The eleven merchant ships of convoy PQ.1 sailed from Hvalfjord, Iceland, on 29 September accompanied by the western local escort – the minesweepers *Britomart*, *Gossamer*, *Leda*, and *Hussar* (until 4 October). The ocean escort was provided by the cruiser *Suffolk*, accompanied by destroyers *Antelope* and *Anthony* (29 September – 4 October). The convoy was met on 10 October by the eastern local escort, the minesweeper *Harrier*, and Russian destroyers *Uritskiy* and *Valerian Kuybyshev*, and the merchant ships arrived safely at Archangel the following day.

PQ.2 (17–30 October 1941)

The seven merchant ships of PQ.2 assembled at Scapa Flow on 16 October[1] having arrived from a number of destinations, principally the Clyde, three days earlier, escorted by the minesweepers *Seagull* and *Speedy*. PQ.2 sailed the following day for Archangel. The ocean escort from Scapa included the cruiser *Norfolk*, destroyers *Icarus* and *Eclipse*, and minesweeper *Bramble*. The convoy was met on 29 October by the eastern local escort, *Gossamer*, *Leda*, and *Hussar*, with Russian destroyers *Uritskiy* and *Valerian Kuybyshev*, and arrived safely in Archangel on 30 October.

QP.2 (3–17 November 1941)

QP.2 of twelve merchant ships sailed from Archangel on 3 November with the local eastern escort, *Bramble*, *Leda*, and *Seagull* (3 to 5 November). The through escort comprised *Norfolk* (3 to 11 November), *Eclipse* and *Icarus* (3 to 17 November). The convoy was met on 11 November by the western local escort, the armed trawlers *Celia* and *Windermere* (11 to 13 November) and arrived safely without incident at Scapa Flow on 17 November, from where the merchant ships dispersed to various ports on the west and east coast of the UK.

PQ.3 (9–22 November 1941)

Convoy PQ.3 should have sailed from Hvalfjord on 4 November. Following reports that the German heavy ships were at sea and could attempt a breakout into the Atlantic on 5 November, the cruiser *Kenya*, with destroyers *Bedouin* and *Intrepid*, sailed from Seidisfjord at 20.55 on 4 November to cover the trawler patrol line west of the Iceland-Faroes minefield and PQ.3 was ordered to remain at Hvalfjord until further notice. When it was confirmed that the German ships were still in their home waters PQ.3, consisting of seven merchant ships and a fleet oiler, finally sailed from Hvalfjord on 9 November escorted by *Hamlet* and *Macbeth*.

The ocean escort *Kenya*, *Bedouin*, and *Intrepid* (all to 20 November) finally joined the convoy on 14 November. The same day *Hamlet* was detached to escort a merchant ship damaged by ice back to Seidisfjord. The eastern local escort, *Bramble*, *Seagull*, and *Speedy* met PQ.3 on 20 November. The convoy arrived at Murmansk at 11.00 the following day, where *Kenya* remained while the convoy continued to Archangel with the eastern local escort, arriving on 22 November.[2]

PQ.4 (17–28 November 1941)

PQ.4 of eight merchant ships departed Hvalfjord at 09.00 on 17 November, escorted by the armed trawlers *Bute* and *Stella Capella* (to 27 November). Cruiser cover between 25 and 27 November was provided by *Berwick*, with destroyers *Offa* and *Onslow*. They should have met the convoy on 20 November but were delayed by the appalling weather conditions. The eastern local escort, *Gossamer*, *Seagull*, and *Speedy* met the convoy on 27 November and PQ.4 arrived safely at Archangel the next day.[3]

PQ.5 (27 November–13 December 1941)

PQ.5 of seven merchant ships sailed from Hvalfjord, Iceland on 27 November escorted by *Sharpshooter*, *Hazard*, and *Hebe*. *Sharpshooter* remained with the convoy all the way through to Archangel, arriving there on 13 December. The escort was joined on 1 December by the cruiser *Sheffield*.

Bramble and *Seagull* joined as eastern local escort on 7 December allowing *Sheffield*, *Hazard*, and *Hebe* to detach to Murmansk where they arrived the following day. The main body of the convoy arrived at Archangel five days later. There was no enemy activity.

QP.3 (27 November–9 December 1941)

The nine merchant ships of QP.3 left Archangel on 27 November escorted by *Hussar* and *Gossamer*. Two merchant ships returned to Archangel. The escort was reinforced by *Bedouin* and *Intrepid* (28 November to 2 December), and *Kenya* (29 November to 3 December) as ocean escort.

The convoy encountered severe weather on passage. It dispersed on 3 December. The Russian merchant ships went on to Kirkwall escorted by *Hussar* and *Gossamer*, arriving six days later. Strong headwinds continued to slow the progress of the British ships as they proceeded to Seidisfjord, where they arrived on 6 December and left three days later for Scapa Flow escorted by *Macbeth* and *Hamlet*, arriving on 12 December.

PQ.6 (8–20 December 1941)

PQ.6 with seven merchant ships left Hvalfjord on 8 December with its western local escort, the armed trawlers *Hugh Walpole*, *Cape Argona*, and *Stella Capella*. They were relieved on 12 December by the cruiser *Edinburgh* and destroyers *Echo* and *Escapade* who escorted the convoy through to Archangel.

Hazard and *Speedy* were scheduled to meet the convoy as eastern local escort, but on 17 December on their way to the rendezvous were attacked by four German destroyers (*Z-23*, *Z-24*, *Z-25*, and *Z-27* sent out to find PQ.6 and lay mines), who mistook them for Russian destroyers. This was the first contact between German warships and a convoy escort. Despite being damaged the minesweepers managed to escape in the gloom under a smokescreen. *Leda* was then sailed to replace *Speedy*, and *Leda* and *Hazard* met PQ.6, which arrived safely on 20 December.

QP.4 (29 December 1941–15 January 1942)

The return convoy of thirteen merchant ships left Archangel on 29 December. Its passage was delayed by ice and it did not reach the open sea beyond the Kola Inlet until 05.00 on 5 January 1942 with its eastern local escort *Leda*, *Seagull*, and *Speedy*, *Bute* and *Stella Capella* (29 December to 9 January). *Bramble* and *Hebe* provided the eastern local escort (29 December to 5 January). Cruiser cover was provided by *Edinburgh* supported by *Echo*, and *Escapade* (5 to 9 January). The escort oiler and one merchant ship had to return to port. The convoy dispersed on 9 January when the merchant ships continued independently. All arrived safely without incident in Seidisfjord on 15 January.

PQ.7A (26 December 1941–11 February 1942)

PQ.7, badly delayed by merchant ship defects, was sailed in two parts. PQ.7A sailed on 26 December and consisted of only two ships, the Panamanian registered *Cold Harbor* and British *Waziristan* (the Convoy Commodore's ship). The ocean escort was held back to accompany the second and larger part of the convoy, PQ.7B, which was to sail on 2 January 1942. The two merchant ships were allocated two anti-submarine trawlers, *Hugh Walpole* and *Ophelia*, as western local escort for the first two days out of port, to be relieved later by the ocean escort *Salamander* and *Britomart*.

The minesweepers failed to make contact before the trawlers parted company, if indeed they ever did. *Waziristan* and *Cold Harbor* arrived south of Bear Island unescorted and then became separated. The *Waziristan* was last seen by the *Cold Harbor* at 16.00 on New Year's Day 1942. The *Cold Harbor* eventually arrived safely at Iokanka, a port between Murmansk and Archangel, on 12 January 1942.

After the end of the war, it was established the *Waziristan* had been attacked and sunk at 06.48 on 2 January about 20 miles south of Bear Island by *U-134*; she was the first merchant ship to be sunk on the North Russia run.

PQ.7B (31 December 1941–11 January 1942)

PQ.7B with nine merchant ships departed Hvalfjord on 31 December, escorted by the trawler *Cape Argona* and anti-submarine whaler *Wastwater*. The ocean escort of destroyers *Icarus* and *Tartar* joined on 4 January and the *Cape Argona* and *Wastwater* then departed. The convoy was not detected and all merchant ships arrived safely at Murmansk on 11 January 1942.

PQ.8 (26 December 1941–17 January 1942)

PQ.8 of eight merchant ships sailed from the Clyde on 26 December 1941, arrived in Reykjavik on 1 January 1942, and sailed[4] again from Hvalfjord on 8 January for Murmansk, escorted by *Harrier* and *Speedwell*. The convoy headed out into the Arctic darkness with just a pale daylight at noon, *Harrier* zigzagging ahead while *Speedwell* brought up the rear. The convoy ran into strong winds and rough seas which went on for forty-eight hours. The ocean escort of *Trinidad*, *Matabele*, and *Somali* joined on 10 January.

The bad weather continued into the following day. The storms then abated, but as the convoy sailed further north the weather became colder and the ships began to enter the ice field – at first scattered, then more concentrated pack ice that eventually stretched to the horizon on all sides. Thereafter the weather improved, giving way to light, variable winds, calm seas and maximum visibility.

The eastern local escort of *Hazard* and *Sharpshooter* joined on 16 January. No enemy forces were encountered until early in the following evening when the convoy was attacked off the Kola Peninsula by *U-454*. The *Harmatris*, the ship of the convoy commodore, was hit amidships by a single torpedo and caught fire. The crew of forty men and seven gunners managed to extinguish the flames and sailed on accompanied by *Speedwell* until *Harmatris* was taken in tow by Russian tugs. She reached Murmansk two days after the main body of the convoy.

After attacking *Harmatris* the U-boat went on to torpedo the destroyer *Matabele*, which blew up and sank with the loss of 236 officers and ratings. PQ.8 was brought into the Kola Inlet in thick fog late on 18 January without further incident. This was the first time a Wolfpack (Wolfpack *Ulan*, of three U-boats, 25 December to 19 January 1942) had encountered an Arctic convoy as a result of intelligence supplied by the German B-Dienst signals intercept and analysis service.

This was also the first convoy to contain an American merchant ship. By 1945 American and Panamanian registered ships would have provided the major contribution to the shipping programme and incurred the highest proportion of losses.

QP.5 (13–19 January 1942)

This return convoy of only four merchant ships sailed from Murmansk at 16.00 on 13 January escorted by the cruiser *Cumberland* (until 16 January), and destroyers *Icarus* and *Tartar* until 19 January, when the convoy dispersed and the merchant ships proceeded independently to their final destinations. *Cumberland* had embarked the Foreign Secretary, Sir Stafford Cripps, for return passage to the UK. The convoy was not detected or attacked and all ships arrived safely on 19 January.

QP. 6 (24 January–2 February 1942)

Convoy QP.6 containing six merchant ships departed Murmansk on 24 January 1942 with the eastern local escort of *Harrier* and *Speedwell* (24 to 25 January), and Russian destroyers *Gremyaschiy* and *Sokrushitelny* (24 to

27 January). The through escort, *Trinidad*, *Somali*, *Bramble*, and *Hebe* joined on 25 January and remained with the convoy until it dispersed on 28 January.

Most of the merchant ships went on to Loch Ewe, arriving by 2 February. They included the British freighter *Empire Redshank*, damaged on 31 January in a bombing attack by aircraft of KG 30, 140 miles north of the Shetlands.

PQ.9/10 (1–10 February 1942)

PQ.9 sailed from Scotland to Iceland in mid-January to be joined by merchant ships from the USA. The convoy was to take nine merchant ships with PQ.10 due to follow, but delays and defects meant just one, the *Trevorian*, was in a condition to sail for Reykjavik on 26 January. PQ.9's intended departure on 17 January was delayed after the Admiralty received reports of a possible sortie by the *Tirpitz*, so it was decided the *Trevorian* should join PQ.9 rather than wait for PQ.10 to be re-formed. A combined convoy of ten merchant ships sailed from Reykjavik on 1 February. The western local escort (1 to 5 February), provided by three armed trawlers was relieved by the through escort of *Faulknor* and *Intrepid* (5 to 10 February), supported by *Nigeria* (5 to 8 February).

The eastern local escort *Britomart*, and *Sharpshooter* joined from Murmansk on 7 February. PQ.9 then passed undetected by aircraft or U-boats in the continuous darkness of the Arctic winter night and arrived safely at Murmansk on 10 February.

PQ.11 (14–22 February 1942)

PQ.11 of thirteen merchant ships sailed from Kirkwall, Orkney, on 14 February 1942 with its western local escort of destroyers *Airedale* and *Middleton* and armed trawlers *Blackfly*, *Cape Argona*, and *Cape Mariato* (14 to 17 February). The local escort was relieved by the ocean escort comprising *Niger*, *Hussar*, *Oxlip*, and *Sweetbriar* (to 22 February). *Nigeria* provided cruiser cover (21 to 22 February).

The convoy averaged a speed of about 8 knots. Rain, fog and snow shielded it from detection by enemy aircraft but also brought great danger; the gale force winds drove sea spray over the ships, forming ice on gun mountings, freezing depth charges to their racks, and threatening the stability of the smaller escorts. As soon as the weather moderated all available crew were set to work to clear the ice with steam hoses, shovels and picks.

The eastern local escort of *Harrier*, *Hazard*, *Salamander* and the Russian destroyers *Gromky* and *Grozny* met the convoy on 22 February. Despite the poor weather conditions, the convoy arrived in Murmansk later that day without further incident.

QP.7 (12–15 February 1942)

Convoy QP.7 of eight merchant ships departed Murmansk on 12 February 1942 with an eastern local escort provided by *Hazard* and *Speedwell* (12 to 13 February), relieved by the ocean escort of *Nigeria*, *Faulknor*, *Intrepid*, *Britomart*, and *Sharpshooter* (13 to 15 February).

The convoy dispersed on 15 February and the ships sailed on independently to Seidisfjord, where all had arrived seven days later. The *Botavon*, *Dartford*, *Empire Halley*, *Jutland*, *Southgate*, and *Stalingrad* went on to Loch Ewe in QP.7A, arriving there on 28 February.

Chapter 3

Phase Two (Part 1):
The Wind of Change, March 1942

P hase Two covers the period from March to September 1942, from PQ.12 through to QP.14 and up to the first suspension of the convoy programme. March 1942 witnessed a significant change in German strategic intent and so the narrative for this phase is presented in two parts, in this and the following chapter.

PQ.12/QP.8 1–12 March 1942

By the beginning of 1942 the German High Command had recognized the strategic significance of supplies to northern Russia and had begun to reinforce their naval and air forces in northern Norway. From March up until the end of that year convoys would be exposed to increasingly heavy air and U-boat attacks, as well as potential attack by surface forces following the deployments of German heavy surface units and destroyers to northern Norway. The Royal Navy's ability to protect the convoys was at the time very limited. The ongoing lack of naval escort vessels and limitations on the endurance of the destroyers due to the difficulties of refuelling at sea meant the ability of the escorts to pro-actively hunt and destroy U-boats and keep them away from the convoys was much impaired. The deployment of German surface vessels against the convoys, whilst perceived by the Admiralty as a major threat, was however constrained by shortages of fuel and the severe operational restrictions placed by the German High Command on their use.

PQ.12 (1–12 March)
PQ.12, consisting of sixteen merchant ships (but SS *Bateau* returned), sailed from Reykjavik for Murmansk at 12.00 on 1 March, with the local western escort of armed trawlers *Angle*, *Chiltern*, *Notts County*, and *Stella Capella* (1 to 5 March). The ocean escort comprised *Oribi* and *Offa*, supported by *Kenya* (5 to 12 March).

The heavy cover force was provided by the 2nd Battle Squadron – battleship *Duke of York*, battlecruiser *Renown*, cruiser *Kenya*, and destroyers *Echo, Eclipse, Eskimo, Faulknor, Fury*, and *Punjabi*, which departed Hvalfjord at 06.00 on 3 March and sailed northwards around Iceland to provide distant cover for PQ.12 and QP.8.

Despite his intention to remain at Scapa Flow with part of the Home Fleet, C-in-C Home Fleet was ordered by the Admiralty to deploy the entire fleet in order to ensure total superiority over *Tirpitz* should she put to sea. He therefore ordered the 2nd Battle Squadron to rendezvous with him on 6 March. He left Scapa Flow two days earlier in the battleship *King George V* with aircraft carrier *Victorious*, heavy cruiser *Berwick*, and destroyers *Ashanti, Bedouin, Icarus, Intrepid, Lookout*, and *Onslow*, and set course to rendezvous with the squadron. At 16.00 *Berwick* was experiencing engine trouble and was detached to return to Scapa Flow, escorted by *Bedouin*.

Following the earlier air reconnaissance reports of a convoy of fifteen merchant ships steering a north-easterly course 70 to 80 miles south of Jan Mayen Island, an air attack was ordered, six U-boats deployed, and a task force comprising the battleship *Tirpitz* and destroyers *Friedrich Ihn, Z-7 Hermann Schoemann*, and *Z-25*, at Trondheim made ready for action.

The German task force sailed from the upper Trondheim fjord on Operation Sportpalast, at noon on 6 March, and steered north to intercept the convoy. About the same time, PQ.12 encountered loose pack ice at 72° N and was forced to turn southeast on a direct course towards the North Cape until the following morning.

At 00.10 the following day C-in-C Home Fleet received a signal from the Admiralty relaying a report from the submarine *Seawolf* of a sighting of the task force. Although this confirmed *Tirpitz* was at sea, it remained unclear whether her intention was to attack the convoy or break out into the Atlantic. The Home Fleet then altered course to the north to close with the convoys. By morning the ice had cleared and the convoy was able to return to its planned course, but escort ship *Oribi* had sustained serious damage to her bow structure due to the ice and two crewmen were washed overboard and lost.

It was planned for PQ.12 and QP.8 to pass each other 200 miles southwest of Bear Island, which they did in visibility of just under a mile, at noon on 7 March, on reciprocal courses northeast and southwest. At the time *Tirpitz* was crossing the mean course of the convoys, astern of PQ.12, and ahead of QP.8, in a position approximately 90 miles from C-in-C Home Fleet. At 16.30, C-in-C Home Fleet received a distress signal from the Russian merchant ship *Ijora* (see QP.8 below) giving a garbled position report, and shortly afterwards received a radio DF bearing of a possible enemy surface vessel which suggested *Tirpitz* was astern of her expected objective, PQ.12. The Home Fleet turned east-southeast for an hour and a half but then, receiving information *Tirpitz* might be expected to remain at sea and operate east of Bear Island, the C-in-C altered course to the east and detached *Icarus* and *Intrepid* to Iceland to refuel.

At 07.40 *Tirpitz* released *Z-25* and *Z-7 Hermann Schoemann* to refuel at Tromsø (approximately 125 miles away), since the weather made it impossible to refuel at sea, and *U-134* and *U-589* were ordered to new attack positions southeast of Jan Mayen. The departure of the destroyers left *Tirpitz* alone about 150 miles south of Bear Island, steering north still in search of PQ.12, which was around 80 miles southwest of Bear Island and proceeding on the northerly course it would follow until midday, when the pack ice forced it to turn again to the southeast. The Home Fleet was 180 miles west of the Lofoten Islands, steaming southwest parallel to and 100 miles south of, QP.8.

Tirpitz turned north at 08.00 to cross the presumed course of the convoy, but at noon a message from the German naval base, Group North, placed the convoy farther west. *Tirpitz* immediately changed course for the new location, but poor visibility, bad weather, lack of air reconnaissance, the vastness of the operational area, and complete ignorance of the enemy's disposition rendered any prospect of success slender. At 10.45 *Tirpitz* turned on to a mean course of 255° and zigzagged down the anticipated route of PQ.12. Luckily for the convoy its change of course from north of Bear Island, due to pack ice, had avoided an encounter with *Tirpitz*. As it was the merchant ships passed clear to the north, undetected even by a searching FW 200 and by nightfall the convoy would be south of Bear Island, some 150 miles beyond *Tirpitz*'s position. The Home Fleet was now 400 miles to the west of Norway and reasonably free from risk of air attack.

At 18.00 the Home Fleet was steering southwesterly when C-in-C Home Fleet received a signal from the Admiralty suggesting *Tirpitz* might be south of Bear Island still searching for the convoys, and at 18.20 acting on this intelligence, they altered course to the northeast, towards *Tirpitz*. At the time the Germans remained unaware that the Home Fleet was at sea. Some fifteen minutes later Group North, the German naval operational command at Wilhelmshaven, advised Admiral Ciliax (task force commander), that it was possible the convoy had turned back three days earlier after the sighting off Jan Mayen Island. (There seems to have been evidence to confirm this, for neither PQ.12 nor QP.8 appears to have been subsequently reported, but it placed the responsibility for continuing the search on Admiral Ciliax's shoulders alone.)

Tirpitz continued to search the convoy route at a speed of 6 to 8 knots until evening. Visibility changed constantly and the search in the area south and southwest of Bear Island proved fruitless. At 20.25 Admiral Ciliax altered course to 191° to rendezvous with his destroyers off Vestfjord before returning to base. Four minutes after Admiral Ciliax had received his earlier unhelpful signal, C-in-C Home Fleet, acting on a suggestion from the Admiralty that the *Tirpitz* was still at sea far to the north, turned the Home Fleet back towards Bear Island. At 21.30 the *Tirpitz* turned onto a southerly course, now moving away from the convoys. Soon after this Admiral Ciliax took the decision to terminate the operation and return to Trondheim. Operation Sportpalast had consumed a large quantity of scarce fuel oil and failed to achieve success.

During the night of 8/9 March the whaler *Shera*, sailing with her sister ship *Svega* in the heavy swell and pack ice in the Barents Sea, capsized. *Svega* rescued three of the *Shera*'s crew, but twenty-seven were lost. The later official board of inquiry report concluded:

> After a full and careful enquiry, with all the witnesses available, into the circumstances attending the loss of HM Trawler *Shera* ... the opinion of the Board is that the loss is attributable to the instability of the vessel, aggravated by a heavy formation of ice ... which resulted in the vessel becoming unstable and capsizing.

During the morning of 9 March a U-boat reported a convoy of ten steamers and four destroyers some 40 miles north of Kola Bay, steering toward Murmansk. This was probably PQ.12, last sighted by the Germans four days earlier, when according to its position at that time it must have been close to Bear Island when *Tirpitz* was in the vicinity. Thus, if the *Tirpitz* task force had been able to scout a wider area or if they had had air reconnaissance it is most likely they would have found the convoy and destroyed a major part of it.

PQ.12 arrived at Murmansk on 12 March escorted by *Harrier, Hussar,* and *Speedwell* as eastern local escort. No merchant ships were lost, but the whaler *Shera* had been lost and the *Oribi* badly damaged by the pack ice.

QP.8 (1–11 March)

QP.8 consisting of 15 merchant ships sailed from Murmansk on 1 March, the Commodore in the *Empire Selwyn.* The convoy was escorted for the first three days by the local eastern escort of *Harrier* and *Sharpshooter* (until dawn) and *Gremyaschiy* and *Grimke* (until dusk). The ocean escort from 1 March comprised just four ships – *Hazard, Salamander, Oxlip,* and *Sweetbriar. Nigeria* sailed the following day, intending to provide close cover until 7 March, but unable to locate the convoy in the bad weather and poor visibility she sailed on to Scapa Flow alone. Close support was provided for a short time by *Kent* and *London.*

For the first three days, the sea was flat calm and covered with ice. On 4 March the convoy ran into gale force 10 southwesterlies followed by westerly winds. Many of the merchant ships with no cargo and very little ballast rode high out of the water. This presented a large surface profile to the wind and reduced their speed. The weather now scattered the convoy and although improved visibility the following day allowed it to reform, the *Larrinaga* and *Ijora* did not reappear.

The improvement in the weather did not last; by noon on 6 March the convoy was again lashed by a force 10 gale with waves 40 feet high and the convoy formation again scattered. The remaining thirteen merchant ships managed to reform in convoy the next day, and at noon, 200 miles southwest of Bear Island in falling snow, passed through the columns of PQ.12.

While the *Tirpitz,* with her escort of three destroyers, was searching for PQ.12 a single merchant ship was sighted. This turned out to be the missing Russian freighter *Ijora,* carrying a cargo of timber, straggling about 100 miles astern of QP.8. Although single vessels were usually avoided, Admiral Ciliax ordered the *Ijora* to be destroyed to prevent her from reporting the presence of the German task force. C-in-C Home Fleet intercepted the *Ijora*'s distress signal but as her location was unclear no assistance was sent. The survivors from the *Ijora* were taken prisoner and subsequently interrogated at the Intelligence Centre in Tromsø.

The merchant ships in the convoy began to disperse to their destinations on 9 March. Four arrived in Akureyri the following day, another on 11 March and nine in Reykjavik that same day, escorted by *Oxlip* and *Sweetbriar.*

Chapter 4

Phase Two (Part 2): Running the Gauntlet, March to November 1942

March 1942 marked a turning point in the conflict. On the 14th Hitler made the Arctic convoys a strategic target of major importance linked directly to the campaign in Russia, as the Anglo-American deliveries of war supplies were 'sustaining Russian ability to hold out'. He declared that it was 'necessary that maritime communications over the Arctic Ocean between the Anglo-Saxons and Russians, hitherto virtually unimpeded, should henceforth be impeded.'

On 31 March, Admiral Erich Raeder declared the commencement of an all-out offensive against convoys carrying vital British and American war goods to Russia. His statement immediately followed the British Admiralty announcement that a strongly escorted convoy (PQ.3) had reached Murmansk despite three air and sea attacks. German newspapers promised that the navy and air force would take the necessary steps to close the Murmansk route. A German naval spokesman announced that the attack was the first act in 'the Battle for the Arctic'.

PQ.13/QP.9 20 March – 3 April 1942

The next two convoys, PQ.13 and QP.9, each of nineteen merchant ships, sailed on 20 and 21 March from Reykjavik and Murmansk respectively, their departure delayed for forty-eight hours due to the presence of U-boats off the Kola Inlet.

The ongoing shortage of suitable warships restricted the size of the anti-submarine escort to two destroyers, a minesweeper and two armed trawlers for the eastbound convoy, and one destroyer and two minesweepers for the westbound convoy, with one cruiser accompanying each convoy to provide close cover and another cruising west of Bear Island in support.

A large heavy cover force provided distant cover over the western half of the route in case the *Tirpitz* and heavy cruisers *Admiral Scheer* and *Admiral*

Hipper sortied against the convoy from Trondheim; five minesweepers and a Russian destroyer reinforced the escorts off the Murmansk coast; no air support was available outside the immediate vicinity of the Kola Inlet.

PQ.13 (10–30 March)

The nineteen ships of PQ.13 sailed from Loch Ewe for Reykjavik at 15.15 on 10 March on the first stage of the passage to Murmansk, escorted by destroyers *Sabre*, *Saladin*, *Lamerton*, and Polish destroyer *Blyskawica*. The convoy ran into heavy weather during the night of 12 March and hove-to for 24 hours, reforming at dawn on 14 March. Several ships and escorts suffered storm damage; one destroyer left, short of fuel, but all the merchant ships finally arrived safely at Reykjavik on 16 March where three small merchant ships, *Lars Kruse* (subsequently returned to Loch Ewe), *Mano*, and *Greenland*, in transit to Iceland detached from the convoy, replaced by a fleet oiler *Scottish American* and two merchant ships, *Ballot* and *Bateau*, which had missed the previous PQ convoy.

During the following days the German Navy made a number of changes in plans for attacking the convoys. On 13 March the chief of the German naval staff announced the Führer's agreement to the proposal to use only U-boats and light naval forces for the time being to attack PQ convoys, and Britain's Commander-in-Chief, Air, instructed the 5th Air Force to give priority to preventing attacks on PQ convoys, both in cooperation with the Navy and independently. The convoys would now have to 'run the gauntlet' of determined German attempts at disruption and destruction.

PQ.13 departed from Reykjavik at 06.45 on 18 March at a speed of just over 6 knots, heading north through the Denmark Strait, accompanied by *Celia*, *Bute*, and *Whitethorn*, but was ordered to return following a report (later proved to be false) that *Tirpitz* had put to sea. The convoy sailed again early on the morning of Friday, 20 March.

In order to protect the convoy against any sortie by *Tirpitz*, *Admiral Scheer*, and *Admiral Hipper*, a heavy cover force comprising battleships *King George V* and *Duke of York*, battle cruiser *Renown*, aircraft carrier *Victorious*, cruisers *Kent* and *Edinburgh* and sixteen destroyers – *Ashanti*, *Bedouin*, *Echo*, *Escapade*, *Eskimo*, *Foresight*, *Icarus*, *Inglefield*, *Ledbury*, *Marne*, *Middleton*, *Onslow*, *Punjabi*, *Tartar*, and *Wheatland*, sailed from Scapa Flow at 14.00 on 22 March to patrol the sea area to the northeast of Iceland.

The ocean escort, the cruiser *Trinidad* with destroyers *Eclipse* and *Fury* joined at 13.30 the next day and the western local escort departed at 14.00.

The armed trawlers *Blackfly* and *Paynter* escorting the whalers *Silja*, *Sumba*, and *Sulla* together with Force Q (the fleet oiler *Oligarch* and escorting destroyer *Lamerton*) joined from Seidisfjord, while *Nigeria* sailed west of Bear Island in support.

On 24 March, the Commanding Officer of *Trinidad* was informed that an attack by German destroyers was expected. During that night the convoy ran into a severe northeasterly gale and was forced to heave-to in the Norwegian Sea for two days. This weather scattered the merchant ships of the convoy across a distance of 150 nautical miles. During the first night of the storm the ships iced up. The ice build-up made the small whalers top heavy and forced them to make efforts to keep their superstructures clear of ice to avoid capsizing, as had happened previously to *Shera* in PQ.12 and was also regarded as the most likely cause of loss of the *Sulla*, which was reported missing having been last seen on the evening of 24 March.

Early the next morning the cover force arrived in its designated patrol area, where it cruised for two days in temperatures of –35° F. That same day *U-445*, *U-589*, *U-454*, and *U-585* were deployed in an attempt to intercept the convoy. Group North had now deduced from earlier intelligence that some PQ convoys sailed east through the Denmark Strait and along the edge of the ice field toward the southeastern tip of Jan Mayen Island. However, the Admiralty, utilizing intelligence gained from Enigma decrypts, was able to provide the SOE with details of the U-boat dispositions and warn of possible air and destroyer attacks. Most importantly the Enigma decrypts confirmed none of the larger enemy surface units had moved north with the destroyers. The Admiralty was therefore able to assure C-in-C Home Fleet that *Tirpitz* was not on this occasion going to put to sea.

On the morning of 26 March the convoy remained very scattered. The merchant ships *Induna*, *Empire Starlight*, *Ballot*, and whaler *Silja* formed up in a small group, survived a strafing attack by a BV.140 reconnaissance aircraft; no damage was sustained. They later met the *Effingham*, *Dunboyne*, and *Mana*. As the Convoy Commodore's ship *River Afton* had lost all contact and continued independently a new convoy was formed under the command of the Vice Commodore in *Induna*.

Aware from *Trinidad*'s signal received late on 25 March that PQ.13 had been scattered by a full gale, and with the Home Fleet itself experiencing gale force conditions that had damaged both *Victorious* and *Tartar*, C-in-C Home Fleet decided he would be unable to provide further assistance to the convoy in its scattered state and so the Home Fleet left its patrol area at 06.00 on 27 March to return to Scapa Flow.

That same morning three merchant ships were sighted by a BV.138 flying boat (*2./KüFl Gr 406*) south of Bear Island and *U-209*, *U-376*, *U-378*, and *U-655* of the Wolfpack *Ziethen* (operated 23–29 March) were ordered to form a patrol line off the North Cape. (Group North was unaware *U-655* had been sunk during the action against QP.9 on 24 March.) The same day the *Eldena*, sailing alone, was joined by three other merchant ships from the convoy,[1] all still in the ice floe where they were safer from U-boats but more vulnerable to air attack, being now within range of aircraft operating from the many bases along the Norwegian coast. Throughout the day, low visibility and foggy weather made it difficult for the escort to find the scattered merchant ships. *Trinidad* searched an area about 100 miles southwest of Bear Island where she was joined by *Nigeria*. Two of the merchant ships were located that evening. The *Eclipse*, 180 miles to the southwest, had one merchant ship in company, whilst *Fury* found and refuelled the whaler *Sumba*, then steered to re-join the convoy.

U-209 made first contact with the convoy at 07.00 on 28 March when it sighted and attacked the Polish merchant ship *Tobruk*, escorted by the trawler *Blackfly*. The encounter was inconclusive; the U-boat missed the trawler with a stern torpedo, and depth charges dropped by the trawler caused no damage. Soon after the ships dropped out of sight in a flurry of snow. By this time the weather was moderating and the day brought clear conditions with good visibility except during the snow squalls. The convoy was still strung out over 150 miles of sea. By 08.00 the *Empire Ranger* was some 80 miles to the east, due north of the North Cape, sailing independently. Forty miles astern was the *Induna* group of six merchant ships with the *Silja*, and 35 miles astern of this group came the *Harpalion* with *Fury*.

At 09.29 enemy aircraft began shadowing *Trinidad* and six merchant ships in the vicinity. Ju.88 dive-bombers attacked the *Induna* between 09.30 and 10.00. She opened fire on one, but it was out of range and flew off without doing any damage.

During the morning the weather improved a little and became clear and sunny with occasional snow showers. In the afternoon Ju.88 bombers of III./ KG 30 carried out several attacks and sank two stragglers from the convoy, the Panamanian merchant ship *Raceland* and British merchant ship *Empire Ranger*. The first attack came shortly after midday. The *Raceland*, sailing alone after being separated from the convoy due to mechanical problems and the heavy gales of 26 March, with a cargo of 9,000 tons of tanks, trucks, and aircraft, was attacked by two Ju.88 dive-bombers about 110 miles northeast of North Cape. Two bombs exploded about twenty yards from the ship on the starboard side, near No 3 hold. There were no direct hits, but the shock from the explosion blew a hole in the starboard side of the hull forward, broke deck fittings and steam pipes, and stopped the engines. The engine room flooded, the ship took a 45° list to port and the crew abandoned ship in two lifeboats. During the night the two boats kept together but became separated the following morning. One lifeboat landed on Norwegian soil on 2 April and the survivors, after spending twenty-four hours on the beach, were rescued by Norwegian civilians and taken to a German naval hospital at Tromsø. They were held there until 20 April then sent to the merchant marine POW camp Milag Nord at Bremen. Thirty-five of the crew of forty-seven were lost and twelve taken prisoner.

The *Eldena* group was now joined by two more merchant ships from the convoy, plus the *Eclipse*, *Blackfly*, and *Paynter*, making nine in all. As they were easing out of the ice field in intermittent snow showers and fog, with visibility ranging from 200 yards to half a mile, though with breaks in the clouds, they caught glimpses of a reconnaissance aircraft.

Several attacks by Ju.88 bombers (III./KG 30) developed during the afternoon. The eastern group (*Induna*) of six merchant ships and *Silja* was dive-bombed twice. At around 13.30 a twin-engined aircraft dived out of the clouds at an angle of 50° and attacked the *Ballot*. The aircraft, thought to be a Me.110, dived with engines full on to a height of 250 feet and dropped two bombs close by before pulling out of the dive. It flew off to port then returned and attacked the *Mana*, dropping four bombs that straddled the ship before flying away. The *Mana* was able to continue with the convoy but the shock from the near misses caused steam leaks in the *Ballot*'s engine room and the engines were stopped. According to a later statement by the Master, half the crew demanded to take to the lifeboats, while the other half promised to remain onboard and attempt to take the ship into port. Sixteen who abandoned ship were picked up later by *Silja*. The engineers were able to stop most of the leaks and get the *Ballot* underway again, but due to problems with the steering gear had to revert to manual steering. The *Ballot* was unable to rejoin the convoy and reached Murmansk independently two days later, on 30 March. After the *Ballot* straggled, the main part of the convoy consisted of nine ships, *Empire Cowper*, *New Westminster City*, *Eldena*, *El Estero*, *Mormacmar*, *Tobruk*, *Gallant Fox*, and *Harpalion*, led by the *Scottish American* (Acting Commodore) and escorted by *Sumba*, *Paynter*, *Hussar*, *Gremyaschiy*, and *Sokrushitelny*,

The *Trinidad*, narrowly missed by three bombs dropped from an aircraft as it dived out of the cloud at 13.18, was persistently dive-bombed by Ju.88s between 13.18 and 13.30. *Harpalion* reported being bombed at about the same time, but no damage was done and she continued on to Murmansk. Fortunately, none of these attacks inflicted serious damage. They were followed by a further series of dive-bomb attacks by varying numbers of aircraft between 13.30 and 14.30 until a snowstorm reduced visibility. No ships were hit and no aircraft damaged. The aircraft then continued searching a wider area until dark.

Mid-afternoon the *Eldena* received a distress message from *Empire Ranger*, reporting being bombed by aircraft. Later that evening *Empire Ranger* reported she was sinking, her crew abandoning ship and heading for the coast. *Blackfly*, ordered by the SOE to search for survivors from the *Empire Ranger*, was lucky not to encounter the German destroyers which, while sweeping to the northwest, had located *Empire Ranger*'s lifeboats and taken all sixty-one survivors onboard *Z-24* as prisoners. *Harrier* and *Oribi* also searched for survivors until the latter located the abandoned lifeboats the following morning. At midnight the group, now reduced to five merchant ships accompanied by *Silja*, ran into the ice field but remained on course.

Following the air reconnaissance reports, the 8th Destroyer Flotilla, led by *Z-26*, with *Z-24* and *Z-25*, left Kirkenes at 16.00 to intercept the convoy. The flotilla was sighted and reported a few hours later by the Russian submarine *K-21*, but she was unable to carry out an attack due to low visibility. The same day the eastern local escort, *Harrier*, *Gossamer*, *Speedwell*, *Hussar*, *Gremyaschiy*, and *Sokrushitelny*, left Murmansk knowing that the convoy was widely scattered owing to gales and *Harpalion* had been bombed.

The main group of convoy PQ.13 was spotted and reported by *U-376* at 03.50 on 29 March. In the early morning *Z-26* located the *Bateau*, a straggler from the convoy. *Z-26* first opened fire, then sank the *Bateau* with a torpedo. *Z-25* immediately went to the sinking position but could only rescue seven survivors from the freezing cold water, who apparently subsequently disclosed a great deal of intelligence about the composition and progress of the convoy and escort. The same morning *Silja* requested *Induna* take her in tow as she was short of fuel and also asked her to embark the sixteen survivors from the *Ballot* rescued earlier. During the morning heavy pack ice was encountered, eventually becoming a solid field that brought the ships to a halt. The other merchant ships, assured *Induna* would be able to extricate herself, turned around and left. *Induna* then turned successfully in the ice field and went alongside *Silja* to embark the survivors from *Ballot*. The tow was resumed until mid-afternoon, when both vessels sailed out of the ice and *Induna* set course for Murmansk.

After rescuing the survivors from the *Bateau*, the German destroyers adjusted their course at 01.40, then again at 05.30. Finding nothing they turned and ran north for three hours before resuming a westerly sweep into increasingly deteriorating weather. The merchant ships were now sailing in two groups about 80 miles apart with four others still unaccounted for. The westerly group of eight merchant ships, escorted by *Eclipse* and *Paynter*, was reinforced at 06.45 on the 30th by *Oribi*, *Gremyaschiy*, and *Sokrushitelny*. At 08.43 *Trinidad* and *Fury* were sailing east to round up the easterly group of four merchant ships.

Just before 09.00 the German destroyers were picked up on *Trinidad*'s radar, 7½ miles ahead, now moving towards her. *Trinidad* opened fire at the leading destroyer, Z-26, a few minutes later at a range of about 4,000 yards and scored several hits, setting her on fire amidships. *Trinidad* then targeted Z-24 but failed to score any hits. As *Trinidad* turned away to evade a spread of seven torpedoes fired by the destroyer, two of which passed as she was turning, she lost sight of Z-24. *Fury* was sailing astern of *Trinidad* and was unable to engage Z-26. During these manoeuvres the ships lost contact with each other, but then *Trinidad* located the fleeing Z-26 and put three of her four gun turrets out of action. *Trinidad* had only been struck two or three times and suffered slight damage during the action. At 10.24, *Trinidad* attempted to torpedo Z-26. Owing to a malfunction (later attributed to a defective warhead firing pistol) the torpedo circled back and struck *Trinidad* on her port side forward of the bridge structure, killing thirty-one of her crew. The forward boiler room flooded with fuel oil which then ignited, causing further major damage and forcing *Trinidad* to break off the action. *Trinidad* was then joined by *Harrier*, *Oribi*, and *Fury*, and taken in tow.

At 11.20 *Eclipse* was attacked by Z-24 and Z-25 and retired damaged by three hits. *Oribi* and *Sokrushitelny*, alerted by the gunfire, joined in the action. The latter fired six salvos at the German destroyers, claiming one hit but then losing contact in a snow squall. *U-376* observed the gunfire but only once sighted a destroyer, which proved to be German. In all, 240 crewmembers of *Z-26* were lost; most perished in the freezing water. *Z-24* and *Z-25* rescued 96 (including the Flotilla Commander and Commander of *Z-26*). Only eight others remained alive and were rescued by *U-376*, and three died of exposure during the following few hours and were buried at sea.

During the day the convoy sailed on unmolested, limited visibility and low cloud giving protection from air attack, but it had not yet arrived at the U-boat patrol line. The western group of eight merchant ships, escorted by the *Oribi* and Russian destroyers passed safely to the south of the enemy destroyers. By the time the surface actions were over, the eastern group of four merchant ships were about to turn southwards. The *Induna* and *Silja* were not clear of the ice until 15.00 that afternoon, when they headed towards Murmansk. But after five hours the towrope parted and *Silja* disappeared from view in a squall.

Induna continued to search for *Silja* until 04.00 the following morning but poor visibility, frequent snow squalls, a rough heavy sea and swell, and a north-northwest force 6 gale all hampered the search. As *Silja* could not be found, *Induna* decided to head for Murmansk to report the missing vessel's position and ask for assistance to be sent. Around 05.00 *Induna*, sailing alone at 10½ knots, steering a course approximately south (true), was sighted and attacked by *U-209*, which fortunately missed her with a spread of two torpedoes. Some three hours later *Induna* was attacked again, this time by *U-376*. No one saw the track of the torpedo, which struck without warning on the starboard side in no. 5 hold, well aft. This contained gasoline and the after part of the ship immediately caught fire, flames shot up to a tremendous height and the ship was violently shaken by the force of the ensuing explosion.

The order was given to abandon ship. Survivors left in two lifeboats, thirty-two in the starboard no. 1 boat, and nine in the port no. 2 boat, with the third mate of the *Ballot* in charge. When the lifeboats were about 200 yards from the ship the U-boat surfaced 300 yards away on the starboard beam, steamed towards the *Induna* and fired a second torpedo. This struck home in no. 4 hold on the starboard side. Again, the track of the torpedo was not seen. The explosion was very loud, there was no flash, but a lot of debris was thrown into the air. A third torpedo missed. The *Induna* started to settle quickly by the stern, rose out of the water by the bow until vertical, then plunged straight down and sank within thirty minutes. The U-boat crew did not question the survivors as they had sighted a submarine periscope. This, although not known at the time, was *U-209* which had pursued the *Induna* after failing to hit her with a spread of two torpedoes at 05.52 and had witnessed the sinking. By the time the survivors in the starboard no. 1 lifeboat were found and picked up by a Russian minesweeper only seventeen of the thirty-two remained alive. A Russian patrol boat later found the port lifeboat. Two of the nine survivors in the second boat died in hospital at Murmansk. Of the sixteen original survivors from the *Ballot*, nine of her crew and two British DEMS gunners lost their lives, just five survived.

The *Empire Ranger*'s boats were found at 08.40 by the *Oribi*, who informed *Harrier* by signal that they showed every sign of having been abandoned by the occupants. There was food, drink, and blankets in the boats so it appeared the occupants had been picked up by some other ship. As no other merchant ship in the convoy or escort had reported picking them up, and as German destroyers were in the vicinity and the German wireless service claimed prisoners had been taken from a merchant ship, their fate appeared obvious. In the meantime, most ships of the convoy headed northeast to evade further air attacks and the German destroyers.

At 10.20 *Gossamer* received instructions from the Senior British Naval Officer (SBNO) to proceed immediately to the assistance of *Induna*. The subsequent search by daylight and during the night, however, proved fruitless and *Gossamer* resumed her patrol the next morning.

Between 10.35 and 10.45, *U-456* attacked the stragglers *Mana* and *Effingham*. *U-456* missed *Mana* with a spread of three torpedoes. A fourth fired at 10.36 struck the *Effingham* amidships on the port side at the no. 4 hold. The *Effingham* came to a stop and the crew of eight officers, twenty-six men and nine armed guards immediately abandoned ship, in rough seas, in two lifeboats, as their ship began to settle by the stern. *U-456* then tried to finish off the *Effingham* with a 'coup de grâce' from the stern torpedo tube at 10.45 but missed, she then lost the *Effingham* from sight in a snow squall while reloading the torpedo tubes. The *Effingham* was attacked a little later by *U-435*, whose first two torpedoes missed their intended target probably because the U-boat miscalculated the anticipated speed – not having realized the ship had been abandoned. A third missile fired at 12.19 hit her in the bow, followed by another two minutes later, and the *Effingham* exploded and sank. The following day, *Harrier*, on patrol off the Kola Inlet searching for stragglers from the convoy rescued the Master, chief mate, and fifteen crew from a lifeboat. Six survivors had already died from exposure. Sixty-five hours after the attack a Russian patrol vessel rescued eleven crew and three armed guards from the second lifeboat; four survivors had died of exposure. *Gremyaschiy*, *Sokrushitelny*, *Gossamer*, *Harrier*, and *Speedwell* now joined the convoy and began dropping depth charges in an attempt to keep the U-boats down.

In the afternoon *Oribi*, *Harrier Trinidad*, *Eclipse* and *Fury* arrived in Murmansk. *Oribi* and *Fury* left immediately to patrol off the Kola Inlet, joined by *Speedwell*. *Oribi* found *Silja* drifting and out of fuel on 30 March. *Silja* was taken in tow by *Harrier* escorted by *Speedwell* and after refuelling the following day was towed into Murmansk by Russian tugs while *Oribi* searched in vain for the straggling *River Afton*. The U-boats were forced to break off their pursuit to avoid running into the defensive mine barrages off the Kola Inlet. Two Russian tugs brought the *Ballot* in to Murmansk the same day.

During the evening of 30 March the convoy of nine merchant vessels sailing in single file near the mouth of the Kola Inlet, at a point just off Kildin Island about 20 miles north of Murmansk, was attacked by a small number of aircraft. Four bombs were dropped ahead of the *Eldena* and two near the *Mormacmar*, one of which caused slight damage.

The eastern group, the *Empire Starlight*, *Dunboyne*, and *Mana*, cleared the ice on 29 March and had a trouble-free run into the Kola Inlet the next day, followed in by the *River Afton*. The western group, *Empire Cowper*, *New Westminster City*, *Scottish American*, *Eldena*, *El Estero*, *Mormacmar*, *Tobruk*, *Gallant Fox*, and *Harpalion*, entered late on 30 March with the eastern local escort, *Oribi*, *Paynter*, *Sumba*, and the two Russian destroyers. Both groups docked on 31 March. *Silja* was the last ship to arrive, towed in on 1 April by *Harrier*.

QP.9 (21 March–3 April)

Convoy QP.9 of nineteen merchant ships sailed from the Kola Inlet on 21 March, with a local eastern escort of *Gossamer*, *Harrier*, *Hussar*, *Niger* and *Speedwell*, and *Gremyaschiy* (to 23 March). The ocean escort (21 March to April 3) consisted of *Offa*, *Britomart* and *Sharpshooter*. *Kenya*, carrying 10 tons of bullion, was to have been in company from the 22 to 27 March, but failed to make the rendezvous. The *King George V, Duke of York, Renown,*

Victorious, *Kent*, and *Edinburgh* supported by sixteen fleet destroyers – *Ashanti*, *Bedouin*, *Echo*, *Escapade*, *Eskimo*, *Faulknor*, *Foresight*, *Icarus*, *Inglefield*, *Ledbury*, *Marne*, *Middleton*, *Onslow*, *Punjabi*, *Tartar* and *Wheatland* provided the heavy cover force (25 to 27 March).

The convoy was not attacked but at 18.35 on 24 March, *Sharpshooter* sighted a U-boat (*U-655*) at a range of 300 yards crossing ahead of her from starboard to port. *Sharpshooter* adjusted course, rammed and struck the U-boat, which turned turtle and sank stern first. The only wreckage observed was two lifebuoys and a canvas dinghy. All forty-five crew were lost.

The convoy had a safe passage and all nineteen merchant ships reached Iceland on 3 April.

PQ.14/QP.10

PQ.14 (26 March–19 April)

The seventeen merchant ships of PQ.14 sailed from Oban at 16.00 on 26 March and arrived in Reykjavik on 31 March. The initial escort included *Ambuscade*, *Blyskawica*, *Bulldog*, and *Richmond*, and armed trawler *Tango*. Three more merchant ships departed Loch Ewe on 27 March in convoy UR.17, and also arrived in Reykjavik on 31 March. An additional five sailed from Loch Ewe in UR.18 on 3 April, arriving in Reykjavik on 7 April.

PQ.14 now with twenty-four merchant ships (the main body had sailed from Oban 26 March and arrived Reykjavyk on the 31st, where they were joined by others), sailed at 14.30 on 8 April with the western local escort, comprising *Hebe*, *Speedy*, *Lord Austin*, *Lord Middleton*, *Chiltern*, *Northern Wave*, and Force Q (the fuelling force – the destroyer *Wilton* and fleet oiler *Aldersdale*).

Within hours of the convoy leaving Reykjavik weather conditions began to deteriorate, the wind coming from the northeast and increasing to gale force with hail and snow flurries, and a falling temperature. The Vice Commodore noted, 'Vessel rolling shipping seawater on the weather side.'[2] The mountainous coast of Iceland to starboard provided some shelter, but the adverse conditions began to cause the merchant ships to become scattered.

The convoy steamed steadily north around the snowbound Icelandic coast, through frequent snowstorms. Fog and icy winds made it difficult for the crew on the bridges of the merchant ships to maintain visibility and frozen snow had to be scraped regularly from the bridge windows. The sea spray froze in the cold air, building up thick layers of ice on every horizontal part of the ships' superstructures, requiring constant chipping off. The ice had to be removed and thrown overboard to avoid ships becoming top heavy and capsizing. This grim weather persisted into the next day with gale force winds and rough seas breaking over the ships. Visibility was very poor due to the driving snow, with an additional hazard at times from pack ice in close proximity; however the speed of the convoy was maintained at 8 knots.

At daybreak on 10 April the wind remained strong with visibility limited by heavy snow. In the poor weather conditions the merchant ships had difficulty maintaining station in the convoy formation and a number were forced to return to Iceland. A small group of six with the *Lord Austin* found themselves separated from the main body and arrived back at Akureyri later that day to await further instructions. Shortly afterwards they were ordered to sail again immediately to rendezvous with the convoy on 12 April. Two of the six (*Hegira* and *Pieter de Hoogh*) conveniently developed engine trouble, but the other four sailed with the *Lord Austin*, out into a sea covered with drifting ice and into heavy snowstorms. They failed to make the rendezvous and returned again to Iceland.

On Saturday, 11 April, the convoy began to encounter thick drift ice and by the following day all the ships in the convoy had entered this field, the polar ice barrier being further south than usual for the time of year. These conditions coupled with the heavy fog made it virtually impossible for the merchant ships to maintain station or to extricate themselves from the icefield. Their slow passage put the convoy about thirty-six hours behind schedule. In the poor visibility and adverse conditions the ships became scattered and many suffered damage to hulls, propellers and rudders. Spray from the turbulent seas rapidly turned to ice in the subzero temperatures on coming into contact with a ship's superstructure, not only fouling moving parts, but also adding irregular and disproportionate weight to the windward side of the vessel, putting the ship at risk of overturning. It was necessary to deploy ice-breaking parties around the clock to counter this threat and keep the ships fully functional. This was difficult and dangerous work; in rough conditions it was not uncommon for ships to roll more than 45° and if a crew member were swept overboard their chances of surviving hypothermia were minimal even if they were recovered alive.

Speedy, *Wilton*, *Hebe*, *Chiltern*, and *Duncton* all sustained ice damage and the anti-submarine gear of the majority of the escort was put out of action.

The main ocean escort group assembled at Seidisfjord on 8 and 9 April, sailed on 11 April, and joined up with the convoy early the following day. Led by the *Edinburgh*, it included *Foresight, Forester, Bulldog, Beagle, Amazon*, and *Beverley, Campanula, Oxlip, Saxifrage*, and *Snowflake*. A cruiser force and a distant cover force provided additional 'stand-off' protection against German surface warships. Cruiser cover (12 to 17 April) was provided by the *Norfolk*, which left Scapa Flow on 10 April to patrol the sea areas about 140 miles southwest of Bear Island, from where she could support either PQ.14 or QP.10.

Distant cover (14 to 16 April) was provided by the battlefleet comprising the *King George V, Victorious, Nigeria, Kent, Faulknor* (D 6), *Onslow* (D 17), *Offa, Escapade, Middleton, Ledbury, Wheatland*, and *Belvoir*, which left Scapa Flow on 12 April.

On Sunday, 12 April, after thirty hours of fog and twelve hours sailing in the heavy polar ice, the main body of the convoy, now reduced to the *Empire Howard, Briarwood, Trehata, Dan-Y-Bryn, West Cheswald, Atheltemplar, Hopemount*, and *Yaka*, was joined south-southwest of Jan Mayen Island by the ocean escort led by *Edinburgh*. The remainder of the merchant ships had returned to Iceland with ice damage or straggled and failed to catch up.

Admiralty reports show the convoy had become divided by the following day, with the more northerly section being shadowed by aircraft. *Wheatland* was detached to Seidisfjord, also arriving on 14 April to relieve *Wilton* (damaged by ice) in escorting *Aldersdale* with ice damage, and detached from PQ.14 on 12 April for Seidisfjord; the corvette *Hebe*, also damaged, was detached the following day to escort her. The minesweeper *Speedy*, another vessel damaged by ice, left PQ.14 on 13 April for Reykjavik. On the way she collected the merchant ships *Seattle Spirit* and *Sukhona* and damaged trawlers *Chiltern* and *Duncton*, arriving at Reykjavik on 15 April. The Naval Officer in Charge (NOIC) Iceland signalled the Admiralty on 13 April: '*Empire Bard* and *Botavon* arrived Akureyri. HMS *Hebe* damaged by ice proceeding Akureyri with HMS [should have read RFA] *Aldersdale*.'

On 15 April it was confirmed nine merchant ships of the original twenty-four, and four naval escorts had returned to Akureyri. NOIC Iceland reported the arrival of the *Arcos, Sukhona, Seattle Spirit, Andre Marti, Exterminator, Pieter de Hoogh, Hegira, Botavon, Empire Bard*, together with the escorts *Chiltern, Duncton, Speedy*, and *Hebe*. He also estimated PQ.14 would now be at least twenty-four hours late in arriving at Murmansk. As the remaining eight merchant ships of PQ.14 steamed towards Murmansk they were sighted east of Bear Island by a German BV.138 flying boat, relieved later by an FW 200 Condor.

From then on the convoy was shadowed at intervals by aircraft, heard directing U-boats to its course. Occasional ineffective bombing attacks were beaten off. One aircraft which flew across the path of the convoy was reportedly badly damaged by anti-aircraft fire from all ships. No ships were sunk, but air and U-boat attacks continued over the next three days. On 16 April the six merchant ships which had lost contact with the main body of PQ.14 – *City of Joliet*, *Francis Scott Key*, *Ironclad*, *Minotaur*, *Mormacrio*, and *West Gotomska* – joined QP.10.

The escort detected U-boats again on the 16th. *Edinburgh*, responsible for guarding the convoy against surface attack and thus unable to assist the destroyers in forming a protective screen around the merchant ships, took up a position 10 miles astern of the convoy while the destroyers dropped patterns of depth charges as they hunted U-boat contacts.

Air attacks intensified and together with U-boat attacks continued through the day. But the weather favoured the escort, and all air and U-boat assaults were beaten off until at 12.45 the convoy was attacked 200 miles north of Norway by *U-403*, which fired a salvo of five torpedoes into the convoy from the starboard side. Two struck the Convoy Commodore's ship the *Empire Howard*. The first hit the boiler room, killing the crew on watch. The second a few seconds later hit the after holds, where the cargo of ammunition was stowed. The *Dan-Y-Bryn* and *Briarwood* avoided the tracks of the other three torpedoes by quick helm action. The *Empire Howard* blew up and sank in just under a minute; there was no time to launch lifeboats. Those crew and passengers above deck jumped over the side and observers on the other ships watched as the *Empire Howard*'s 'tween decks cargo of army trucks slid from her port side into the sea.

The crew on the American freighter *West Cheswald*, in the station immediately astern of the *Empire Howard* and in the same column, described feeling an explosion so violent the men of the engine-room watch thought their own ship had been hit. The *West Cheswald* yawed and reeled from the concussion, pumps shook on their base plates and almost stalled, paint flaked from the bulkheads. The reverberations of the blast echoed around the engine room and fire room, and men opened their mouths wide trying to relieve the eardrum pain. Those on deck saw a pillar of fire several hundred feet high and nearly as broad rise from the sea where the *Empire Howard* had been, while fragments of wood, steel, and other debris from the pillar rained down into the sea.

Those survivors who leapt into the sea were initially protected from the icy waters by a film of oil on the surface, released from the ship's ruptured fuel tanks. Unfortunately they were not sighted by the crew of the trawler *Northern Wave*, as she appeared out of the mist firing depth charges in an effort to sink the U-boat. Only those some distance from the exploding depth charges survived the shock waves, the remainder died of internal injuries or broken necks.

The SOE ordered *Lord Middleton*, sailing close to the *Empire Howard* and *Northern Wave*, to pick up survivors. Despite an engine defect preventing her from going astern, the *Lord Middleton* managed to pick up eighteen including the ship's Master, while *Northern Wave*, having abandoned her attack, rescued around thirty.

The Convoy Commodore, three of six signalmen and telegraphists, three DEMS gunners and eighteen members of the *Empire Howard*'s crew were lost. The Commodore was last seen in the water smoking a cheroot while holding on to wreckage. The *Empire Howard*'s Master afterwards attributed survival in the freezing sea to a protective covering of oil from his ship's ruptured bunker tanks, giving some insulation. Unfortunately, only nine of the eighteen rescued subsequently survived. The water temperature when the *Empire Howard* sank was 29° F. The Master, the last man to be rescued, later reported:

> Everyone was conscious when taken out of the water, but many of the men lost consciousness when taken into the warmth of the trawlers. Nine of the men died on board the Lord Middleton soon after being picked up. They were all given a small mouthful of spirits and that made them sleep. These unfortunate men went to sleep and did not wake up again.[3]

The Master and chief engineer were later decorated for their bravery and fortitude. Chief Engineer John Porteous received the MBE, and the Master, Captain Henry Downie, a King's Commendation. The awards were announced in the *London Gazette* on 18 August 1942. The citation for John Porteous read:

The ship was torpedoed and sank at once. Survivors clung to wreckage in icy water, sometimes being 'lifted bodily' by the bursting of depth charges by which the escort was attacking the enemy U-boat. The Chief Engineer, an 'elderly' man, set a splendid example of endurance. He kept up the hearts of the survivors and they owe their lives largely to his inspiration.

The Master, Henry John McDonald Downie, was also amongst a number of masters commended for 'Brave Conduct' when 'their ships encountered enemy ships, aircraft, U-boats or mines'.

Throughout the remainder of that day (16 April), U-boats tried to get past the escort to attack the convoy, which carried out various emergency turns and wheels. At around 05.00 on 17 April, thirty minutes after the *Sokrushitelny* and *Gremyaschiy* transferred from QP.10 to PQ.14, a number of Ju.88s appeared and attacked the main body of PQ.14. One, as it passed overhead, was fired on by *Briarwood*'s anti-aircraft guns and last seen making off trailing smoke. The attack, lasting ten minutes, was unsuccessful, and broken off due to low visibility. No ships were hit and no damage done.

The last lone straggler from PQ.14, the tanker *British Corporal*, carrying a cargo of aviation fuel, arrived back in Akureyri on 18 April, the same day the Battlefleet, the *King George V, Duke of York, Victorious*, and *Nigeria*, escorted by the *Somali* (D.6), *Faulknor* (D.8), *Onslow* (D.17), *Middleton, Ledbury, Lamerton, Hursley, Bedouin*, and *Matchless* arrived back at Scapa Flow.

The remaining seven merchant ships of PQ.14, escorted by *Edinburgh, Foresight, Forester, Bulldog, Beagle, Amazon, Beverley, Campanula, Oxlip, Saxifrage, Snowflake, Lord Middleton, Northern Wave, Sokrushitelny*, and *Gremyaschiy*, finally arrived without further incident off the entrance to Kola Inlet at 07.55 on 19 April and anchored just after midday. By 18.00 the merchant ships had berthed and begun to discharge their cargoes. The stragglers who had joined QP.10 reached Iceland on 21 April.

QP.10 (10–21 April)

QP.10 of sixteen merchant ships, escorted by *Oribi, Punjabi, Fury, Eclipse, Marne, Speedwell, Blackfly*, and *Paynter*, and the eastern local escort comprising *Harrier, Gossamer, Hussar, Gremyaschiy*, and *Sokrushitelny*, left Murmansk at 17.00 on 10 April for Iceland. The cruiser *Liverpool* left Murmansk the following day to catch up and escort the convoy, joining them early on 12 April.

The first attack developed at 13.30 on 11 April. A pack of Ju.88s appeared, approaching from astern at around 400 feet. One dropped down to 200 feet and attacked the *Empire Cowper*, whose gunners opened fire and launched two PACs (parachute and cable anti-aircraft devices). The Ju.88 took avoiding action and dropped its bombs some 30 to 40 feet from the ship. Another two bombers then attacked, one each from port and starboard, dividing the *Empire Cowper*'s anti-aircraft defences. Three 500lb bombs dropped by the starboard aircraft penetrated *Empire Cowper*'s no. 3 hatch and exploded in the empty hold directly adjacent to the boiler room, blowing a huge hole in the port side of the ship and damaging the starboard hull. With a force 7 wind blowing and a heavy sea running the engines were stopped, the *Empire Cowper* gradually lost way and drifted behind the convoy. Two lifeboats were launched but the port boat was dropped, throwing eight crewmen into the sea. Two smaller boats were then launched. Forty-two of the crew abandoned ship in two lifeboats but the Chief Officer and eight crew remained stranded on board when their lifeboat broke away from the side of the ship. The *Empire Cowper* was then attacked yet again and the remaining crew manned their guns. The Ju.88 machine-gunned the ship, dropped two bombs into no. 2 hold and began to attack the two lifeboats, but was driven off when two more PACs were fired. As it flew low overhead the Ju.88 was then shot down by the *Empire Cowper* gunners. *Paynter* rescued the occupants of the lifeboats and went alongside the *Empire Cowper* to take off the remaining crew. The freighter was left on fire, low in the water. The American freighter *Stone Street* received bomb damage in the same attack but was able to return to the Kola Inlet. Fortunately, a heavy snowstorm ended the air attacks.

Heavy ice disrupted the convoy formation on 12 April and reduced its speed to 4½ knots. Later that night the convoy, fifty-six hours out of Murmansk and 140 miles north of North Cape, was detected by *U-435*. In the early hours of the following morning aircraft were heard homing U-boats onto the convoy. *U-436* attacked at 01.00, firing a torpedo at the Russian freighter *Kiev*. The Convoy Commodore signalled for a series of 'emergency turns'. *U-436* heard one torpedo hit after a running time of forty-eight seconds and observed three lifeboats after surfacing at 02.15. The *Kiev* sank within seven minutes. Five crew were lost, the remainder and eight passengers (family members of Soviet Embassy employees in London) were picked up after thirty minutes by *Blackfly*, but a female crew member died from her wounds. The survivors were later landed in Iceland.

The escorts searched for *U-436* but it made good its escape. Around thirty minutes later the Panamanian freighter *El Occidente* was hit in the engine room by one or two torpedoes from *U-435*, the damage almost breaking her in two. She sank stern first within two minutes, leaving no time for the crew to launch lifeboats. The survivors, forced to jump overboard, were picked up by *Speedwell* about thirty minutes later and landed at Reykjavik. Nine bodies were also recovered and later buried at sea.

QP.10 now reformed and took a westerly course to skirt the ice to the south of Bear Island. As dawn broke on 14 April an FW 200 appeared, circling the convoy out of range of its guns. At 05.00 the freighter *Harpalion* observed three Ju.88s approach, then circle warily for about an hour before the first air attack came, carried out by around twenty Ju.88s just after 06.00. Eight bombs were dropped within 50 yards of *Harpalion* but did no significant damage. Minutes later four more bombs were dropped just 20 yards from her, but did these not explode, allowing her time to escape from the target area.

At about 07.30 another pair of Ju.88s appeared. One attacked from ahead and one from astern, each dropping four bombs which exploded 50 yards off the port bow without causing any damage. Minutes later a single Ju.88 flying at around 200 feet dropped four bombs close to the *Harpalion*'s stern. The force of the explosions lifted the stern out of the water, damaged the steering gear and broke the rudder post, leaving the rudder useless. The crew attempted to rig an emergency rudder, but while *Harpalion* was stopped astern of the convoy four Ju.88s bombed and machine-gunned her. None struck her but the crew were now running out of ammunition and the decision was taken to abandon ship. The lifeboats were machine-gunned as they pulled away, but no harm was done. *Fury* picked up the survivors, then tried but failed to scuttle *Harpalion* with gunfire, leaving her on fire with the decks awash. Three hours later her abandoned wreck was located by *U-435*. The last of a spread of three G7a torpedoes fired at 15.35 struck aft, and *Harpalion* sank slowly by the stern at 15.50.

Four aircraft and a U-boat shadowed the convoy during the morning of 13 April. At noon *Eclipse* attacked the U-boat. Three attacks resulted in dark patches in the water but there are no records of any U-boat sunk on this date. *Z-7 Hermann Schoemann*, *Z-24*, and *Z-25* made another attempt to locate the convoy but were forced by the poor weather to suspend their search and return to port.

Six stragglers from PQ.14 joined QP.10 – *City of Joliet*, *Francis Scott Key*, *Ironclad*, *Minotaur*, *Mormacrio*, and *West Gotomska*. *Eclipse*, with damage to her hull, dropped astern to escort another straggler from PQ.14. *Sokrushitelny* and *Gremyaschiy* transferred from QP.10 to PQ.14 at 04.30.

The following day *Liverpool* and *Kent* departed, *Kent* to Scapa Flow arriving there on 20 April and *Liverpool* first to Seidisfjord to fuel on 19 April, then on to arrive at Scapa Flow 21 April.

Eleven merchant ships and six stragglers from PQ.14, escorted by *Oribi*, *Marne*, *Punjabi*, and *Fury* arrived in Reykjavik on 21 April. Four vessels had been sunk by enemy action and one had returned to Murmansk.

PQ.15 (10 April–5 May)

The main section of PQ.15, with nineteen merchant ships, sailed from Oban on 10 April for Reykjavik to be joined by another six waiting at Hvalfjord. PQ.15 then departed for Murmansk on 26 April with a very strong naval escort. Between 26 April and 5 May the western local escort comprised *Bramble*, *Leda*, *Seagull*, *Cape Palliser*, *Chiltern*, *Northern Pride*, and *Vizalma*, all of whom remained with the convoy throughout the voyage. The remainder of the close escort (*Somali*, *Matchless*, *Venomous*, *St Albans*, *Boadicea*, *Badsworth*, *Ulster Queen*, and *Sturgeon*) sailed from Seidisfjord to join the convoy at sea on 28 April, together with the fuelling force (Force Q – *Ledbury* and fleet oiler *Grey Ranger*). The ocean escort was also reinforced by *London* (30 April to 1 May) and *Nigeria* (30 April to 2 May). A heavy cover force – *King George V*, *Victorious*, *Kenya*, *Belvoir*, *Hursley*, *Inglefield*, *Lamerton*, *Martin*, *Middleton*, *Ledbury*, *Marne*, *Oribi*, and *Punjabi* sailed from Scapa Flow on 27/28 April to cruise south of the convoy route.

Since the strength of the Home Fleet had been depleted in order to find ships for the forthcoming invasion of Madagascar, the heavy cover force was reinforced between 4 April and 16 July 1942 by a number of USN warships. This was a significant development, being the first occasion on which United States Navy ships operated as part of the Home Fleet, and was particularly appropriate as fifteen of PQ.15's merchant ships were American and one Panamanian. The US Navy force under the command of Rear Admiral R. C. Giffen consisted of the battleship *Washington*, cruisers *Tuscaloosa* and *Wichita*, and destroyers *Madison*, *Plunkett*, *Wainwright*, and *Wilson*.[4] This was also the first convoy to be protected by a CAM (catapult aircraft merchant) ship, the *Empire Morn*.

Submarines protected both convoys. *Sturgeon* provided close submarine escort from 28 April until noon on 1 May when she left to join *Truant*, *Unison*, *Uredd* (Norwegian), *Minerve* (Free French), and *Jastrzab* (Polish), which were deployed off the Norwegian Coast from 28 April to provide cover against the German surface forces at Trondheim; and joined later by *Trident*, who accompanied PQ.15 as far as longitude 5° East.

On 28 April the destroyer escort of *Badsworth*, *Boadicea*, *Matchless*, *Somali*, *Venomous*, and the Norwegian *St Albans*, joined together with *Ulster Queen*. The convoy steamed north along the west coast of Iceland, across the Arctic Circle and on northeast towards Bear Island, then southeast around the north cape of Norway into the Barents Sea. The weather remained favourable, though almost twenty-four hours of daylight exposed the convoy to greater risk of attack. PQ.15 was detected and reported by enemy reconnaissance aircraft when approximately 250 nautical miles southwest of Bear Island and 200 miles northwest of Tromsø, but was not to become the focus of enemy attention for another two days, as the westbound QP.11 remained within close range of the air bases in northern Norway.

The convoy suffered its first air attack at around 20.00 on 30 April off the North Cape. An eyewitness on the American freighter SS *Mormacrey* described it:

> Only four planes attacked but it seemed like many more. Most of the action concentrated on the vulnerable corners of the convoy. One plane showed disdain for our defenses and flew low between our column and the adjacent column. This was the gun crew's first opportunity to fire in combat and it revealed how ineffective our fire power was. No planes were downed. Several bombs were dropped, but no hits were scored. As suddenly as the raid began, it ended.

Another eyewitness on the *Alco Cadet* recalled: 'First air attack. Dive-bombed and high-level bombing. Four bombs fell close to starboard side with minor damage.'

No ships were damaged. The merchant ships and escorts opened fire with every available gun, with the *Botavon* credited with shooting down an aircraft which crashed into the sea ahead of the convoy.

The convoy suffered a second attack[5] later that evening when six Ju.88s[6] appeared out of the fog flying at about 2,000 feet. In the limited visibility they were heard before they were seen but fortunately they were detected by

Nigeria's Type 281 radar, so all ships were at their first degree of readiness when the attack began. The CAM ship *Empire Morn* had her Hurricane fighter ready to launch but it was judged the scale of the attack did not justify its use.

As the approaching aircraft came under a controlled 4-inch anti-aircraft barrage from *Ulster Queen* and *Nigeria*, with spasmodic fire from the rest of the escort, their formation broke up. The planes manoeuvred individually around the convoy and made a number of high-level dive-bombing attacks (later described as a 'ragged and very poorly executed', possibly due to the intense cold) between the snow squalls. They attacked singly or in pairs and appeared to drop only single bombs as no *sticks* (ie, groups of two or more bombs) were seen. A few bombs fell near an armed trawler astern of the convoy. Half an hour later one Ju.88 came close to reaching an effective bombing position over the convoy. It attacked through the cloud from off the port bow of the *Ulster Queen*, then flew over the convoy at a height of about 800 yards. The Master of the *Southgate* reported seeing bombs drop near one escort, and three distinct flashes as they exploded. The escorts and *Southgate* opened fire causing the aircraft to bank away, descend dead ahead of the convoy, and crash into the sea. The Ju.88 received the full force of all the ships' close-range weapons, but it is not clear from the varying accounts which ship or ships should be credited with the result. The *London Gazette* despatch credits the kill to the *Southgate* which altered course slightly to avoid the aircraft wreckage, then passed close by but saw no survivors in the water. No merchant ships were damaged during this attack. The volume of AA fire put up by the escort and convoy was described by the Rear Admiral, 10th Cruiser Squadron, as 'impressive' and later credited as largely responsible for the fact that with the exception of the near miss, none of the attacks was 'pressed home'.

The first serious incident of the passage occurred just before 14.00 on 1 May. The distant cover force was cruising to the south of the convoy routes when, in poor visibility, the *King George V* travelling at a speed of 25 knots crashed into the destroyer *Punjabi*'s port side just aft of the engine room. The force of the impact sliced straight through the hull of the *Punjabi*. Her stern sank almost immediately and as it went down the ready-use depth charges stacked on the stern rails exploded, causing severe internal bruising to survivors in the water and the stern section to sink more rapidly.

The forward section remained afloat for forty minutes giving *Martin* and *Marne* sufficient time to go alongside and rescue five officers and 201 ratings. Unfortunately, many survivors were pulled from the sea unconscious due to the effects of the intense cold and could not be revived; a total of 49 were killed. The explosion also caused extensive damage to the hull and internal compartments of the *King George V* – unable to continue, she was relieved by the *Duke of York*.

After the attack, just before midnight on 1 May, Admiral Burrough signalled the Admiralty in London:

> The convoy has been under constant observation by enemy a/c who worked in relief by pairs. Attack by 6 JU. 88 developed at 22.17. No damage to convoy. A/C shot down.

The following day the Polish submarine *Jastrzab* (part of the cover force), a very long way from her designated patrol area, was accidentally attacked by *Seagull* and *St Albans* and forced to surface before being identified as 'friendly'. Badly damaged and unseaworthy, she was sunk by *Seagull* using her 4-inch gun after the crew were taken off. Seven of her crew of forty-two were killed outright or died of their wounds.

Shortly before midday the westbound QP.11 came in sight and as it moved away the enemy focus switched to PQ.15, the shadowers returned and radio transmissions were intercepted indicating a U-boat was reporting the convoy's position.

The convoy was attacked again at around midnight on 2/3 May by six He.111 torpedo bombers from I./KG 26. They flew in low on the convoy's starboard bow in 'line ahead' then turned to approach in formation at a height of about 50 feet, wing tip to wing tip, about 60° on the starboard bow of the convoy. When the sighting of the approaching aircraft was confirmed, *Ulster Queen* blew a long blast on her foghorn, hoisted the signal 'air attack imminent' and commenced a 4-inch gunfire barrage.

The Master of the freighter *Southgate* later reported:

> I saw 6 planes approaching the convoy on the starboard bow, five of which were flying in formation at an angle of 45 to 50 degrees and the sixth came in independently and flew along the starboard side of the convoy.
>
> The planes were flying low and appeared to be Ju.88s.

The two leading ships in the starboard column immediately opened fire with their guns causing two of the aircraft to turn away; the other stood on, one of them firing across the convoy in our direction.

Unfortunately, due to the *Ulster Queen*'s station between columns 3 and 4 of the convoy the 4-inch barrage could not be sustained at a low enough angle of fire and was checked almost at once when the firing arcs became badly obscured by the superstructures of two merchant ships.

As soon as they dropped their torpedoes the aircraft zoomed up clear of the ships, masking the anti-aircraft fire. One hit by the *Ulster Queen* passed a few hundred yards ahead of the ship and crashed in flames 200 yards on her port bow. Another, as it turned away to pass down the starboard side of the convoy, flew off emitting smoke and losing height but was not seen to crash. Although the *Ulster Queen* sighted only three aircraft, three more were positively sighted by observers on other ships with a better view.

On first sighting the aircraft the Convoy Commodore ordered the signal 'emergency turn' to starboard to be made. Unfortunately, before the manoeuvre could be completed, one torpedo struck his ship (the *Botavon*) on the starboard side forward and others in quick succession struck the *Jutland* and *Cape Corso*. This was initially taken to be a conventional bomb attack as there was no previous experience of torpedo attacks against the Arctic convoys. When interviewed later, the Master of the *Southgate* expressed surprise he had heard no bombs dropping and was considerably amazed when he saw the Commodore's and Vice Commodore's ships – *Botavon* and *Jutland* – suddenly swung right round to starboard and begin to sink, the *Botavon* by the bow and *Jutland* by the stern. He then spotted the wake of a torpedo that entered the port bow of the ship astern of the *Southgate*, the *Cape Corso*, and realized this must have been an aerial torpedo attack, though he had not actually seen any torpedoes launched. As the aircraft which torpedoed the *Cape Corso* flew low across the bows of the *Southgate* her gunners opened fire, shooting off the aircraft's port wing – it then burst into flames and crashed into the sea.

In his interview report, the Master of the *Cape Race* mentioned he had not seen the torpedo which hit the *Cape Corso* as it passed under the stern of his ship. He had been unable to take any avoiding action simply because there was no time to do so, the attack being over in minutes. He thought the aircraft might have dropped torpedoes in the hope of hitting any ship in the convoy rather than targeting one particular vessel. He recalled:

The *Cape Corso* went down in a few minutes, but the *Botavon* and *Jutland* sank more slowly. Also, with these two last merchant ships there was not the usual column of water thrown up when the torpedoes entered the ship's side.

The *Jutland* was carrying a cargo of 1,560 tons of military stores, including 500 tons of cordite and 300 tons of ammunition. Hit by one torpedo she settled lower in the water, but fortunately for the crew the warhead did not explode and the ship, although disabled, remained afloat. The Master, fifty-three crew and eight passengers abandoned ship and were quickly picked up by *Badsworth*; only one passenger was lost. The *Jutland*, although abandoned, remained afloat until at 02.14 on the 3rd she was found, torpedoed, and sunk by *U-251*. At 16.00 in the same area, *U-703* reported finding a large area of wreckage and salvaged a lifebelt marked 'JUTLAND – GLASGOW'.

The *Botavon* was the ship of the Convoy Commodore. When on sighting the approaching aircraft the Commodore ordered the emergency turn to starboard, the Master of the *Botavon* had also given the order 'hard to starboard' to bring his ship head on to the attacking aircraft, in an attempt to 'comb' (turn into the track of) the torpedoes. But before this manoeuvre could be completed he saw a torpedo coming towards his ship from the starboard bow. It appeared to circle in towards her, then struck amidships in the after end of no. 2 hold, just forward of the bridge. There was a very loud explosion with a large column of black water thrown up into the air. Although there was no flame, smoke or smell the crew on the bridge were showered with seawater and with lumps of coal thrown up from the ship's bunkers by the force of the explosion.

After the explosion the *Botavon* listed slightly to starboard and commenced to settle by the bow. The Chief Officer gave the order, 'Away to the boats, lads' and the confidential books were thrown overboard in a weighted box. The crew abandoned ship in four lifeboats and two liferafts. The ship's decks and rails were heavily covered in ice, which made the process of abandoning ship risky and illustrates just how severe weather conditions were at the time. By the time the Master left the forward well deck was only a foot above water. As the crew of the *Botavon* rowed away from their sinking ship, they saw the *Jutland* going down by the stern. In the noise and confusion of the attack they had not realized any other ships had been hit.

The Master's Admiralty Post-Convoy Interview Report gives the number of crew as seventy-three including Commodore Anchor, six naval staff, four naval gunners and two army gunners and states there were no casualties. This however appears incorrect as two engine room staff were subsequently recorded as lost. A further nineteen survivors being repatriated from North Russia onboard *Trinidad* were lost on 14 and 15 May, when she was attacked by Ju.88 bombers and severely damaged before being scuttled with three torpedoes by the destroyer *Matchless*.

The Master and crew of the *Botavon* were in their lifeboats for about half an hour before being picked up by *Badsworth*. *Cape Palliser* rescued the Commodore and his yeoman of signals. As the *Botavon* did not appear to be sinking very rapidly the Master and the Chief Officer of *Badsworth* agreed she should be sunk. *Badsworth* then fired six 4-inch HE rounds into the wreck, which still did not sink; she then moved closer in and fired a depth charge under the hull of the *Botavon* which finally sank at around 04.30.

The *Cape Corso* was the most unfortunate of the three merchant ships torpedoed. When the torpedo detonated, she blew up almost immediately in a single blinding flash. Those aboard the *Cape Palliser* described seeing the *Cape Corso*

> explode and disappear in a purple flash. All that was left afterwards was a mass of floating debris of deck cargo; everything else had gone to the bottom of the sea.

The Master, thirty-eight crew and eleven DEMS gunners were lost. Amazingly six survivors (who must have abandoned ship or been thrown clear immediately before their ship was attacked) were rescued from rafts by *Cape Palliser*.

It was established at a later date that the aircraft involved were He.111 H-6 torpedo bombers of the Luftwaffe's I *Gruppe*, Kampfgeschwader 21./KG 2. This was apparently the Luftwaffe's first ever successful aerial torpedo-bomber attack on an Arctic convoy. Of the six aircraft, two were shot down and one damaged.

PQ.15 was continuously shadowed all that day of 3 April and attacked again at around 21.00 in the evening. The weather was clear, the cloud base at about 500–1,000 feet when *Ulster Queen* spotted a formation of four Ju.88s and two reconnaissance aircraft approaching, flying low on the horizon at a range of about 7 miles on the starboard quarter. *Ulster Queen* sounded the usual alarms and opened up a controlled fire with her 4-inch guns, supported by *Badsworth*. The formation immediately split up to approach from different sectors, some aircraft using the cloud cover for concealment. This made it difficult for the observers to assess the number of aircraft taking part. At least two Ju.88s (later identified as from KG 30) were spotted, although up to four more were heard in the clouds above.

The combined fire from the *Ulster Queen* and *Badsworth* kept the enemy aircraft out of bombing range. One Ju.88 hit by the 4-inch barrage from *Ulster Queen* was seen to crash into the sea. The arrival of Russian fighter aircraft drove off the remainder. Official reports later suggested the attack was badly carried out and hampered by low cloud. No bombs fell near the convoy and attacks were only made on small escort vessels. The *Cape Palliser* was badly shaken by a near miss when dive-bombed by a Ju.88. Two bombs dropped, one falling directly into the ship's wake about 50 feet astern, while the shock wave from the second was felt throughout the ship, causing damage to the engine mountings and cracking the plummer block (pedestal supporting the mounting for the propeller shaft).

The convoy continued towards Bear Island. The escorts kept both the shadowers and U-boats at bay and no further air attacks took place. By the 5th however the weather had worsened and a southeast gale developed bringing heavy snow, conditions which fortunately provided the convoy with excellent protection for the remaining part of the passage. PQ.15 reached the Kola Inlet at 22:00 on 5 April without further loss.

At 2300/B[7] on the 5th, Senior Officer 1st Minesweeper Flotilla signalled the Admiralty:

PQ.15 arrived Murmansk. Regret to report loss of *Botavon*, *Jutland*, *Cape Corso* as a result of attack by six torpedo aircraft at 2327 May 2nd in position 73N, 19.40E. Attack carried out in good conditions and aircraft appeared to be led in well by leader who may not have carried torpedo. Indications that shadowing submarine may have surfaced and fired torpedoes at same time. One aircraft destroyed and possibly one other. 136 survivors including Commodore. Convoy bombed at 2230 May 3rd in position 73N, 31.51E. Minor damage from near miss to *Cape Palliser* only. One Junkers 88 shot down. Attack badly carried out and hampered by low cloud. Convoy continuously shadowed by one or more aircraft and or one or more U-boats to 36E. U-boats driven off successfully by screening force forcing them to dive and firing depth charges in vicinity.

The convoy was considered a success despite the difficult conditions. The long hours of daylight had exposed the convoy to air attack, but the poor weather provided some measure of protection and relief for the vulnerable merchant ships, deterring further attacks.

Two of the merchant ships' masters were later decorated for their skill and bravery. Captain Harry Austin of the *Southgate* and Captain John Henry Reardon Smith of the *Botavon* each received the OBE. The citation in the *London Gazette* on Tuesday, 27 October 1942 read:

> The ships formed part of an important North Russian convoy, which was subjected to very heavy enemy attacks. Both Masters showed consistent courage and devotion to duty throughout. They handled their ships with great skill and, in the course of a series of close and heavy air assaults, directed their armament to such good effect that they destroyed two enemy aircraft.

Both men also received the Lloyds War Medal for Bravery At Sea.

QP.11 (28 April–7 May)

Convoy QP.11 consisting of thirteen merchant ships and escort oiler, sailed from Murmansk at 14.00 on 28 April with its eastern local escort, *Kuibyshev*, *Sokrushitelny*, *Gossamer*, *Harrier*, *Hussar*, and *Niger* (28 to 29 April), which escorted the convoy for the first 300 miles then returned to Murmansk.

The ocean escort comprised *Amazon*, *Beagle*, *Beverley*, *Bulldog*, *Campanula*, *Oxlip*, *Saxifrage*, and *Snowflake*, and *Lord Middleton* (28 April to 7 May), augmented by *Foresight* and *Forester* (28 to 30 April). *Edinburgh* left Murmansk the following day carrying five tons of Russian gold bullion and joined on 30 April, sailing 15 miles ahead to fend off any attack by German destroyers. Distant cover was provided by *King George V*, *Duke of York*, *Victorious*, *Kenya*, *Belvoir*, *Escapade*, *Faulknor*, *Hursley*, *Inglefield*, *Lamerton*, *Marne*, *Martin*, *Middleton*, and *Oribi*.

The convoy was sighted and reported by a Ju.88 reconnaissance aircraft and a U-boat in the afternoon of 29 April, approximately 150 miles northeast of Vardoe, then shadowed and reported during the night.

In the afternoon of 30 April *Edinburgh*, having just joined the escort for QP.11, was attacked twice by *U-456* whilst taking position ahead of the main body. The initial attack failed but in the second two torpedoes struck her on the starboard side. The first hit amidships and the second blew away the stern structure including the rudder. Although *Edinburgh* was able to use her port propeller shafts, steering by engines was impracticable in the prevailing weather conditions. Little progress could be made. *Forester's* first attempt to tow the damaged cruiser failed when the rope broke. On *Forester's* second attempt *Edinburgh* took the *Foresight* in tow, enabling *Edinburgh* to steer a steady course.

The eastern local escort of *Harrier, Gossamer,* and *Niger,* which had returned to Murmansk, sailed together with the *Hussar, Gremyaschiy,* and *Sokrushitelny,* Russian guard ship *Rubin,* and tug to escort the *Edinburgh. Foresight* and *Forester* stayed with *Edinburgh* until the minesweepers arrived, when the Russian tug took over the tow.

U-456 and *U-589* shadowed the *Edinburgh* group and although the Kriegsmarine faced a fuel shortage the German Flag Officer Northern Waters despatched the destroyers, *Z-7 Hermann Schoemann, Z-24, and Z-25* from Kirkenes in the early hours of 1 May to attack the group.

Later that morning the convoy came under torpedo-bomber attack 150 miles east of Bear Island, but no ships were hit. U-boats were detected shadowing the convoy, but there were no attacks until 03.13, when *U-589* fired a spread of two torpedoes at the convoy and heard a detonation after five minutes. The victim was the Russian freighter *Tsiolkovsky,* damaged and later sunk as a straggler by *Z-24* and *Z-25. Lord Middleton* rescued fourteen survivors from *Tsiolkovsky's* crew of forty-nine.

The German destroyers made five attacks on the convoy during the day but were prevented from closing in on it by the skilful manoeuvring of the escort. After a series of actions lasting four hours, during the first of which *Amazon* was badly damaged, the German destroyers abandoned their attempt to attack the convoy and set off in pursuit of *Edinburgh.* In the meantime, the SOE had taken the merchant ships into the ice field, where they remained for seven or eight hours and where the German destroyers could not follow as their thin hulls would have been damaged by the ice.

The German destroyers located *Edinburgh* with her escort again on the morning of 2 May, in low visibility and extreme cold. They first attacked *Hussar,* the tow was immediately slipped and *Edinburgh,* unable to steer, circled slowly at about 8 knots.

Aggressive offensive action by the destroyers and minesweepers initially kept the German destroyers at bay and in the ensuing battle *Edinburgh* managed to hit and disable *Z-7 Hermann Schoemann,* while *Forester* and

Foresight engaged *Z-24* and *Z-25*. *Forester* was badly damaged in the exchange of fire. Torpedoes fired by *Z-24* at *Forester* missed, but one went on to strike and fatally damage *Edinburgh*, she being unable to take avoiding action. *Foresight*, the last effective destroyer, was then hit, badly damaged and stopped in the water. The German destroyers however broke off the action to rescue the crew and scuttle *Z-7*, before returning to Kirkenes. The surviving crew from *Edinburgh* were taken aboard *Harrier* and *Gossamer*, and *Foresight* was ordered to sink *Edinburgh* with her last torpedo.

The rest of QP.11's voyage saw unsuccessful attacks on the convoy by U-boats. The twelve remaining merchant ships arrived in Iceland on 7 May.

PQ.16/QP.12

PQ. 16 (21 May–1 June)

The thirty-five merchant ships of PQ.16 sailed from Reykjavik for North Russia at 01.00 on 21 May with the western local escort, *Hazard* (to 31 May), *St Elstan* and *Lady Madeleine* (to 24 May), *Retriever* (returned to port, unable to keep up), and *Northern Spray* (to 25 May). At that time of year there was no darkness and all the ships could be clearly seen in their respective stations making good speed in ideal sailing conditions, although the temperature was dropping, the sea temperature having fallen to 36°F. The perpetual daylight of the Arctic summer made it easier to spot and deter U-boat attacks, but equally left the convoy more exposed to aerial detection and bombing.

The ocean escort assembled at Seidisfjord and joined on 23 May. It comprised *Ashanti* (Senior Officer) and *Martin* (all from Home Fleet), ORP *Garland* (British ship transferred to Poland in 1940), *Achates*, *Volunteer*, with *Honeysuckle*, *Roselys*, *Starwort*, and *Hyderabad*, from the Western Approaches Command (all to 30 May), the anti-aircraft ship *Alynbank* (to 31 May), and submarines *Trident* and *Seawolf*. In addition, a fuelling force, Force Q (the destroyer *Ledbury* and fleet oiler *Black Ranger*) was provided to support the escorts of both PQ.16 and the returning QP.12.

Due to the ongoing perceived threat from German surface vessels, PQ.16 and QP.12 were protected by a cruiser cover force and a distant cover force. The cruiser cover force under Rear Admiral Commanding, Tenth Cruiser Squadron, comprising *Nigeria*, *Kent*, *Liverpool*, and *Norfolk*, escorted by *Onslow*, *Oribi*, and *Marne*, left Hvalfjord on 22 May to escort PQ.16 (23 to 26 May) with orders not to proceed east of 12° E unless it could ensure contact with heavy enemy forces.

The distant cover force, battleships *Duke of York* (Commander-in-Chief) and *Washington* (Commander, Task Force 99), aircraft carrier *Victorious*, cruisers *Wichita* and *London*, destroyers *Faulknor* (D8), *Intrepid*, *Icarus*, *Eclipse*, *Fury*, *Blankney*, *Lamerton*, *Middleton*, and *Wheatland*, left Hvalfjord early on 23 May to cover PQ.16. The destroyers USS *Wainwright*, *Mayrant*, *Rhind*, and *Rowan*, had already arrived at Seidisfjord to fuel and when they had joined the Battlefleet the *Faulknor*, *Intrepid*, *Fury*, *Icarus*, and *Eclipse* detached on 24 May to top up, rejoining the fleet later the same day. *Middleton*, *Lamerton*, *Wheatland*, and *Blankney* then left in turn for Seidisfjord. The escort was supported by a fuelling force, Force Q (RFA *Black Ranger* with *Ledbury*), which left Seidisfjord to join the escort of PQ.16 early on 23 May. Five submarines were on patrol to the south of the convoy, in addition to the two who sailed with PQ.16.

As an additional protective measure, all the merchant ships of PQ.16 carried barrage balloons for anti-aircraft defence. An additional degree of anti-submarine protection as far as longitude 10°E was provided by four flying-boats from Iceland; and SBNO North Russia was authorized to adjust the sailing time of QP.12 by up to twenty-four hours either way to take advantage of weather unsuitable for German air reconnaissance. The Russians promised to cover the passage of these convoys with a large-scale offensive by 200 Army bombers on the aerodromes of northern Norway, but in the event were only able to deliver one small attack, which took place after the enemy's main attacks on the convoy had been completed. Owing to the evident inability of the Russians previously to ensure air cooperation in the Barents Sea, C-in-C Home Fleet had requested RAF reconnaissance and long-range fighter aircraft be stationed in North Russia to provide the convoys, during the worst part of their passage, with anti-submarine patrols, fighter protection and reconnaissance against surface attack. Unfortunately, the number of aircraft in Coastal Command was insufficient to meet any of these requirements and the convoys had to continue on their hazardous passage with virtually no air protection.

The convoy suddenly ran into a very thick fog at midnight on 23/24 May but the speed of the merchant ships continued unaltered. The destroyers had considerable difficulty in locating the convoy, now divided into two sections in the fog, and the convoy was unable to reform and proceed under escort until 00.30 on 25 May.

At 05.35 the cruiser cover force reached a position halfway between convoys PQ.16 and QP.12, then turned west to join PQ.16. The cruisers, formed up in two divisions, sailed between columns 5, 6, and 7 respectively of the convoy formation whilst the destroyers reinforced the escort screen.

The Luftwaffe planned several aerial reconnaissance sorties to locate the convoy. Protected by persistent banks of cloud and fog, however, it was not sighted until 06.30 on 25 May when it was spotted by an FW 200, 120 miles east of Jan Mayen Island, and also probably reported by a U-boat. For the next five days the convoy would be continuously shadowed.

At 13.45 PQ.16 passed the westbound QP.12 and came within range of the Luftwaffe aircraft based in northern Norway. Soon afterwards an air battle would begin and last throughout virtually the whole of the rest of the passage. The presence of U-boats was detected at 15.00. *Martin* reported sighting a surfaced U-boat 7 miles on the starboard bow of the convoy and carried out an attack, but the U-boat crash-dived. No enemy attacks took place for twelve hours.

That evening in the continuing daylight, at around 20.35, the first air attacks developed when seven He.111 torpedo bombers of KG 26 and six Ju.88 dive-bombers of III./KG 30 carried out alternate sorties. Bombs were dropped close to a number of merchant ships including the *American Robin*, *City of Joliet*, and *Michigan*. Near misses also damaged two merchant ships but no torpedoes found their intended targets. The *Empire Lawrence* launched her Hurricane fighter, which set one He.111 on fire and severely damaged another before it was unfortunately shot down by the over-enthusiastic gunners on the American freighter *Carlton* and crash landed in the sea. The wounded Hurricane pilot bailed out and was picked up by *Volunteer*. Two Ju.88s were shot down. The only damage to merchant ships was a fractured steam pipe, ironically in the *Carlton* – the result of a near miss. She was subsequently detached to return to Iceland towed by *Northern Spray*.

The anti-submarine escort chased off the U-boats, and the cruisers' anti-aircraft fire held off the air attacks, succeeding in destroying some enemy aircraft. Later the convoy passed through drifting ice, which further deterred the U-boats. The day closed with an ineffectual attack carried out by twelve Ju.88s between 23.15 and 23.30.

All attacks on 25 May had been repulsed but just after 03.00 the next morning, about 200 miles southwest of Bear Island, the freighter *Syros* was hit on the port side by two torpedoes from *U-703*. The first struck the *Syros* abreast of her funnel in the engine room; the second hit at the no. 2 hold, causing the ammunition in the cargo to explode. The *Syros* broke in two and sank in just over a minute. The eight officers, thirty crew and two USN armed guards were unable to take to the lifeboats as both those on the port side had been destroyed by the explosions and the others could not be launched in time. The survivors abandoned ship in three liferafts or jumped overboard and clung to wreckage until picked up by *Hazard* and *Lady Madeleine*, to be landed later at Murmansk. Two died of exposure and were buried at sea. The Master, two officers, eight crewmen, and one armed guard were lost.

By 27 May the convoy was sailing even closer to the German airfields in Norway; the weather was fine and clear with thin layers of cloud to conceal aircraft from sight. The first air attack of the day in the early hours of the morning was carried out by a number of dive-bombers. Two flew in low and dropped several bombs, which missed the merchant ships and fell into the sea. Neither dive-bomber appeared to be hit by the heavy anti-aircraft fire and no merchant ships were damaged. The convoy's course was then altered towards the southeast for a couple of hours to avoid heavy pack ice. A second series of air attacks began at 10.30, when the convoy was approximately 100 miles southeast of Bear Island, and continued intermittently throughout the day. The first casualty occurred during the second attack at 13.10, when the American freighter *Alamar* suffered a bomb strike at the after end of no. 4 hold on her port side. Her deck cargo of high-test gasoline immediately caught fire and she began to settle rapidly in the water. The crew of eight officers, twenty-eight men and nine armed guards abandoned ship after thirty minutes and were picked up from their lifeboats by *Starwort*, *St Elstan*, and *Trident*. The latter was ordered to sink the disabled ship and did so with two torpedoes (for one hit) at 14.19.

Five minutes after the attack on the *Alamar*, the American freighter *Mormacsul* was attacked by seven dive-bombers with four bombs dropped from 5,000 feet. Two near misses ruptured the hull, killing the one officer and two crew on watch below, while a third bomb hit the ship on the port side. The surviving ten officers and twenty-nine crew, along with nine armed guards, abandoned ship in three lifeboats and three liferafts. One of the lifeboats capsized but *Starwort* and *St Elstan* rescued forty-five survivors thirty minutes after they abandoned ship. Both merchant ships sank approximately 250 miles due west of the North Cape and 50 miles south of Bear Island. During the attack the freighter *American Robin* was straddled by seven bombs and the *Mauna Kea* shaken by several near misses.

At 14.20 the CAM ship *Empire Lawrence* was targeted by a formation of six Ju.88s which approached from astern. Hit by one bomb in her no. 2 hold *Empire Lawrence* pulled out of her place in the convoy. As the Master sounded the emergency alarm to signal 'abandon ship' she listed heavily to port and began to sink. With the port lifeboats jammed in the davits or blown away by the explosions the crew made for the lifeboats and rafts on the starboard side. As they were doing so and as *Lady Madeleine* approached to take them off if necessary, three dive-bombers attacked from astern. Eyewitness accounts describe four or five bombs falling, followed by the ship splitting into three parts and sinking. The crew of the *Lady Madeleine* heard the bombs dropping but were unable to move their ship away from the scene. The resulting explosions covered the trawler with falling wreckage and enveloped her in suffocating brown smoke, but fortunately no damage was done. There were also reports one aircraft might have crashed onto the foredeck of the *Empire Lawrence*.

In the general noise and confusion, the crew of *Lady Madeleine* initially thought their own ship had been hit. When minutes later the smoke cleared away there was no sign of the *Empire Lawrence*. As *Lady Madeleine* circled to pick up the sixteen survivors she was heavily attacked with bombs and machine-gun fire. (There are some dramatic accounts that describe an enormous explosion and machine-gunning of survivors in the water, but had this been true the *Lady Madeleine* and her entire crew could not have survived.) A number of survivors were also picked up by one of *Lady Madeleine*'s sea boats and transferred to *Hyderabad*, just arrived on the scene. Twelve of the crew of the *Empire Lawrence* and three DEMS gunners were lost.[8] It was later concluded that at least three of the six bombs aimed at the *Empire Lawrence* must have been direct vertical hits, which had passed through the holds and penetrated the bottom of her hull.

Bombs also struck the Russian ship *Stari Bolshevik* on the foredeck, setting drums of paint and oil on fire; flames leapt high into the air and great clouds of smoke rolled out. It took thirty-six hours for the crew to extinguish the fire with water and steam. Near misses during the midday attacks damaged the *Empire Baffin*, ORP *Garland*, and *City of Joliet*. *Empire Baffin* suffered from several near misses – her propeller, driveshaft and bearings were damaged, and she developed a leak in her stern gland. The chief engineer spent three days and nights in the shaft tunnel tending to the bearings. She was successfully repaired and returned to service. *City of Joliet* was badly damaged when a near miss off the starboard side sprang her hull plates. The pumps were unable to cope with the resultant flooding and the crew eventually abandoned ship at 05.40 the following day. In two lifeboats, the crew were later picked up by *St Elstan* and *Roselys* and taken to Murmansk.

The CO of the escort subsequently wrote:

> Great courage and determination was shown by the smaller escort vessels in rescuing survivors from the ships sunk, though subjected to deliberate heavy dive-bombing while doing so.

Soon after these attacks the ice conditions allowed for a more northerly course and at 14.35 the SOE ordered the convoy to steer 060°, as there appeared to be more cloud in that direction and he hoped the increased distance from the enemy's airfields might reduce the possibility of air attacks next day. Attacks continued that day, however – the next at 15.25, by seventeen Ju.88s carried out in bright sunshine, clear blue sky and perfect visibility was fortunately ineffective and no ships were hit, although the *Massmar* was 'near missed'.

A second attack followed almost immediately, carried out by an estimated eight torpedo bombers. The *Lowther Castle* was torpedoed and sunk by an HE.111 of I./KG 26,[9] and the Convoy Commodore's ship, the *Ocean Voice*, received a direct hit that set her on fire and tore away 20 feet of her steel plating abreast of no. 1 hold to within a couple of feet of the water line. Fortunately, the sea remained calm and she was able to continue to her destination.

Commenting later on these events, the SOE, Commander Onslow wrote:

> I had little hope of her survival [commenting on the *Stari Bolshevik*], but this gallant ship maintained her station, fought her fire, and with God's help arrived at her destination. … The escort's stocks of ammunition were beginning to run low; yet there were three more days, and twenty-four-hour days, too, to be endured. … We were all inspired by the parade-ground rigidity of the convoy's station-keeping, including the *Ocean Voice* and the *Stari Bolshevik*, who were both billowing smoke from their foreholds.

During the rest of the afternoon there was a lull in the action except for one ineffective attack by eight Ju.88s, which approached the convoy from the starboard beam at 19.00 but then sheered off to circle astern without dropping any torpedoes. Forty-five minutes later heavy dive-bombing recommenced, accompanied by attacks by the torpedo bombers. The *Empire Purcell*, on her maiden voyage, was hit in the no. 2 hold by a pair of bombs. The resultant explosion set her on fire, while two near misses exploded alongside. Hatches and beams were blown into the air, the bunker bulkhead collapsed, and an avalanche of coal ran into the stoke hold. Water was already flooding the engine room through fractured ship's side valves and the duty engineers stopped the main engines. Aware the cargo of ammunition might explode at any moment the Master ordered the crew to abandon ship. However, the cold had stiffened the ropes so the falls on one lifeboat ran slack, dropping the lifeboat and throwing its occupants into the numbingly cold sea. Six men lost their lives in this incident and two more died in the confusion. The Master and three of his officers succeeded in lowering the remaining lifeboat and pulling clear before the *Empire Purcell* blew up with a stunning explosion, and *Hyderabad* and *St Elstan* rescued the survivors despite deliberate bombing attacks. The five men trapped under the capsized lifeboat were all rescued, one after another, by Able Seaman William Thompson.

For his most gallant action William Thompson was later awarded the George Medal. The citation in the *Supplement to the London Gazette*, 6 October 1942, read:

> When the ship was sunk the port forward lifeboat, after being lowered, capsized, taking with it Thompson and five other men. Thompson extricated himself and then, despite the extreme cold of the water, repeatedly dived under the boat until he had got all the others. He managed to get them on the boat's keel, and later they were picked up.

At 20.20 *Trident* went alongside the *Empire Purcell* but the salvage attempt had to be abandoned following fresh air attacks. The *Empire Purcell* was left on fire and is believed to have sunk shortly after.

There were no further attacks that day as heavy cloud after 22.00 screened the merchant ships from further attacks, but two BV.138 floatplanes were seen continuously circling the convoy. The outlook appeared grim; five merchant ships had been lost, the *City of Joliet* left sinking by the bows and *Ocean Voice* not expected to remain afloat much longer. The badly damaged

Polish destroyer *Garland* was detached to make her own way at high speed to Murmansk where she arrived on 29 May.[10]

The anti-aircraft ship *Alynbank* recorded attacks by 108 aircraft and 120 explosions of sticks of bombs or torpedoes during the day. The dive-bombing attacks were described as pressed well home from broken cloud at 3,000 feet, the aircraft assisted by an intermittent filmy haze at an altitude of about 1,500 feet which made them very difficult to spot. The He.111s circled the convoy in groups, keeping out of gun range, while the Ju.88s climbed high above the convoy to hide above the broken cloud.

More attacks followed, but no more losses were suffered. During the evening of 29 May the eastern local escort of *Bramble*, *Leda*, *Seagull*, *Niger*, *Hussar*, and *Gossamer* joined the convoy. The convoy split up later that night. Six merchant ships escorted by the minesweepers, with *Alynbank* and *Martin*, were diverted to Archangel (which had just become ice free) in order to ease the load on Murmansk's bomb-damaged facilities, to which the main body now headed. There was a final air attack while the two convoys were still in sight of each other, but no damage to either group of ships.

The Murmansk section of twenty-two merchant ships, escorted by *Ashanti*, *Achates*, *Volunteer*, *Honeysuckle*, *Starwort*, *Hyderabad*, *Roselys*, *Trident*, *Seawolf*, *Hazard*, *St. Elstan*, and *Lady Madeleine* and three Russian destroyers arrived at Murmansk on 30 May. The eastern local escort of *Bramble*, *Leda*, *Seagull*, and *Gossamer*, together with *Martin*, arrived the following day and *Alynbank* and six merchant ships arrived at Archangel on 1 June.

Twenty-seven of the thirty-five merchant ships in the convoy succeeded in reaching port, one returned, and seven were sunk. The American freighter *Steel Worker* was sunk on 3 June during a bombing raid on the harbour at Murmansk.

At 0254/B on 31 May the First Sea Lord, Sir Dudley Pound, signalled C-in-C Fleet and AOC Coastal Command:

> We congratulate all concerned on their magnificent exploit in fighting convoy P.Q. 16 through to North Russia in the face of all the enemy could do in the air, and at sea.
>
> Request this may be passed to the Commodore, Officers and men of the allied merchant navies and allied forces concerned.

The long hours of daylight had robbed the U-boats of their tactical advantage. Only one of the seven ships sunk – the *Syros* – was accounted for by a U-boat

(*U-703*) while the aggressive anti-submarine tactics of the escort resulted in a number of U-boats receiving varying degrees of depth-charge damage.

QP.12 (21–29 May)

Convoy QP.12 consisting of fifteen merchant ships including a fleet oiler, sailed from the Kola Inlet at 19.30 on 21 May, escorted by the local eastern escort – *Bramble, Leda, Seagull, Gossamer, Grozny,* and *Sokrushitelny* (21 to 23 May) as far as 30° East. The cruiser cover force and distant cover force were the same as for PQ.16. One merchant ship, the *Hegira*, returned to Murmansk on 23 May with engine defects. The Russian merchant ship *Kuzbass* also returned, date and reasons not known. Both ships sailed again with QP.13.

The ocean escort, *Inglefield, Escapade, Boadicea, Venomous, St Albans, Badsworth, Ulster Queen, Harrier, Northern Wave, Northern Pride, Vizalma,* and *Cape Palliser,* joined on 26 May. The cruiser cover force *Nigeria* (CS.10), *Liverpool, Norfolk, Kent, Onslow* (D17), *Icarus,* and *Marne,* also joined the same day together with Force Q and covered QP.12 until 28 May when *Kent* proceeded to Hvalfjord and the remaining ships to Scapa Flow, all arriving 29 May. After oiling QP.12's destroyer escorts, Force Q was detached on the 27th to Scapa Flow, but later diverted to Sullom Voe where it arrived on 30 May, going on to Scapa Flow the following day.

Enemy aircraft and U-boats reported QP.12 on 25 May but in the event there were no attacks, German attention being focused on PQ.16. However, *Empire Morn*'s Hurricane pilot was killed when his parachute failed to open as he ditched alongside the convoy, after having shot down a shadower.

On 27 May *Venomous, Badsworth, Ulster Queen,* and three merchant ships detached and proceeded direct to the Clyde where they arrived on 30 May, *Ulster Queen* continuing on to Belfast the same day. The main body of QP.12 arrived at Hvalfjord on 28 May. Although the convoy had been shadowed by both aircraft and by U-boats no attacks developed and after a comparatively uneventful passage the fifteen merchant ships of QP.12 arrived intact at Reykjavik on 29 May.

Of the fifty merchant ships in PQ.16 and QP.12 which set out on the double journey, only seven were lost. 'This success was beyond expectation', wrote Admiral Tovey, who gave high praise to the officers and men of both escorts and merchant ships. Admiral Dönitz himself paid tribute to the work of the Allied escorts and admitted his favourite weapon (the U-boat) had failed him. The Luftwaffe had, with great exaggeration, claimed that the convoy was totally destroyed. This misled Dönitz into recommending aircraft rather than U-boats should be used against the summer convoys. The Commander of *Onslow* urged many more CAM ships, or an escort carrier and more anti-aircraft ships be included in the escort of future convoys. It was recognized, in face of the air strength now deployed by the enemy in north Norway, that anti-aircraft defence against surface attack must take equal status with anti-submarine measures.

PQ.17 (27 June–24 July)

PQ.17, comprising thirty-four merchant ships together with Force Q (escort oiler RFA *Grey Ranger* and destroyer *Douglas* to 2 July), and the rescue ship *Zaafaran*, sailed from Hvalfjord on 27 June, escorted by *Halcyon*, *Britomart*, *Salamander*, *Lord Middleton*, *Lord Austin*, *Ayrshire*, *Northern Gem*, and submarine *P.615*. The close escort was reinforced on the 30th by *Palomares*, *Pozarica*, *Keppel*, *Leamington*, *Wilton*, *Ledbury*, *Fury*, *Offa*, *Lotus*, *Poppy*, *La Malouine*, *Dianella*, submarine *P.614* and the rescue ships *Rathlin* and *Zamalek* from Seidisfjord.

A cruiser cover force comprising *London* and *Norfolk*, American cruisers *Wichita* and *Tuscaloosa*, with destroyers HMS *Somali* and USS *Rowan* and *Wainwright*, protected the convoy between 2 and 4 July. Heavy cover against any sortie by the German heavy surface ships was provided by the battleship *Duke of York*, American battleship *Washington*, aircraft carrier *Victorious*, the cruisers *Nigeria* and *Cumberland*, with destroyers *Faulknor*, *Onslaught*, *Middleton*, *Escapade*, *Blankney*, *Martin*, *Marne*, and *Wheatland*.

Shortly after leaving Iceland the *Richard Bland* ran aground and turned back. Part of the convoy ran into drifting ice in the Denmark Strait on 29 June. Four merchant ships were damaged and one, the *Exford*, returned to Iceland. The *West Gotomska* and RFA *Grey Ranger* both suffering defects also returned. The convoy, now reduced to thirty-three merchant ships, was re-routed further north to keep at a greater distance from the enemy air bases in north Norway.

On 1 July, following news that the port of Murmansk had been damaged by heavy bombing the previous day, the convoy's destination was switched to Archangel. During that morning, shortly after the convoy entered the open sea, PQ.17 was sighted and reported by *U-456*. PQ.17 and QP.13 then passed each other shortly after noon. After PQ.17 was sighted and reported it was shadowed almost continuously by enemy aircraft and U-boats. An initial air attack by torpedo-bombers in the evening of 2 July was unsuccessful.

The first successful air attacks on PQ.17, executed by a number of He.115s from KG 906, began at 03.15 on 4 July about 35 miles northeast of Bear Island. One torpedo dropped at about 800 yards range passed between the American freighters *Carlton* and *Samuel Chase*, and went on to strike the American freighter *Christopher Newport*, amidships on the starboard side. The resulting explosion tore a large hole in the hull and flooded the engine room, killing three of the crew on watch below and destroying the steering gear. The freighter continued veering to port, crossed the bows of ships in two other columns, then headed off in the opposite direction before coming to a halt. Seven officers, twenty-nine crew and eleven armed guards abandoned ship in the two port lifeboats, the starboard lifeboats having been destroyed. *Britomart*, sent to investigate whether the ship could be saved, reported the engine room and stokehold flooded. *Zamalek* picked up the survivors within fifteen minutes. An attempt by *P.614* to sink the *Christopher Newport* failed and she remained afloat; a later attack by *U-906* was also unsuccessful. At 08.08 *U-457* found and sank the abandoned ship.

Despite clear weather the next attacks did not develop until around 18.30, when the convoy was some 800 miles northwest of Archangel. The first by Ju.88 bombers from KG 30 was unsuccessful. The second at around 20.15 was carried out by twenty-five He.111s of I./KG 26. Although every ship in the convoy opened fire, the aircraft pressed home their attack. Torpedoes dropped by the leading He.111 bounced on impact with the surface, disappeared, then a few seconds later hit the *Navarino*, which was immediately engulfed in smoke as one torpedo struck amidships under her bridge on the starboard side. The resultant explosion, though described as not very loud, generated a great deal of water with all the (coal) bunkers thrown into the air and every window in the wheelhouse and bridge shattered. The *Navarino* listed to 40° and the keel rose out of the water on the starboard side as water flooded no. 3 hold. The engine room telegraph jammed and the *Navarino* veered sharply to port. Two lifeboats hastily lowered capsized. The starboard lifeboat got away with most of the crew. The Master, left on board with four gunners and an ordinary seaman, returned to the port lifeboat as the ship was righting herself and managed with great difficulty to lower it into the water. *Britomart* later sank the abandoned hulk of the *Navarino*. *Rathlin* and *Zamalek* picked up the Master and crew.

The following wave of He.111s attacked the *William Hooper*, which was carrying 8,486 tons of military stores, including trucks, ammunition and tanks as deck cargo. She was hit on the starboard side in the engine room by one of two torpedoes. The subsequent explosion blew engine parts and debris through the funnel and the engine room skylight, killed three crew on watch below and set fire to the settling tank. Seven of the complement of eight officers, thirty-four crew and sixteen armed guards panicked and jumped overboard, followed by the remaining crew who abandoned ship in three lifeboats and two liferafts. Forty-four survivors were picked up forty minutes later by *Rathlin*, and eleven by *Zamalek*. An attempt an hour later by *Halcyon* to sink the hulk by gunfire was unsuccessful and she remained afloat. The *William Hooper* was found at 23.00 by *U-334* whose first attempt at a *coup de grâce* was with a torpedo that failed to function, while a second a few minutes later missed. The U-boat then shelled and sank the wreck with gunfire.

Aerial torpedoes also damaged the Russian tanker *Azerbaijan*, whose female crew particularly distinguished themselves in their response to the attack. The *Azerbaijan* was transporting linseed oil to Archangel when targeted by dive-bombers and torpedo bombers – she was heavily damaged and her cargo caught fire. In the immediate aftermath lifeboats were lowered and some crew abandoned the ship, which soon became engulfed in smoke, with those remaining onboard tackling the fires. When they realized that the ship was not sinking, the occupants of the lifeboats were recalled to help extinguish the flames. Although it was thought the ship would become a total loss she eventually caught up, returned to her station in the convoy, and arrived at Archangel òn 24 July.

The air attack was over by 20.25. Apart from the *William Hooper* and *Navarino*, only the *Azerbaijan* in the centre of the convoy astern of the *River Afton* had been torpedoed. The SOE later commented that the Russian tanker was found to be 'holed but happy and capable of 9 knots'. She eventually reached port. The convoy and escort defended themselves and each other with splendid discipline, and with good results. All felt 'provided the ammunition lasted, PQ.17 could get anywhere'. Four enemy aircraft were shot down during this attack.

That evening of 4 July, at about the time PQ.17 was repelling the torpedo-bomber attack, the First Sea Lord called a staff meeting at the Admiralty in London to discuss the perceived threat to the convoy from the *Tirpitz*, now known to have joined the *Scheer* in Altenfjord. He calculated, on the basis of the available information and the assumption the heavy ships were at sea, a surface ship attack on the convoy could occur any time after 02.00 the following morning. It seemed to the naval staff this outcome could only result in the cruisers, convoy and close escort being overwhelmed. On the other hand, the convoy still had 800 miles to run, and enemy aircraft and U-boats would find things much easier for them if the convoy dispersed. The risk of surface attack was held to be the greater of the two dangers. Although the latest intelligence assessment concluded *Tirpitz* had not sailed from Altenfjord, the First Sea Lord sent a signal at 21.11 (without consulting C-in-C Home Fleet, who was supposed to exercise direct operational control), ordering Rear Admiral Commanding, 1st Cruiser Squadron (CS1) to 'withdraw to the westward at high speed'. This was followed 12 minutes later by a further signal prefixed, 'Immediate' to CS1, which read: 'Owing to threat of surface ships convoy is to disperse and proceed to Russian ports.' At 21.36 came a further signal: 'Most Immediate. My 21.23 of the 4th, Convoy is to scatter.' This last was taken by the recipients to indicate an attack by *Tirpitz* was imminent. The merchant ships were immediately ordered to scatter, the escorting destroyers to join the cruiser cover force and the rest of the escort to proceed independently to North Russia.

With the majority of the escorts now ordered to return to Scapa Flow, only the close escort of anti-aircraft auxiliaries, corvettes, minesweepers and armed trawlers was left to protect the scattered merchant ships. The rescue ship *Zaafaran*'s medical officer, who had been on deck dealing with eight Russian survivors when the Admiralty signal came ordering PQ17 to scatter due to the imminent arrival of German heavy surface craft, recalled:

> As our ship was 4 miles astern after picking up survivors, we had an excellent view of the situation. The signal to scatter had been received about half an hour previously. To port and ahead, the merchant ships were spreading out fan-wise, full steam ahead and belching smoke. To starboard, the destroyers were in line ahead and disappearing at top speed. On either beam was a sinking ship, and astern could be seen the wreckage of two enemy aircraft. The smoke of the battle was drifting away over the quarter.

At 23.00 the *Palomares*, now senior escort vessel, signalled the escorts: 'Scatter and proceed independently.' Sometime later her Chief Officer realized this left the *Palomares* as denuded of anti-submarine protection as the merchant ships. *Britomart* seven miles to the north was then signalled to 'Close' and 10 minutes later instructed, 'Take station on my Port beam, one mile. Course 077°, 11½ knots.' Soon after, *Palomares* ordered *Halcyon* to take station on her other beam. *Britomart's* CO later observed:

> It seemed wrong my anti-submarine minesweeper was being used only to escort a heavily armed anti-aircraft ship. But the CO of the *Palomares* seemed more concerned with the safe passage of his ship than the merchant ships. The anti-submarine vessels were of course afforded excellent AA protection in this way.

In the afternoon of 4 July the *Empire Byron*, a new Liberty ship on only her second voyage, carrying 2,455 tons of military stores, 6 vehicles, 30 tanks and 15 aircraft, had been torpedoed and damaged by an He.111 of II./KG 26. Now a straggler, she was attacked again at 07.15 on 5 July, this time by *U-703* which launched two torpedoes at a range of two miles. The target speed was misjudged and both torpedoes missed, as did a second salvo. Around one hour later *U-703* fired a fifth torpedo which hit the *Empire Byron* in the engine room and the crew began to abandon ship. Twenty minutes after the attack the ship's boiler exploded, tearing a gaping hole in the hull, and the *Empire Byron* sank within minutes. Three crew, six DEMS gunners and one passenger were lost. The Master, forty-two crew, twelve DEMS gunners and six passengers were picked up by *Dianella* and landed at Archangel on 16 July.

The American freighter *Carlton*, carrying a cargo of 5,500 tons of tanks, TNT, ammunition, fuel, and food was the next victim. The *Carlton* had been spotted by *U-88* at around 07.00 and pursued for three hours before the U-boat fired a torpedo, which struck the ship but did not detonate. At 10.15 a second missile struck the starboard side amidships, entered a tank containing 5,000 barrels of Navy special fuel oil and ignited the cargo. The resultant blast collapsed the forward boiler room bulkhead and after bulkhead of no. 2 hold. The two starboard lifeboats were destroyed, and no. 3 hatch cover blown away, dispersing the cargo of flour from the hold all over the deck. The burning wreck of the *Carlton* sank on even keel by the bow in ten minutes. Two men on watch in the engine room were killed. The remainder of the complement of eight officers, twenty-six crew and eleven armed guards abandoned ship in one lifeboat and four liferafts later lashed together. Ten hours after the attack German seaplanes landed near the survivors and took eighteen crewmen, and eight armed guards prisoner. (By 17 July all had been transferred to Milag Nord, the merchant marine POW camp near Bremen.) On the 9th, a British aircraft dropped food for the remaining fourteen crew and three armed guards. At 19.30 on the 13th *U-376* appeared, offered the men medical assistance which they declined and supplied details of their position, plus a compass, charts, biscuits, water, blankets, and cigarettes. Nineteen days after the attack the survivors made landfall at Tufjord, Norway near the North Cape. The first assistant engineer had already died of exposure and the remaining sixteen survivors were now captured by the Germans and arrived at Milag Nord on 27 August.

The survivors of the *Carlton* subsequently provided their German captors with valuable information on the convoy and cargos carried by the merchant ships, giving them a propaganda coup. Twenty-seven were later repatriated, arriving in New York aboard the Swedish motor passenger ship *Gripsholm* on 21 February 1945. The others remained at Milag Nord until after the end of hostilities.

The next casualty an hour later that day (5 July) was the *Peter Kerr* which, after the convoy dispersed, proceeded in company with the *Earlston*. At about 13.00 lookouts on the *Peter Kerr* spotted seven torpedo bombers and five dive-bombers approaching from the southeast. The *Peter Kerr* by altering course, using speed and a zigzag path, at first successfully avoided the torpedoes. During the following two hours the aircraft dropped thirteen torpedoes before the attacks ended. Four Ju.88 dive-bombers then appeared from the southeast and commenced an assault from about 4,000 feet. Around thirty bombs were dropped. Three hit the ship and set fire to no. 3 hold, the radio room, and deck cargo. The force of the explosions destroyed the steering gear as well as instruments and steam lines on the bridge. The *Peter Kerr* began to flood after the hull was damaged by a near miss off the port bow. The Master secured the engines five minutes after the first hit. Bombs struck at the no. 5 and no. 6 hatches and set fire to the cargo in the holds. The crew abandoned ship in two lifeboats, where they remained for seven days before they were rescued by a Russian patrol boat and taken to Murmansk. The *Peter Kerr* burned for eleven hours after the final attack, then exploded and sank.

About ninety minutes later the American freighter *Honomu*, sailing alone in the Barents Sea with a cargo of 7,000 tons of food, steel, ammunition and tanks, was torpedoed by *U-456*. One torpedo struck the starboard side at no. 3 hold. The subsequent explosion destroyed the boiler room, killed two crew on watch below and cut off all power. As the *Honomu* began to settle in the water a second torpedo struck the no. 4 hold and she sank by the stern within ten minutes. Nineteen of the seven officers, twenty-eight crew, four British DEMS gunners and two Navy signalmen managed to launch a lifeboat, while twenty others scrambled onto four liferafts. The Master was taken off the no. 5 raft into the U-boat as a prisoner. The crew of the *U-456* then handed out meat and bread to the survivors. The lifeboat set sail with the four rafts in tow.

On 14 July the survivors were spotted by a patrolling Russian Catalina flying boat, and late that evening *Salamander* and *Halcyon* were despatched from Murmansk on a rescue mission. After a three-day search only the four liferafts were found, the Chief Officer having decided on 16 July to cut the rafts loose and continue alone in the lifeboat. On 18 July twenty-one survivors were rescued and taken to Murmansk. The Chief Officer's decision to go it alone was to prove fateful: when at 10.13 on 28 July, *U-209* picked up five crew and three British DEMS gunners from the lifeboat and took them as prisoners to Norway they had been without food for six days. Two officers, eight crewmen and one British DEMS gunner had died of exposure in the boat.

The next ship to be attacked, at around 15.00, was another American freighter, the *Pan Kraft*, laden with TNT, 5,000 tons of crated aircraft parts and a deck-load of bombers. Sailing along the ice-barrier that afternoon, 6 miles astern and within sight of the *Bellingham*, she was bombed from over 4,000 feet by three Ju.88s, part of a flight of six guided to their victim by two FW 200 reconnaissance aircraft. The *Pan Kraft* had been visible for miles because of her smoky engines, steaming along on a straight course without any attempt at zigzagging as the drifting ice allowed no room for evasive action.

The Master rang 'General Quarters' at 15.00 when the lookouts heard enemy aircraft approaching; the sun was dead astern and visibility unlimited. Three Ju.88s each dropped a single bomb as they flew overhead. These fell as near misses but close to the port side of holds 1, 3 and 4. The concussions ruptured the steam and oil lines. The duty watch secured the main engines within ten minutes. After the third bombing run the *Pan Kraft*'s Master took the decision to abandon ship. According to survivors he gave no direct orders to that effect but was seen along with the Chief Officer to be among the first to take to the lifeboats. The second officer remained onboard to supervise the evacuation, as eight officers, twenty-eight crew and eleven armed guards began leaving in four lifeboats. The wireless operator remained at his post long enough to broadcast the 'Air attack' signal and to add, 'Hit by bombers'. Then he left the ship in haste making no attempt to destroy the confidential British papers in his office. A Ju.88 roared in low as the last lifeboat was about to pull away and sprayed the decks of the deserted ship with incendiary bullets. The boats pulled away from the *Pan Kraft* leaving her to her fate. *Lotus* rescued the survivors within the hour and fired three or four HE rounds into the ship. The second mate later died of bullet wounds and one seaman of shrapnel wounds while in a lifeboat. Left on fire *Pan Kraft* suffered an internal explosion, blew up, and sank some hours after the attack.

After the convoy dispersed *Salamander* steamed east with *Zaafaran*, and *Ocean Freedom*. Just after 14.30 they were joined by RFA *Aldersdale*, then at around 15.10 shortly after the attack on the *Pan Kraft*, lookouts spotted a group of four enemy aircraft approaching from astern and all guns were manned and made ready for action as the aircraft started to circle. Suddenly two planes broke away from the formation and started a run in from the stern. One flew down to low level and dropped three bombs which exploded under the stern of the *Aldersdale*, causing extensive damage to the engine room, boiler room and after pump room, totally disabling the engines and breaching the hull in the engine room. Due to the engine damage, the fact *Aldersdale* was now stopped and taking in water, and the proximity of the enemy aircraft, the Master gave the order to abandon ship. This was carried out in good order, the crew getting away in three of the lifeboats. They quickly started rowing towards *Salamander*, about two miles to the south as she made her way towards the stricken *Aldersdale* to pick up survivors. Luckily there had been no casualties.

The Master of the *Aldersdale* and CO of the *Salamander* agreed the minesweeper should go alongside the stricken oiler to see if she could be towed. A group of volunteers from *Aldersdale*'s crew reboarded to make a rapid survey of her condition but quickly realized the damage was too severe to attempt a tow and returned to *Salamander*. It was then decided to sink the *Aldersdale* but after gunfire and depth charges she was still afloat. *Salamander*'s CO thought it was too dangerous to remain in the area given enemy units were still operational and left the scene. When last sighted the *Aldersdale* appeared to be settling quickly by the stern.

Later the following evening a reconnaissance aircraft sighted the hulk of the *Aldersdale* drifting in the Barents Sea. Recognizing the value of her cargo the German Navy gave consideration to a salvage attempt, but this proved impracticable and the order was issued for her to be sunk. At 11.40 on 7 July the drifting wreck was pinpointed by *U–457*, which surfaced and fired on her with HE and incendiary shell. The *Aldersdale* broke in two and sank within twenty minutes.

After this the next target was *Zaafaran*, an attack that straddled her by a stick of three bombs. One hit on the waterline close to the engine room and caused extensive damage to the hull – *Zaafaran* quickly flooded and sank within eight minutes. The crew and passengers took to two lifeboats. After fifty minutes *Zaafaran*'s sister ship *Zamalek* arrived to pick up survivors, bringing *Britomart* as anti-submarine protection. All but one of *Zaafaran*'s crew (an Army DEMS gunner) and all passengers were saved. *Zamalek*, *Ocean Freedom*, and *Britomart* now continued on after the *Palomares Halcyon*, while astern of them *Salamander*, having abandoned her attempts to finish off *Aldersdale*, struggled to catch up.

At 17.00 the Luftwaffe sighted the cruisers and destroyers of CS1's force, so CS1 judged it safe to break radio silence to report his course and position to C-in-C Home Fleet. This was the moment C-in-C Home Fleet first discovered the cover force was no longer with the convoy.

Another group of merchant ships was attacked about the same time. The first, the British *Bolton Castle*, had steered a northeasterly course in order to keep beyond range of the German air bases and had joined the Dutch merchant *Paulus Potter*, and American freighter *Washington*, the latter already leaking from previous attacks. A fourth merchant ship, the American freighter *Olopana* had been with this small group but was unable to keep up and gradually dropped back out of sight. The other three ships headed north but early the following morning, finding their route blocked by the ice barrier, turned east along the edge of the ice. After a few hours of steaming they again found their route blocked by ice and were forced to head southeastwards, sailing ever closer within range of the German airfields in northern Norway.

During the afternoon of 5 July the group was attacked several times, about 175 miles east-northeast of Bear Island, by Ju.88 aircraft from III./KG 30. The first came at around 17.00 when lookouts sighted a lone Ju.88 flying overhead at around 13,000 feet. The Ju.88 dive-bombed and machine-gunned the *Washington*, bombs falling about 15 yards off the ship's starboard quarter. The *Washington*, shaken but undamaged, transmitted an 'Air attack' signal and reported her position.

Half an hour later a starboard lookout reported several Ju.88s approaching. One swooped down on the *Washington*. Several of the bombs dropped were near misses, the explosions lifting the hull partly out of the water. More Ju.88s followed, dropping a total of twenty-one bombs, all of which fell into the sea close by. There were no direct hits, but the near misses disabled *Washington*'s steering gear and she began to take in water. Her Master gave orders to abandon ship, the radio operator broadcast an SOS and the crew took to the lifeboats.

The aircraft now turned their attention to the *Bolton Castle*, attacking from several directions and different altitudes simultaneously. The Master made no attempt to take evasive action as an aircraft dived out of the sun and dropped three bombs directly onto his ship. The second penetrated the no. 2 hold containing several hundred tons of cordite.[11] For a moment the *Bolton Castle* forged on as if ignoring the direct hits; she did not shake and the Master did not even hear the detonation as the bombs exploded in the hold. But as he looked through the bridge windows the world suddenly went green: a brilliant flash blinded him and he heard a roar lasting some seconds, like a mighty waterfall. The cargo of cordite had ignited – not as an explosive with shattering violence, but 'like a giant Roman candle'.

The survivors in the *Washington*'s lifeboats saw the mushroom cloud rise from the *Bolton Castle*'s position barely a quarter of a mile away and feared the worst, but as the cloud drifted away they saw she was still afloat. The heat from the fire had melted the steel hull, the hatch cover had vanished, the bridge windows had buckled, twisted and melted in the heat. The hold where the cordite had been stowed was now empty and began to flood rapidly – the order was given to abandon ship and the crew took to the lifeboats.

At the same time the dive-bombers attacked the *Paulus Potter*, carrying 2,250 tons of general cargo, ammunition, 34 tanks, 15 aircraft and 103 trucks. Two bomb hits disabled her steering gear and the crew immediately abandoned ship in four lifeboats, believing their ship was about to sink. In the event the abandonment was premature and proper procedures not followed. Eight Ju.88s descended to a few feet above the waves and flew over the three merchant ships, firing incendiary rounds into their hulls.

The freighter *Olopana* arrived some two hours later in response to the *Washington*'s SOS, anxious to rescue the survivors of the three stricken merchant ships seen burning on the horizon. She reached the *Washington*'s boats first but the traumatized survivors, convinced it was only a matter of time before the unescorted *Olopana* was also sunk (she was indeed sunk on 8 July, see below), refused to set foot on another merchant ship. *Olopana* then approached the survivors from the *Paulus Potter* in their four lifeboats, one a motorboat. They also declined the offer of rescue and were given cigarettes, bread and lubricating oil. The *Paulus Potter*'s lifeboats then cast off to join the *Washington*'s lifeboats, heading for Moller Bay. The lifeboats from the *Bolton Castle* were seen sailing away to the south, they too showed no desire to contact the *Olopana*, who then sailed off to the north.

The abandoned *Paulus Potter* had failed to sink. On 13 July the hulk was found drifting by *U-255*. A boarding party from the U-boat, unable to restart the ship's engines as the engine room was flooded, searched her and removed blankets, cigarettes and other useful materials, including a heavy box containing classified documents they found on the bridge. This should have been thrown overboard when the crew abandoned ship. The U-boat finally sank the *Paulus Potter* at 08.25. The following day the crew of the *Paulus Potter* met survivors from the *Washington* and they rowed southwards, to find and board the abandoned, grounded *Winston-Salem*. All were later rescued by a Russian whaling vessel and on 17 July transferred to the *Empire Tide*, anchored in the Matochkin Strait. Three days later the *Empire Tide* would join the small convoy of five merchant ships and eleven escorts for Archangel, where the convoy arrived four days later.

The next casualty was the *Fairfield City*, carrying 7,400 tons of war supplies. When PQ.17 dispersed the *Fairfield City* sailed on with three other American merchant ships – *Daniel Morgan*, *John Witherspoon*, *Benjamin Harrison*, and a few naval escorts, which left them at around 13.00 on 7 July. Just after 15.00 that afternoon, three Ju.88s found the group and began an attack. The first cluster of bombs fell close to *Fairfield City*'s starboard side. Those released by a second Ju.88 hit the afterdeck and those from the third struck the bridge, killing two officers and six crewmen but sparing the helmsman. The survivors abandoned ship in the no. 1, no. 2 and no. 3 lifeboats and a life raft. The burning wreck of the *Fairfield City* sank soon after, taking its cargo of tanks to the bottom. The no. 1 lifeboat, fitted with an engine, took the others in tow toward Novaya Zemlya where thirty-four survivors landed four days later. The trawler *Ayrshire* rescued them on 12 July and on arrival at the Matochkin Strait transferred them to several other merchant ships.

Later that afternoon, at around 17.45, the British merchant ship *Earlston*, carrying 2,005 tons of military stores, 195 vehicles, 33 aircraft and a steam launch as deck cargo, sailing alone after the loss of the *Peter Kerr*, was attacked and bombed by a number of Ju.88 aircraft of III./KG 30 returning to their base at Banak. Three 'near misses' off the ship's bow damaged the hull and caused some flooding. A fourth bomb that fell into the sea off the port side caused further damage, stopping the engines. An 'air attack' distress signal was broadcast, and the crew ordered to abandon ship. As they pulled away in the two lifeboats, they could see steam pouring from the engine-room ventilators and the *Earlston* settling lower in the water. They had scarcely put a quarter of a mile between themselves and the ship, fearing the explosives in no. 2 hold would detonate, when two U-boats surfaced within a few moments of each other on the *Earlston*'s starboard bow – one of them most probably *U-456* (which three hours before had torpedoed the American freighter *Honomu*). Apparently three U-boats had been stalking the *Earlston* because a short while later a third, *U-334*, surfaced and fired two torpedoes. The first struck beside the after mast; the *Earlston* listed slightly but remained afloat. The second fired from closer range missed. A third struck in the no. 2 hold and was followed by a violent explosion. The *Earlston* then broke in two and her bow section sank almost at once, followed by the stern.

The Master and three DEMS gunners taken prisoner by *U-344* had a lucky escape when two bombs dropped by a Ju.88 damaged the U-boat's steering so that it was unable to submerge. *U-334* was escorted back to Neidenfjord by *U-456*. The second officer and twenty survivors from the *Earlston* landed on the Rybachi Peninsula seven days later and the Chief Officer and twenty-six survivors arrived on Norwegian-occupied territory.

The American freighter *Daniel Morgan*, carrying 8,200 tons of steel, food, explosives, and tanks was the next victim. After the convoy dispersed, she set out with four other merchant ships for Archangel. At around 18.00, the small group was attacked several times for over an hour by five Ju.88 aircraft from III./KG 30, with approximately eighty bombs dropped. The *Daniel Morgan*, zigzagging in an attempt to throw off the attackers, suffered thirty near misses. The attacks by the first three Ju.88s were unsuccessful.

Three bombs dropped by the fourth aircraft fell close to the starboard side, ruptured the hull plates between nos 4 and 5 holds and caused them to flood. The *Daniel Morgan* took an immediate list to starboard and began to settle in the water. As she tried to escape, she was intercepted by *U-88* who fired a torpedo into her port side amidships and observed a plume of smoke as the torpedo hit. A few minutes later a second torpedo struck the engine room, putting the main and steering engines out of commission. The eight officers, thirty-one crew and fifteen armed guards abandoned ship in three lifeboats, one of which capsized killing two crew, a third died later from concussion. The ship sank stern first shortly afterwards. The U-boat Captain questioned the Master and crew and ordered them to follow the U-boat, which they did until it pulled away. The survivors were rescued by a Russian tanker, *Donbass*, and landed at Murmansk.

After the PQ. 17 convoy had scattered at 22.30 the previous evening, the British freighter *River Afton*, the ship of the Convoy Commodore carrying 2,314 tons of military stores, 36 tanks, 12 vehicles and 7 aircraft, kept religiously to her northeasterly 'scatter course' until she met the ice-barrier, then in thick fog groped her way eastwards making for the coast of Novaya Zemlya. Suddenly, just after 21.00 on 5 July, she was torpedoed by *U-703* northeast of the Kola Inlet. The first torpedo detonated in the engine room below the water line. The *River Afton* gradually slowed down but initially showed no signs of sinking. As the order to abandon ship was being given some gunners were already struggling to lower the starboard lifeboat, the port lifeboat having been destroyed by the blast. Other seamen launched two liferafts but these promptly floated away with no one on them. At this moment *U-703*'s second torpedo struck the engine room, killing the crew on watch below. The starboard lifeboat was capsized by the force of the blast and the DEMS gunners were thrown into the sea. *U-703* then turned away to the west, but as the *River Afton* had still not begun to sink twenty minutes after the first torpedo had struck home, *U-703* fired a third at 10.22. This struck cleanly on the starboard side of no. 5 hold – *River Afton* then blew up, broke in two and sank.

Twelve crew, eight DEMS gunners, two RN staff members and one passenger were lost. The Master, the Convoy Commodore, twenty-six crew, one DEMS gunner, three naval staff members and one passenger were later rescued by *Lotus* and landed at Matochkin, Novaya Zemlya. Three of these survivors were later lost during their repatriation aboard *Leda*, torpedoed and sunk by *U-435* in QP.14 on 20 September 1942.

Meantime *U-255* had been pursuing the American freighter *John Witherspoon*, carrying a cargo of 8,575 tons of ammunition and tanks, for some thirty-six hours, the ship having successfully avoided attacks by aircraft for the previous five days in her dash for the White Sea. At 16.40, 20 miles from the shore of Novaya Zemlya, *U-255* fired a spread of four torpedoes. The first struck the *John Witherspoon* on the starboard side between no. 4 and no. 5 holds, followed by a second about one minute later which struck underneath the bridge. At 16.55, two *coups de grâce* were fired, striking the port side amidships and breaking the hull in two, and the *John Witherspoon* sank within thirty minutes. After the second explosion the Master ordered the crew to abandon ship. By the time the third torpedo struck the eight officers, thirty-one crew and eleven armed guards had already done so, in three lifeboats and one liferaft. One seaman fell overboard and drowned. The U-boat approached the lifeboat of the Master, asked for him and about the cargo, offered food and water, promised to send a message for the survivors, gave directions to the nearest land and then left. *La Malouine* rescued thirty survivors. Sixteen crew and three armed guards in the other lifeboat were trapped in the ice for fifty-three hours, unable to break their boat free. They were finally rescued in a heavy fog by the *El Capitan* on 8 July, when her chief mate spotted the lifeboat after hearing the tone of a bosun's pipe.

Mid-afternoon on the 6th, the crew of the American freighter *Pan Atlantic* spotted a reconnaissance aircraft shadowing their ship. After several hours it disappeared and about three hours later a single Ju.88 dive-bomber from II./KG 30 attacked. Two bombs struck forward of the well deck at the no. 2 hold. The 3,000 tons of explosives in the hold detonated and blew the bow off. There was no time to send an SOS and the *Pan Atlantic* sank within three minutes.

The crew abandoned ship in two lifeboats with the Master in the no. 1 lifeboat. The U-boat surfaced and asked for the Master, but the crew hid him in the bottom of the boat under a blanket and told the U-boat commander he had been killed when the ship was hit. The commander believed their account, told the crew he was sorry some men had been killed, gave them bread, sausage and directions to the nearest landfall then left.

U-88, fresh from sinking the *River Afton*, had also been hunting the *Pan Atlantic* that morning and afternoon. During the morning she had fired two torpedoes at the *Pan Atlantic*, both of which had missed. At 18.45, she surfaced and radioed to Narvik to complain 'her victim' had now been 'sunk by an aircraft'. Both *U-88* and *U-703*, which had also been following the ship, salvaged provisions from the freighter's flotsam. *Lotus* rescued the *Pan Atlantic*'s surviving crew and armed guards nine days later on 15 July and transported them to Murmansk.

The first ships to sight Novaya Zemlya on the morning of 6 July were *Palomares*, *Britomart*, *Halcyon*, *Salamander*, and *Zamalek* (now carrying 153 survivors), together with the *Ocean Freedom*. *Britomart* was sent ahead to carry out an anti-submarine sweep as the convoy passed the difficult entrance into the Matochkin Strait and to make contact with the Russian authorities at the settlement of Lagerni. This was done and by half-past two the remaining ships of the *Palomares* Group had followed *Britomart* in and anchored off Lagerni. Two hours later, the CO of the *Palomares* called a conference of the COs of the other escorts and Master of the *Ocean Freedom* to discuss whether they should attempt to break out into the Kara Sea or wait a time before attempting the shorter west coast route into the White Sea and Archangel. There was concern the Matochkin Strait might be blocked by ice, so the Walrus seaplane picked up two days previously was sent on a short reconnaissance flight, which confirmed the Strait was indeed icebound.

Shortly afterwards the *Palomares* Group was joined by *Pozarica*, *Poppy*, and *La Malouine*. Although it was not known if the surface threat had reduced, *La Malouine* was sent out to look for any merchant ships in need of assistance and returned that evening with four – *Hoosier*, *Samuel Chase*, *El Capitan*, and *Benjamin Harrison* – which arrived at the anchorage in deteriorating weather. Shortly before midnight *Lotus* arrived with Commodore Dowding, two of the *River Afton*'s crew and another seventy-eight survivors from the *River Afton* and *Pan Kraft*, whom she had subsequently rescued. At dawn on 7 July the *Lord Austin*, *Lord Middleton*, and *Northern Gem*, arrived in the Matochkin Strait.

The next victim was another American freighter. After the convoy dispersed, the *Alcoa Ranger*, loaded with 7,200 tons of steel, armour plates, flour, and nineteen tanks as deck cargo, steamed on independently hoping to escape detection and attack. At 07.40, *U-255* fired a spread of two torpedoes at two freighters. Both missed due to the range of about 6,000 yards, but another fired at 09.27 struck the *Alcoa Ranger* on the starboard side at the no. 2 hold, opening a large hole and causing the freighter to list heavily to starboard. The eight officers, twenty-six crew and six British DEMS gunners abandoned ship in three lifeboats, fifteen minutes after the attack. *U-255* then surfaced and headed towards the second freighter which had stopped but then made its escape, so *U-255* returned to the *Alcoa Ranger* to question the survivors. She then shelled the *Alcoa Ranger* from a distance of about 100 yards with at least 60 rounds (some survivors reckoned as many as 150), until she sank by the bow at 12.00. Two lifeboats landed at Novaya Zemlya later the same day, and one a week later on 14 July. The survivors were subsequently rescued by Russian patrol boats and taken to Archangel.

At 13.00 Commodore Dowding called a conference of the masters of the five merchant ships and the escort vessels aboard the *Palomares*, while *Lotus* maintained an anti-submarine watch on the entrance to the Strait. Some masters advocated their ships remain in the anchorage until the hue and cry died down, arguing the high cliffs on either side of the Strait afforded some protection from dive-bombing. The warships' officers, and particularly the anti-aircraft ships' masters, took the view that as a force of German destroyers was out hunting for them, once one aircraft spotted the seventeen ships in the Strait the enemy could mine the entrance or block it with submarines and indulge in an orgy of high-level bombing. While the sea outside the Strait was invariably foggy, the Strait itself seemed to enjoy unusually fine, clear weather. The other ships' masters argued that the last signals received from the Admiralty in London could only mean German surface ships were out searching for them; and the escort vessels' COs agreed that the two AA ships should be able to create a sufficient diversion. Commodore Dowding had in the meantime radioed to Archangel a request they be given fighter escort for the latter part of their journey.

In the end it was decided to form up a small convoy to depart that evening on the hazardous and difficult passage south towards the White Sea, and a message was passed to SBNO Archangel via the local Russian radio station. At 19.00, *Lotus* led *Palomares*, *Pozarica*, *Halcyon*, *Salamander*, *Britomart*, *Poppy*, *La Malouine*, *Zamalek*, *Ocean Freedom*, *Samuel Chase*, *Hoosier*, *El Capitan*, *Benjamin Harrison*, *Lord Austin*, *Lord Middleton*, and *Northern Gem* out to sea. The convoy ran into dense fog in which the group became dispersed; the freighter *Benjamin Harrison* lost contact and returned to the anchorage.

The British freighter *Hartlebury*, carrying a cargo of 6 vehicles, 36 tanks, 7 aircraft and 2,409 tons of military stores, had been sighted mid-afternoon on 7 July by *U-255*. Sailing close inshore, due south past the entrance to Matochkin Strait and shadowed for several hours, she was hit at around 18.30 by two of three (some accounts say four) torpedoes fired by *U-355* and a third hit came two minutes later. The first blasted a large hole in the deck outside the crew's quarters. The second threw up a wave of water over the bridge. The ship listed heavily and both engines stopped. The decks had been 'corrugated' by the force of the explosion and the boilers blowing off steam. The first torpedoes killed six mess attendants and the Master had to be freed from underneath debris.

Before the Master could order the crew to abandon ship, there was a rush for the two lifeboats. Each could hold thirty-six men. The ship had a total complement of fifty-nine including the gunners and naval signals staff. Unfortunately, the force of the second torpedo explosion had crushed the starboard lifeboat. The crew then ran to the port lifeboat, whether this was their allocated station or not and began struggling with the release gear. As the panicking crew lowered the lifeboat it capsized, throwing the occupants into the icy sea, while others jumped into the water to try to reach the liferafts.

The *Hartlebury* was settling fast and listing to starboard. Ten minutes after the first four torpedoes were fired she was hit by a fifth. A plume of spray and smoke billowed 400 feet into the air, with the funnel and pieces of superstructure blown into the sea. The force of the explosion broke *Hartlebury*'s back, she immediately took a violent list to port and sank over the bow within ten minutes, 17 miles from Britwin Lighthouse, Novaya Zemlya. A total of twenty-nine crew, seven DEMS gunners, and two RN signalmen were lost. The Master and twelve survivors landed at Pomorski Bay. Seven others made it to the American freighter *Winston-Salem* aground at North Gusini Shoal, Novaya Zemlya, from where they were rescued by a Russian survey ship and transferred to the *Empire Tide*. All were later transferred to *La Malouine* and landed at Archangel on 25 July.

The next merchant ship to be attacked was the *Olopana*. After the convoy scattered, the *Olopana*, carrying 6,000 tons of explosives, gasoline, and with trucks as deck cargo, headed towards Novaya Zemlya, hoping to reach Archangel. At 01.00 on 8 July, about 10 miles west of Moller Bay, she was attacked by *U-255*, a single torpedo hitting her on the port side in the engine room. The resultant explosion blew in all the bulkheads and extinguished the lights, as water poured from the main deck into the crew accommodation area. The starboard lifeboat was thrown into the air and all its fittings and equipment blown out. The *Olopana* settled immediately in the water but did not sink, allowing the survivors among the eight officers, twenty-eight crew and five armed guards to abandon ship on four liferafts. One officer, two armed guards and four crewmen were lost, including three on watch below. The U-boat surfaced about fifteen minutes after the initial attack and shelled the *Olopana* with twenty rounds before she sank by the bows around twenty minutes later. The U-boat crew questioned the survivors, gave them directions to make land and asked if they had enough food and water before leaving the area. The survivors, fourteen of them suffering from frostbite, landed at various points in Novaya Zemlya. Some were rescued and flown by a Russian Catalina flying boat to the Matochkin Strait, where they boarded the *Empire Tide*, others were rescued by the crew of the *Winston Salem*, and a third group by the ice breaker *Murmanez*.

The fog thickened again during the afternoon of 8 July. Commodore Dowding's little group of ships steamed on, hugging the coast and hoping to pass east of Kolguyev Island. At 16.30 they encountered an extensive ice field which broke up the convoy formation for several hours as the ships blundered about. The *Ocean Freedom* severely damaged her bow when she hit the ice, and *Zamalek* was stuck on an ice ridge for some hours. The convoy eventually reformed on a westerly course.

In the early hours of 9 July, *Britomart*, *Halcyon*, and *Lotus* broke out of the fog and ice, sighting the *Samuel Chase*, *Ocean Freedom*, *Lord Middleton*, and *Northern Gem* some 40 miles ahead. The *Salamander*, *El Capitan*, *Hoosier*, *Lord Austin*, *Poppy*, *La Malouine*, *Zamalek*, *Palomares*, and *Pozarica* also sailed into clear weather and found the remaining twenty-nine survivors from the *John Witherspoon* who had been adrift in two lifeboats for three days. Two boatloads of survivors from the *Pan Atlantic* were also found and rescued. At 11.00 the *Palomares* Group was sighted by aircraft and three U-boats homed in on it. The group knew they were being tracked, but the escorts lacked sufficient fuel to attempt a counterattack and were forced by the ice onto a course which left them steaming southwest towards the enemy airfields in Norway, in bright sunshine with 20-mile visibility and light winds. Freighters *Bellingham* and the Russian *Donbass* and rescue ship *Rathlin* arrived at Archangel.

A third group had comprised the trawler *Ayrshire* and three merchant ships *Silver Sword*, *Troubador*, and *Ironclad*. On receiving the third order to scatter on 4 July, the CO of *Ayrshire* had decided that as he was heading north to the Arctic ice shelf, there was nothing to prevent him from escorting any merchant ships he met, and so he had gathered up the three and proceeded northward.

On the morning of 5 July they had reached the southern edge of the Arctic ice fields and turned east, closely following the edge of the pack ice. Using the *Troubador* with her stiffened bows as an icebreaker the *Ayrshire* shepherded the ships 20 miles into the ice field, until they could make no further progress. They hove to, stopped engines and banked their fires so that smoke from the fireboxes would not give away their location to any patrolling aircraft. The CO of the *Ayrshire* formulated a defence: using the *Troubadour*'s cargo of drums of white paint the crews painted all the vessels white, covered the decks with white linen, and arranged the Sherman tanks on the decks in a defensive formation, with their main armament loaded. There they remained until late in the afternoon of 6 July when, undetected, they headed out of the ice and took an easterly course along the edge of the ice fields heading for the coast of Novaya Zemlya.

At around midnight on the night of 9/10 July, around forty Ju.88 aircraft from II and III./KG 30 attacked the *Palomares* Group about 65 miles northeast of Iokanka. The Ju.88s approached from different directions while *U-255* observed the action from astern. Their primary target was the American freighter *Hoosier*, loaded with 5,000 tons of machinery, explosives, and tanks as deck cargo. The first stick of three bombs dropped into the water about 50 yards from her port bow, a second fell 5 feet from the boat deck inflicting considerable damage, the third fell on the port side 20 yards abaft of the beam. The shockwaves from the explosions damaged the steam pipes and oil lines, sprang some of the hull plates and disabled the engines. The chief engineer went below to determine if the ship could continue to be operated, but concluded it could not. Aircraft were still flying overhead and *U-255* remained on the surface, at a distance of about 8½ miles. The eight officers, thirty-four crew and eleven armed guards abandoned ship in four lifeboats and were picked up by *Poppy*.

Despite the continued presence of enemy forces, the CO of *La Malouine* decided to attempt to take *Hoosier* in tow and sent a salvage party including the ship's engineers back on board. The operation was abandoned and the salvage party recovered when the *U-255* was seen to be shadowing them, now at a reduced distance of 4 miles. The corvette's attempt to sink the *Hoosier* with gunfire failed. Her burning and drifting wreck was later hit by one torpedo from *U–376* but remained afloat. A second shot missed and *Hoosier* finally sank by the bow after being hit in the engine room five minutes later.

The Panamanian freighter *El Capitan* was dive-bombed in two separate attacks. In the first at around 02.00 a Ju.88 dropped three bombs, two to port and one to starboard about 40 feet astern, the blast opening up the seams in the after-peak tank and the gun crew's quarters. Although damaged by these near misses the *El Capitan* sailed on.

Ju.88 dive-bombers attacked *Zamalek* for around three hours. Shortly before 03.00 a heavy bomb detonated just 20 feet from her starboard side; the engines stopped, she gradually lost way and fell out of the convoy. Although by this time the air attacks had ceased no ships were sent back to her assistance, but one hour later the engineers had made good the damage and she was able to rejoin the group.

The second attack on *El Capitan* took place at 05.30 when a Ju.88 from II./KG 30 dropped three bombs. None caused any damage but a further three dropped by a second plane exploded close to the starboard side of the engine room and abreast of the bridge. The engines stopped, and the *El Capitan* slowed to a halt. The shock waves blew in the sea valves, ruptured the fuel and water pipes to the main engines, demolished the bulkhead in the no. 4 hold, and wrecked the starboard side of the engine room. As no. 4 and no. 5 holds began flooding, the *El Capitan* began to settle aft.

The first officer volunteered to go below to see for himself what had happened; the engine-room telegraphs were broken, and the voice-pipe produced no reply. He found the stoke hold flooded to a depth of 4 feet, the sea valve blown in, and the fuel and water pipes to the main engines ruptured. The third engineer emerged drenched in black fuel oil and water, shouting that the water was coming up to the fires. Recognizing that the situation was irrecoverable the Master destroyed the ship's classified documents and ordered all hands to prepare to abandon ship. The thirty-seven crew, eleven armed guards, and nineteen survivors from the *Washington* were picked up by *Lord Austin* and later landed at Archangel. An attempt by *Lord Austin* to sink the *El Capitan* was unsuccessful and she was abandoned, to be torpedoed and sunk by *U–251* later that day. There were now no merchant ships left in the *Palomares* Group.

At around 11.00 on 11 July, sixteen Ju.88s attacked the second group of merchant ships – the *Samuel Chase* and *Ocean Freedom*, with their escorts

Lotus, *Halcyon*, *Britomart*, *Lord Middleton*, and *Northern Gem*. During this attack, which lasted ninety minutes, *Samuel Chase* suffered two direct hits and three near misses, her main steam line was broken, and she came to a standstill. The group then split in two. *Britomart* and *Northern Gem* escorted the *Ocean Freedom*. *Halcyon*, rather than abandoning *Samuel Chase*, took her in tow whilst *Lord Middleton* provided anti-submarine cover. The two vessels made a steady 5 knots south to the White Sea, ready to cut the towrope should they be attacked. After some hours the Americans, encouraged possibly by the example of the little 1,000-ton minesweeper, managed to restart their engines and finish the journey under their own steam. In recognition of *Halcyon*'s assistance, the Master of the *Samuel Chase* requested the minesweeper be allowed to escort him into harbour, which she did.

Both groups continued to fight off air attacks. In the late afternoon Russian Hurricane fighters at last provided air cover. *Hazard* and *Leda* appeared to escort *Britomart*, *Halcyon*, *Samuel Chase*, *Ocean Freedom*, *Lotus*, *Lord Middleton*, and *Northern Gem* into Archangel, where they arrived later that day.

The same day, *Ayrshire*, *Silver Sword*, *Troubador*, and *Ironclad* arrived in the Matochkin Strait. (They had reached a bay on the north island of Novaya Zemlya the previous day and after lying up for 24 hours, sailed out again for the Matochkin Strait.) Here they found the American freighter *Benjamin Harrison*, and the damaged *Azerbaijan*, at anchor. The CO of *Ayrshire* went ashore and with some difficulty persuaded a Russian signal station to report their arrival to the authorities at Archangel.

On 14 July the survivors of the *Paulus Potter* encountered those from the *Washington* and together they rowed south towards Novaya Zemlya, where they found the abandoned American freighter *Winston-Salem*, deliberately run aground. They boarded the vessel and ate their first proper meal in ten days. Later they were rescued by a Russian whaling vessel and on 17 July transferred to *Empire Tide*, anchored in the Matochkin Strait. Three days later *Empire Tide* would join the small convoy of five merchant ships and eleven escorts that left for Archangel, where they arrived four days later.

When Commodore Dowding heard five more merchant ships had reached a safe haven in the Matochkin Strait he organized a rescue force and sailed from Archangel on 16 July in *Poppy*, accompanied by *Lotus* and *La Malouine*. After a stormy voyage they reached Byelushya Bay in southern

Novaya Zemlya, where they found twelve survivors from the *Olopana* camped ashore. A little further up the coast they found the *Winston Salem* aground southeast of North Gusini Nos, where she had provided a refuge for survivors from *Hartlebury* and *Washington*. As she was stuck hard and fast on a reef and would require powerful tugs and time to be refloated Dowding left her there and pressed on to Moller Bay, where he found the *Empire Tide*. She had also run aground but had freed herself and was accommodating a large number of survivors from other merchant ships. Dowding distributed the survivors amongst the three corvettes and left for the Matochkin Strait, instructing the Master of the *Empire Tide* to be ready to sail with him when he returned.

Hazard and *Seagull* left Archangel on 19 July to sweep ahead of the merchant ships arriving at Archangel from the Matochkin Strait.

On arrival at the Matochkin Strait on 20 July, Commodore Dowding found *Silver Sword, Ironclad, Troubadour, Benjamin Harrison, Azerbaijan*, and *Ayrshire* at anchor. He immediately organized another convoy and all sailed on that evening, the Commodore aboard the Russian icebreaker *Murman*. He planned to collect the *Empire Tide* the following day then head south for Archangel. The next day *Bramble, Leda, Hazard, Dianella*, and *Pozarica* left Archangel to meet Dowding's group and escort them into Archangel.

Commodore Dowding's convoy of six merchant ships, escorted by *Bramble, Pozarica, Lotus, Poppy, La Malouine, Dianella, Hazard, Seagull*, and *Ayrshire* arrived at Archangel from the Matochkin Strait on 24 July. *Empire Bard* and *Troubador* arrived the same day. The survivors from the *Carlton* (sunk by *U-88* on 5 July) reached the North Cape of Norway, where they were taken prisoner. During their ordeal in the lifeboat one man died, not long before they came ashore.

The last survivors from the *Honomu*, five crew and three British DEMS gunners, were rescued from their lifeboat at 10.13 on 28 July by *U-209* and taken as prisoners to Norway. Two officers, eight crewmen and one British gunner had died from exposure while in the lifeboat. The same day, the *Winston Salem*, aground in Novaya Zemlya, was refloated with the help of two Russian tugs and reached Archangel on 29 July, the last survivor of PQ.17 to arrive.

The Luftwaffe claimed their raids on PQ.17 over a period of five days had sunk 8 merchant ships (actually 7) totalling 48,218 tons and damaged 8 others (actually 13) totalling 54,093 tons, and U-boats subsequently sank

11 of the damaged vessels – two survived. Luftwaffe units carried out 202 sorties during which they expended 60 torpedoes and 212 tons of bombs for the loss of 5 aircraft. U-boats sank 6 merchant ships.

Two weeks elapsed before the results of these attacks and the fate of the various merchant ships of the convoy became fully known. Of 36 merchant ships (excluding the fleet oiler and rescue ship), 3 returned to port, 22 (excluding the fleet oiler and rescue ship), were sunk, only 11 arrived. Of these, two British, four American, one Panamanian and two Russian reached Archangel, and two American, the *Samuel Chase* and *Benjamin Harrison* arrived at Murmansk. The total deliveries amounted to 70,000 tons (64,000 short tons) out of the 200,000 tons (180,000 short tons) despatched from Iceland. Losses included 3,350 military vehicles, 430 tanks, and 210 aircraft.

Prime Minister Winston Churchill later described the event in *The Second World War* (Vol IV, p. 237) as: 'One of the most melancholy naval episodes in the whole of the war.'

QP.13 (26 June–8 July)

The thirty-five merchant ships of QP.13 departed from Murmansk and Archangel. The Archangel section of twelve merchant ships left on 26 June, escorted by the *Intrepid* (26 June to 3 July), *Garland*, *Starwort*, *Honeysuckle*, and *Alynbank* (all to 7 July), and the eastern local escort, *Bramble*, *Seagull*, *Leda*, and *Hazard* (26 to 28 June).

The Murmansk section of twenty-three merchant ships sailed on 27 June, escorted by *Inglefield* (to 3 July), *Achates*, *Volunteer*, *Niger*, *Hussar*, *Hyderabad*, *Roselys*, *Trident* (to 1 July), *Lady Madeleine* and *St. Elstan* (all except *Niger* to 7 July), with *Grozny*, *Gremyaschiy*, and *Kuibyshev*, were proceeding with the convoy as far as 30° East (to 28 June).

The two sections of the convoy joined up at sea on 28 June when the eastern local escort of *Grozny*, *Gremyaschiy*, *Kuibyshev*, *Bramble*, *Hazard*, *Leda*, and *Seagull* departed and QP.13 proceeded westwards in very low visibility. The convoy was sighted by aircraft and shadowed by a U-boat, but no attacks took place since PQ.17, the eastbound laden convoy, remained the focus of German attention.

On 4 July the convoy split into two sections. *Alynbank*, *Achates*, *Volunteer*, *Garland*, *Starwort*, *Honeysuckle*, and *Hyderabad* proceeded east of Iceland with the sixteen merchant ships bound for Loch Ewe, whilst the remaining nineteen merchant ships (bound for the USA) escorted by *Intrepid*, *Inglefield*, *Niger*, *Hussar*, *Roselys*, *Lady Madeleine*, and *St Elstan* sailed for Reykjavik.

At 19.00 the convoy was approaching the northwest coast of Iceland in five columns. The weather was bad, visibility under one mile, with rough seas and a force 8 wind from the northeast. No sightings had been taken since 2 July and the convoy's estimated position calculated by 'dead reckoning' was in doubt. At 19.10 the *Niger*'s senior officer (Commander A. J. Cubison) suggested to the Convoy Commodore that the convoy formation be reduced in width from five to two columns to pass between the coast at Straumness and the British minefield to the northwest of Iceland. Course was then altered on a dead reckoning basis supported by depth soundings.

At 21.00 Commander Cubison in *Niger* went ahead to look for land, leaving *Hussar* in position to provide a visual link with the convoy. From the depth soundings taken, Commander Cubison estimated the convoy had passed the North Cape of Iceland and so ordered a southwest course to try to make a landfall. Cautiously making his way through the mist and cloud he suddenly saw what appeared to be a steep cliff looming up in the murk, thought to be the North Cape. It seemed the convoy had altered course too soon and if they maintained that course they would run into the coast. To avoid this, he immediately signalled the convoy to turn back on to a westerly course. Hardly had the convoy swung back onto the new course when a clearance in the weather showed that what had been taken for a cliff was in fact a large iceberg. But the mistake was to prove their undoing – at 22.40 *Niger* hit a mine and blew up. The force of the explosion tore her bottom out and broke her back. *Niger* capsized and sank within a few minutes. The Commanding Officer, eighty officers and ratings, and thirteen passengers, survivors from *Edinburgh* were lost; there were only three survivors.

Thick fog had reduced visibility to 500 yards and the accompanying merchant ships thought a U-boat or surface raider attack was in progress. As they too sailed on into the minefield four were sunk and two seriously damaged. The American freighter *Massmar* fouled two mines and sank; seventeen of her twenty-six crew, and five of her nine armed guards were lost, along with twenty-two merchant seamen and four armed guards amongst the forty-five passengers she was carrying (survivors of the *Alamar*, sunk in convoy PQ.16) – *Roselys* rescued the survivors. Another American freighter *Hybert* also fouled a mine and was abandoned. As her forty-six crew (including eleven armed guards) and twenty-six passengers (survivors from the *Syros*) abandoned ship, the *Hybert* drifted into a second mine – the *Lady Madeleine* and *Roselys* rescued the survivors. The American *John Randolph* then fouled two mines and broke in two; five of her thirty-eight crew were killed, but none of the twelve passengers or twelve armed guards were lost; other ships in the convoy rescued the survivors. The *John Randolph's* stern section sank but the bow section was later recovered and salvaged. The *Heffron* also fouled two mines and was abandoned; one crewman died in the process. *Roselys* rescued thirty-six crew, two Navy signalmen and twenty-three passengers. The *Heffron* sank very early the next morning. The Russian merchant ship *Rodina* struck a mine; her Master, thirty-eight crew and a number of civilian passengers were lost; twenty-six were rescued by *St Elstan*. The American freighter *Richard Henry Lee* was damaged but suffered no casualties among her crew of thirty-four and nine armed guards. Another American freighter the *Exterminator*, also hit a mine and was seriously damaged but reached Reykjavik on the 7th. *Hussar* obtained a shore navigational fix and led the remaining ships of the convoy out of the minefield. The rescue operation lasted six and a half hours. Of 580 crew and passengers over 200 were lost.

Twelve merchant ships of the convoy with *Hussar*, *Roselys*, *Lady Madeleine*, and *St Elstan* arrived at Reykjavik on 7 July, two more came in on 9 July and the salvaged section of the *John Randolph* a day later. The Loch Ewe Section – QP.13(U), of sixteen merchant ships escorted by *Alynbank*, *Achates*, *Garland*, *Starwort*, *Honeysuckle*, and *Hyderabad* – arrived on 8 September.

PQ.18 (2–21 September)

This was the first convoy escort strengthened to counter air, U-boat, and surface ship attack with a sixteen-ship fighting destroyer escort (FDE) to reinforce the close escort of corvettes and trawlers. The escort included a carrier group, the *Avenger*, carrying twelve Sea Hurricane and three Swordfish anti-submarine aircraft to provide additional protection, with two destroyers. As frequent German air reconnaissance of the Icelandic ports had been reported, it was decided to sail PQ.18 direct from Loch Ewe.

The convoy of thirty-seven merchant ships (including RFA *Atheltemplar* and with two fleet oilers bound for Force Q, *Grey Ranger* and *Black Ranger*)[12] and one rescue ship sailed from Loch Ewe on 2 September, escorted by *Eskdale*, *Farndale*, *Campbell*, *Mackay*, *Arab*, *Duncton*, *Hugh Walpole*, *King Sol*, and *Paynter*, which would accompany the convoy as far as the Denmark Strait off the coast of Iceland, reached on 8 September.

In the afternoon of 6 September *Montrose*, *Echo*, and *Walpole* from Hvalfjord reinforced the escort to provide additional defence against the U-boat threat. The convoy was running twenty-four hours behind schedule as bad weather slowed its progress. The *Beauregard* returned to Loch Ewe with engine trouble and PQ.18 finally arrived at the rendezvous point off Iceland thirty-six hours later than planned.

The Western Approaches local escort was relieved on 7 September by the second stage close escort group *Malcolm*, *Achates*, *Bergamot*, *Bluebell*, *Bryony*, *Camellia*, *Harrier*, *Gleaner*, *Sharpshooter*, *Cape Argona*, *Cape Mariato*, *Daneman*, and *St Kenan*. The escort was further reinforced by *Alynbank*, *Ulster Queen*, and submarines *P.614* and *P.615*, which sailed from Hvalfjord that morning escorting eight merchant ships and three motor minesweepers (MMS) *90*, *203* and *212* (each towed by one of the trawlers) being delivered to the Russian Navy.

Three merchant ships, the *Oremar*, *San Zotica*, and *Gateway City*, which sailed with the main body of PQ.18 from Loch Ewe, went into Reykjavik at 19.00 escorted by the trawler *Arab*. The addition of the Icelandic contingent on 7 September brought the total number of merchant ships up to forty-one, in excess of the ceiling of forty set by the Admiralty, and so the *Richard Basset*, with engine trouble and unable to keep up, was ordered to return to Hvalfjord.

During the night of 7/8 September the weather deteriorated and by daybreak on the 8th four merchant ships had fallen behind. The convoy reformed by noon and proceeded on a northerly course keeping just south of Spitzbergen, skirting the edge of the ice barrier and taking it within 400 miles of the German air bases in northern Norway – just within range.

The convoy was first sighted by enemy aircraft late on the 8th but would not be shadowed from the air again until 12 September, protected in the meantime by cloud and low visibility.

On the morning of 9 September the convoy was joined by part of the ocean escort, led by *Scylla*, and half the FDE, Force B – *Milne*, *Faulknor*, *Impulsive*, *Intrepid*, *Marne*, *Martin*, *Fury*, and *Meteor*, plus the Carrier Force – *Avenger*, *Wheatland*, and *Wilton*. The eight destroyers of Force A – *Onslow*, *Onslaught*, *Opportune*, *Offa*, *Eskimo*, *Somali*, *Ashanti*, and *Tartar* – sailed direct from Akureyri to refuel at Lowe Sound, Spitzbergen, from Force P – RFAs *Oligarch* and *Blue Ranger* guarded by *Oakley*, *Cowdray*, *Windsor*, and *Worcester*, which arrived on 10 September from Scapa Flow. *Scylla*, *Milne*,

Martin, *Meteor*, and *Intrepid* left to fuel in Spitzbergen, whilst *Faulknor*, *Fury*, and *Impulsive* fuelled from Force Q (RFAs *Grey Ranger* and *Black Ranger*). *Sharpshooter*, *P.614*, and *P.615* joined at midday from Seidisfjord.

From 12 to 22 September PQ.18 and QP.14 were continually shadowed by Wolfpack *Trägertod*, with an estimated eight U-boats in contact at any time. Around 21.00 on 12 September *U-589* was detected and sunk ahead of the convoy by the destroyer *Faulknor*.

The first U-boat attack took place on 13 September when PQ.18 was 150 miles northwest of Bear Island and about to turn into the Barents Sea. Shortly before 09.00, the *Stalingrad* and *Oliver Ellsworth* were torpedoed by *U-408*. The Commodore ordered the convoy to make an 'Emergency turn' after the first attack but too late to save the second ship.

The *Stalingrad* (Master A. Sakharov) one of six Russian merchant ships in the convoy, was hit amidships on the starboard side at the coalbunker. A column of fire rose into the air and the boilers exploded. The *Stalingrad* is estimated to have sunk in under four minutes. Crew and passengers abandoned ship in the port lifeboats, all those on the starboard side having been destroyed by the force of the explosion. One boat capsized causing further casualties. Sixteen crew and five passengers were reported lost (some accounts differ), the survivors being rescued by MMS *90* and MMS *203*. The Master, last to leave his ship, spent forty minutes in the freezing water before he was picked up. Nevertheless, he later served as a river pilot for the convoy on reaching North Russia and was subsequently awarded the Distinguished Service Cross.

The American Liberty ship *Oliver Ellsworth*, not yet three months old, loaded with ammunition and a deck cargo of aircraft, sailing in the same column but two stations behind, steered hard to port to avoid the *Stalingrad* but was hit by a second torpedo in her starboard side between no. 4 and no. 5 holds. (It was later established *U-408* fired three torpedoes; one hit the *Stalingrad* and two missed. Unfortunately, one of these latter two struck the *Oliver Ellsworth*.) The engines were stopped and the eight officers, thirty-four crew and twenty-eight USN armed guards abandoned ship in four lifeboats within fifteen minutes of the strike, fearing the cargo would explode. But the *Oliver Ellsworth* maintained headway, causing both starboard lifeboats to swamp. One of the port lifeboats then struck a raft and sank. The survivors in the remaining lifeboats began to search for and pick up those who had jumped overboard. All were rescued within the hour by the *St Kenan*. At 09.45, after the rescue action was complete, *Harrier* set the *Oliver Ellsworth* on fire with eight 4-inch HE rounds. Fifteen Russian survivors were transferred from MMS *203* to *Harrier*. All the rescue ships rejoined the convoy by about 11.00. At 11.15 the *Oliver Ellsworth* sank stern first.

The first series of air attacks came at 15.00 while the screen was reforming on the return of *Scylla* and five destroyers, 450 miles from the German air stations. In the preliminary attack six Ju.88 aircraft dropped bombs through gaps in the clouds, from a height of about 4,000 feet; in the misty conditions and low cloud no ships were lost or damaged and no enemy aircraft hit. This may however have been designed as a diversion, as when the attackers were sighted *Avenger* launched a number of Hurricane fighters which were then left out of position when the main attack developed thirty minutes later.

Over forty torpedo bombers, Ju.88s and He.111s, each armed with two torpedoes, attacked from the starboard bow at low altitude, undetected by radar so giving little more than visual warning of the attack. This whole body of aircraft was described as spreading from ahead of the convoy round the starboard side to the quarter and approaching in line abreast. According to the Convoy Commodore, Rear Admiral E. K. Boddam-Whetham,

> [They were] like a huge flight of nightmare locusts: flying 30 to 40 feet above the water, and keeping such good station 100 to 150 yards apart that, says Rear Admiral Burnett, it was impossible to break them up.

The aircraft attacked the starboard wing of the convoy, a few passing ahead and flying down either side of *Scylla*, which steamed out ahead to respond, and came under an intense barrage of AA fire from the escort and merchant ships. As the largest number appeared to be coming in on the bow, the Convoy Commodore ordered a 45° emergency turn to starboard to bring the merchant ships head on to the enemy aircraft and reduce the target profile, but the two starboard columns either 'wheeled' or did not turn at all, leading Rear Admiral Burnett to believe the Commodore had purposely refrained from altering course.

One of the first merchant ships to be hit was the British *Empire Stevenson*. The torpedo detonated her cargo of munitions and eyewitnesses described how the ship, 'went up' in a tremendous explosion, with first a yellow flash, then a great red cloud of smoke and flame ascending to a height of more than 3,000 feet.

Some commentaries record sailors on several ships in the convoy who were temporarily unable to comprehend what had happened to the *Empire Stevenson* such was the enormity of the explosion when the torpedo struck, describing how the ship quite literally,

> disappeared without a trace, in an instant, a plume of smoke seeming to rise thousands of feet into the air, followed by the acrid smell of burnt oil and a tell tale oil slick on the sea where seconds before the ship had been.

Several also commented on how quiet it all seemed after the strike. The Chief Officer of the *Ocean Faith*, sailing off the port bow of the *Empire Stevenson*, recalled:

> She was attacked and blew up. But a strange thing, we never heard any explosions from her, it was one huge flash – the ship wasn't there – and it was just as though one minute the ship was there and the next minute there was floating debris and soot on the surface of the sea – it was incredible. ... it was obvious that there were no survivors.

He was correct; all fifty-nine crew – forty-one merchant seamen and eighteen DEMS gunners – were killed.

The next victim, the Panamanian registered *Africander* carrying machinery and a deck cargo of six tanks and five aircraft, was hit by two aerial torpedoes dropped from around 150 feet. These struck the starboard side aft of no. 3 hold causing her to settle slowly by the stern. Her engines were immediately shut down. There was no fire, but the force of the explosion disabled the steering gear and ruptured the watertight bulkheads and she sank by the stern within a few minutes. There were no casualties among the crew of twenty-five and eleven USN armed guards, all of whom abandoned ship in the lifeboats despite being machine-gunned by enemy aircraft.

The American freighter *Wacosta*, sailing in the same column and immediately astern of the *Empire Stevenson*, bore the brunt of the blast when the latter blew up. The force of the explosion devastated the *Wacosta*'s superstructure, and burning debris showered down on the decks. The force of the explosion damaged much of the ship's machinery and the engines stopped. Whether she could have survived will never be known since a torpedo then struck and penetrated no. 2 hatch without touching the water. A series of explosions were heard, a hole was blown in the ship's side, and she began to sink immediately by the bow. Fortunately, there were no casualties. All of the thirty-five crew and eleven USN armed guards were rescued by the *Harrier* and later transferred along with survivors from other ships to *Scylla*.

The Russian cargo steamer *Sukhona* was torpedoed in the same attack. Little is known of her cargo or crew. She was abandoned while still under way, the crew were rescued by MMS *90* and later transferred to the rescue ship *Copeland*. The *Sukhona* was later lost to sight in snowstorms, and it is not known when or where she sank.

The next victim, the British freighter *Empire Beaumont*, was on her maiden voyage. Although most of the other merchant ships hit were in columns 9 and 10, she was sailing at the head of column 4 towards the port side of the convoy, away from the main thrust of the attack. When torpedoed she caught fire but did not sink, giving the majority of the crew time to abandon ship and take to the lifeboats. *Sharpshooter* rescued thirty-three survivors (some accounts say *Copeland*, but this is not verified – they may have been transferred to her subsequently). Twenty-eight were later transferred to *Scylla* and five landed at Archangel for transfer to the *Empire Bard*. Five crew and two DEMS gunners were lost. The *Empire Beaumont* was left on fire with her forecastle head awash and was still afloat at 16.45, but it was later concluded she had sunk by 18.30.

The American freighter *Oregonian*, sailing as the leading ship at the head of the outer starboard column, was hit by three aerial torpedoes. These destroyed the entire starboard side of the ship, flooded the engine room and caused her to list to starboard. Lifeboats were lowered but the *Oregonian* capsized and sank almost immediately, before many of the crew could get clear. Twenty-two sailors, including the Master and seven USN armed guards were killed. Fourteen survivors were picked up by MMS *212* (other accounts say *St Kenan*).

The next casualty was the American freighter *John Penn*. Very little is known of her history or cargo. She had previously experienced problems in keeping up with the convoy and narrowly avoided being sent back to Iceland; unfortunately, her luck now ran out. She was hit by two torpedoes, the first striking starboard amidships and the second in the starboard bow. Three of the engine room crew were killed. The engines stopped and she began to settle in the water. Thirty-seven of the crew of forty and the twenty-five men of the USN armed guard abandoned ship and were rescued by *Harrier*. There were reports she might not have been seriously damaged and that both ship and cargo might have been saved had the crew not abandoned ship prematurely, but given her condition and the difficulty of salvage under hostile conditions the decision was taken to sink her with five rounds of 4-inch shell fired by *Harrier*. She was last seen at about 18.15 settling by the stern, but it is not known where or when she sank.

The Panamanian registered *Macbeth*, with a cargo of war supplies, foodstuffs, and deckload of tanks, sailing astern of the *Oregonian*, was attacked by an He.111 from the starboard bow at a height of about 80 feet. The aircraft released two torpedoes at close range and banked away unscathed. These struck the *Macbeth* in the starboard side below the waterline, rendering her helpless; the crew abandoned ship and left her sinking slowly by the head. Thirty-eight crew and eleven USN armed guards were rescued by MMS *90* (other accounts say *St Kenan*). *Harrier* attempted to sink the wreck by shellfire. Again, it is not known where or when the *Macbeth* sank.

Overall, the attack had been extremely successful, decimating the starboard side of the convoy formation, sinking six of the remaining seven, and two from the middle of the convoy – the *Empire Beaumont*, *John Penn*, *Empire Stevenson*, *Wacosta*, *Africander*, *Oregonian*, *Macbeth*, and *Sukhona*. In thirteen minutes the Luftwaffe had sunk or fatally damaged eight ships for the cost of five aircraft; the heaviest defeat ever suffered by a British convoy in a single air attack. Despite exaggerated claims made for the numbers of enemy aircraft shot down, official German records confirm only four He.111s shot down and ditched in the sea after the first attack. Two aircrews were rescued by air-sea rescue aircraft and one by *U-457* but the latter drowned when the U-boat was sunk on 16 September by *Impulsive*. The fourth aircrew was not found.

Many ships had narrow escapes. Captain McLeod, Vice Commodore in the *Dan-Y-Bryn*, reported no fewer than six torpedoes running more or less parallel to his ship after she completed her 45° emergency turn. The attack left the American freighter *William Moultrie* the only merchant ship in the starboard column – always the side from which the attacks were made – and there were now gaps inside the convoy formation where vessels had been sunk. The Master of the *William Moultrie*, Captain Hopkins, demanded his ship – carrying more TNT than most – be placed in a safer position, so she was allowed to exchange with the British *Goolistan* (later lost in QP.15). The Commodore informed Captain Hopkins the only difference he could see between 4,000 tons of TNT and 2,000 tons was a fractional part of a second should his ship be hit.

The Chief Officer of the *Ocean Faith* was convinced more controlled firing could have shot down more torpedo bombers. The aircraft that torpedoed the *Empire Beaumont* flew directly across the *Ocean Faith* almost at masthead height. The crew saw the aircraft coming straight at the ship's bridge, where the gunners were operating twin Colt machine guns. Had those on the side nearest the approaching aircraft not stopped firing and ducked he concluded they would have very likely shot it down, but their reaction was perhaps understandable in the circumstances. There was such a lot of crossfire going on and it was difficult in the confusion to differentiate between the enemy aircraft and the Hurricanes, even though the Hurricanes had one engine and the He.111s two; events were happening too quickly.

There are many accounts at this point of ships in the convoy receiving collateral damage from friendly fire. The air was filled with anti-aircraft shell and machine gun bullets from the naval and merchant ships as the aircraft flew through the columns at low altitude. The resulting crossfire from friendly ships proved almost as much of a hazard as the enemy air attacks and several merchant ships were damaged by what was described as 'indiscriminate' firing from vessels in adjacent columns. As the torpedo bombers were flying at below masthead height the superstructures of the nearby merchant ships obstructed the gunners' aim. Consequently, many ships had their upper works riddled with machine-gun bullets and larger calibre shells. The captain of the *Ulster Queen* later described how it had been:

> The wild firing of some of the merchant ships was at times highly dangerous, being particularly noticeable amongst the Americans – indeed *Ulster Queen* had one man at 'Y' gun very slightly wounded and sustained her only damage in this manner.

Commodore Boddam-Whetham in his convoy report commented in similar vein:

> It was a most unpleasant sight when every US ship in the vicinity opened fire on the CAM Ship's Hurricane although the ship was in middle of the convoy, and everyone had been warned about it.

At 16.15 the convoy was attacked again, this time by the eight He.115s of K.Fl.Gr.406. No ships were hit and no damage done. One He.115 was reportedly shot down by the convoy's anti-aircraft barrage (though this is not confirmed by Luftwaffe records). The remainder dropped torpedoes at long range; these were easily evaded. During this attack the Sea Hurricanes were diverted to search for a shadowing BV.138, which shot down one Sea Hurricane of 802 Squadron FAA without receiving any apparent damage.

The last torpedo-bomber attack of the day came at 20.35 when it was almost dark, with the convoy reformed in eight columns. About a dozen He.115s of 1/906 approached from ahead, attacking in small groups for half an hour or so. No ships were hit, and no damage done. Luftwaffe records indicate one He.115 was lost.

It is difficult to imagine how the crews of the ships in PQ.18 viewed the start of the new day on 14 September, on their long voyage to Archangel. No doubt some were thinking of their good fortune to have survived the mass attacks of the previous day and of those who had been lost, while also contemplating anxiously the dangers this new day might bring.

At 03.10 BST, on 14 September when the convoy was southwest of Bear Island (Bjørnøya), Norway, steaming at a speed of 8½ knots, the fleet tanker *Atheltemplar*, trailing half a mile astern of the convoy, was torpedoed by *U-457* which had slipped within the protective escort screen. Fortunately, the torpedo struck in the engine room on the port side just missing the fuel storage tanks, having already passed under the rescue ship *Copeland* and just astern of *Bryony*. *U-457* then dived and passed directly under the convoy, the sound of its propellers masked by the noise of the vessels on the surface, and escaped.

Immediately after the torpedo struck the crew heard a dull explosion and the *Atheltemplar* swung to starboard. None of the crew appeared to have seen the track of the torpedo, but the Master reported observing a large patch of oil astern covering an area of about 100 square feet, probably the ship's own diesel oil. Hanging over the furthest edge of this patch, 200–300 feet astern of the vessel, a blueish-coloured flame about two feet high burned for fully ten minutes. The force of the explosion blew away the port after lifeboat, badly fractured the Bofors Gun platform, but caused surprisingly little other visible external damage. However communication between the bridge and the engine-room was lost, the ship's telegraph jammed, all the lights failed, the engine-room and stokehold began flooding, and the engines stopped. The tanker then began to settle very rapidly by the stern. The crew did not fire an emergency signal rocket or send a wireless SOS signal, knowing the other ships would have seen that the *Atheltemplar* had been torpedoed.

The Master ordered the crew to take to the lifeboats. As the port after boat had been destroyed some of the designated occupants went round to the starboard after boat, and others to the port midships boat. There was some difficulty in launching the starboard after lifeboat. Ice had filled the plughole and frozen the blocks. The starboard midships boat was lowered successfully but broke adrift with only three occupants. The remainder climbed into the port midships boat, about thirty men. At this point the senior second engineer, emerging from his cabin, heard shouting from below. He looked down into the engine-room but could see nothing through the steam and oil fumes, other than that it was flooded with water and fuel oil to well over the top of the engines – a depth of about 25 feet. Shining a torch down the engine-room skylight to see if he could spot where the shouts were coming from, he noticed all the ladders including the emergency escape ladder had been destroyed. Word that men were still in the engine-room was passed to the second officer, engaged in clearing the starboard after lifeboat for lowering and still having difficulty due to the accumulation of ice. The junior third engineer was then sent back to the senior second engineer's assistance. After shouting into the engine-room he located the assistant engineer trapped in the forward starboard wing. The Chief Officer had intended to assist the second officer with lowering the lifeboat but on hearing there were still men in the engine-room went there to join the rescue party. They discovered a second man, one of the firemen, was also trapped. A rope was lowered down through the skylights into the engine room to the assistant engineer. By this time the starboard after lifeboat was at last successfully lowered into the water. Its crew were ordered to remain alongside with their boat to await the return of the rescue party and the rescued men. All this time the *Atheltemplar* was slowly settling by the stern. The second officer then joined the rescue party, accompanied by another assistant engineer and one of the DEMS gunners.

The trapped assistant engineer managed to catch the rope lowered into the engine room, but it was not long enough for him to make it fast round himself. A second rope was let down, but he lacked sufficient strength to hold on and be hauled up on deck. With the aid of these ropes, however, he did manage to reach the engine room athwartship beam, about 15 feet immediately below the skylight by then awash with oil and water. The same ropes were then used to assist the fireman on to the strongback, but he lacked the strength to climb on to it from the oily water. The second officer now secured the lifeboat embarkation ladder and lowered it through the skylight into the engine room. The assistant engineer made a fresh attempt to climb up but slipped and fell back exhausted. The Chief Officer then went down the ladder. He tied one rope round the assistant engineer and another round the fireman. The rescue party hauled the assistant engineer up while the fireman was being made secure. The Chief Officer then went back up on deck to assist in hauling the fireman up. But the fireman was a very heavy man and his clothes were soaked in oil – as they hauled, the rope holding him slipped under his arms and was then pulled up over his head. When he was just six or seven feet away from the skylight and safety he slipped through the rope and fell onto the beam. By now unconscious he was unable to help himself. Although the water level in the engine room was still rising, the Chief Officer descended again and secured another line round the fireman. Whilst the rescue party on deck were pulling on the rope he freed the man's leg which had become trapped between some pipes and the beam. The fireman was at last successfully hauled to the top by means of the motorboat falls. The whole rescue party then assisted in the tricky task of bringing him out through the skylight.

Rear Admiral (Destroyers) had earlier directed that if *Atheltemplar* could still steam the *Sharpshooter* was to tow her to Lowe Sound on Spitzbergen. Although the tanker was settled low in the water it was evident she was not actually sinking (oil tankers retained buoyancy so long as the cargo tanks were not breached) and given the strategic value of her cargo there was benefit in attempting a salvage operation even though she could no longer steam under her own power. *Harrier* therefore passed her a tow wire but this broke owing to the swell. A second tow wire was secured to the stern of the tanker – by now only about a foot above the water. *Harrier* briefly took the *Atheltemplar* in tow with a view to taking her on to the Kola Inlet, but as there were still at least five U-boats in contact with the convoy it was decided not to continue without an adequate escort (under the circumstances very unlikely). A further attack was almost certain and the risk of losing the towing ship and both the ships' companies could not be justified. The Master of *Atheltemplar* and CO of *Harrier* agreed the tanker was likely to remain afloat if left abandoned (there was also the possibility she might be salvaged by the enemy). The CO of *Harrier* therefore very reluctantly signalled RA (D) his intention to sink her and was ordered to do so. At this point the destroyer *Tartar* arrived from an anti-submarine hunt and was delegated the task of sinking the *Atheltemplar*.[13]

Harrier left to rejoin the convoy now about 12 miles ahead and the survivors were instructed to remain below deck to keep her centre of gravity low. When *Atheltemplar*'s Master went back up on deck he saw his ship on fire. *Tartar* had thrown a depth charge under the tanker and must also have fired one or two shells into her oil tanks, as heavy columns of smoke were rising into the air. At noon he could still see the smoke from his old ship; this was the last he saw of her. There were now about 200 survivors on board *Harrier* and at 13.00 a number were transferred to *Scylla*, with the rest of the *Atheltemplar* survivors from the *Sharpshooter*. Just after the transfer another high-level bombing attack developed but the survivors, still kept below decks, saw nothing of it. *Tartar* left the *Atheltemplar* burning, yet she would not sink. Later that day at around 14.30, *U-408* came across the capsized and drifting wreck north of Bear Island and sank her with the 88mm deck gun.

By midday on 14 September the weather was clear and calm with 8/10 cloud cover at 2,000 feet and the convoy was between Spitzbergen and Hope Island. The first sighting of enemy aircraft came at 12.35 when one of *Avenger*'s Swordfish aircraft spotted groups of planes approaching at very low level below the radar. *Avenger* went to action stations and flew off three sections of Hurricanes. The first attack developed at 12.40 when twenty-two Ju.88s of III./KG 26 approached in an extended line across the broad front of the convoy. They flew through the escort screen then split into two groups to systematically attack the *Avenger* from both sides of the convoy. Lookouts on the ships saw twelve planes coming down outside on the port wing with the remaining eight passing between the starboard columns. Apparently at the last moment, the formation leader realized the *Avenger* had fighters deployed, the carefully rehearsed attack was abandoned, and the leading torpedo bombers attempted to reform a defensive line. Three Ju.88s were shot down and two damaged by anti-aircraft fire during this phase.

Avenger steamed out ahead of the convoy to gain greater freedom to manoeuvre whilst launching more Hurricanes, and *Wilton* and *Wheatland* put up a covering AA barrage. The *Ulster Queen* also steamed out to meet the main attack. The fighters drove off some of the attackers while AA fire made others drop their torpedoes at long range. No ships were hit.

The Germans lost eleven aircraft. Rear Admiral Burnett, in Battle History Summary 22, para 47, commented:

> It was a fine sight to see *Avenger* peeling off Hurricanes, whilst streaking across the front of the convoy from starboard to port inside the screen with her destroyer escort blazing away with any gun that could bear, and then being chased by torpedo bombers as she steamed down on the opposite course to the convoy to take cover. Altogether a most gratifying action.

As the aircraft approached the Commodore had ordered an emergency turn 45° to port to 'comb' the torpedoes' tracks and there were no casualties (as recorded in his report). The second attack broke up soon after penetrating the escort screen with some aircraft dropping their torpedoes at a range of 4,000 yards before turning away. By 12.45 this latest phase of the attack had ended with two more enemy aircraft shot down, no ships hit and no damage done. Almost immediately however, twelve Ju.88 torpedo bombers of I./KG30 arrived overhead and commenced shallow dive-bombing out of the clouds, mainly on the port side of the convoy where their target again was the *Avenger*. After the first attack *Ulster Queen* just had time to circle back to her position, no. 4 in the 2nd column, to open fire on these aircraft which were about fifteen minutes too late to synchronize their activity with the previous attack. This second onslaught lasted from 12.50 to 14.10 and consisted of individual bombing runs by small groups of Ju.88s, coming down out of the cloud at 6,000 feet to drop their bombs at 2,000 feet. The escort opened fire whenever bombers appeared below cloud cover. At about 13.25 two bombs dropped by a Ju.88 exploded off the *Avenger*'s port side. Other ships of the escort also had narrow escapes – the *Ulster Queen* was near missed by two bombs exploding 30 yards off her port bow. *Gleaner* had a similar experience, with two bombs dropping 50 yards off her starboard beam. Another two bombs fell within the formation of the convoy but no damage was done and one Ju.88 was damaged.

The *Avenger* was steaming off the convoy's starboard quarter with four Hurricanes up when the third attack developed around 14.05. Twenty-two He.111s from I./KG 26 supported by 18 Ju.88s from III./KG 30. The 'firing arcs' on the *Ulster Queen* were masked by the superstructures of the ships in the port wing column as she steamed out to the flank of the convoy to engage the aircraft. Still flying low, the majority retained their torpedoes for use against *Avenger* but were unable to find a suitable release point. Some of the torpedoes dropped ran into the tracks of the merchant ships in the convoy. No 'emergency turn' was ordered, as the merchant ships were not the direct target. Many torpedoes were seen to pass harmlessly down through the convoy, but at 14.15, the *Mary Luckenbach* was hit as she crossed the track of a torpedo running in from the starboard side. Commodore Boddam-Whetham later recalled in his official report:

> She completely detonated. A huge column of blue and grey smoke went up to the cloud base and there mushroomed out.

> A number of ships were hit and damaged and casualties were sustained from this explosion. *Nathanael Greene* thought she had been torpedoed and is much damaged but managed to complete the voyage with the help of her pumps.

The *Mary Luckenbach* was carrying a cargo of munitions including 1,000 tons of TNT. When the torpedo struck she disintegrated in a huge explosion. Little was left when rescue craft arrived to look for survivors.

A number of merchant ships sailing close to the *Mary Luckenbach* suffered varying degrees of collateral damage. The explosion shook the nearby *Scoharie* as though she had been torpedoed, throwing men flat on the deck. Fragments of hot steel crashed down on them from bow to stern. The *Nathanael Greene* sailing on the port side of the *Mary Luckenbach* had just changed course to avoid the track of one of several aerial torpedoes. The commander first thought his ship had been hit and ordered the crew to lifeboat stations, but countermanded the order when it became apparent there was no immediate danger. All the same, the *Nathanael Greene* did suffer significant damage. The shockwave from the explosion threw the gunners from their stations, damaged most of the deck cargo, blew hatches from their fittings, broke porthole windows, damaged bulkhead doors, the ship's hospital, crockery, and other fittings and knocked the ship's compasses out of adjustment. Several of the crew and armed guards were injured and one crewman was reported missing, blown overboard. Despite all this the *Nathanael Greene*'s main engine remained functional and she continued on to Archangel.[14]

The force of the explosion, terrific noise and vibration also made some of those on the *Ocean Faith* think their ship had been hit. Shrapnel from the

Mary Luckenbach rained down on them, puncturing the hulls of the steel lifeboats, while the shockwave flattened ventilators, sprang radiators from the bulkheads, smashed crockery and threw compasses out of true.

Various eyewitness accounts survive of the moments before and after the *Mary Luckenbach* was hit:

> The plane came in to about 300 yards before dropping its torpedoes and then swept on. As it passed, the ship's gunner raked it fore and aft and bright tongues of flame flickered from its starboard engine. It dipped, recovered, dipped again and seemed just about to crash, when its torpedoes reached their mark and the ship simply vanished into thin air. It took the plane with it.

> A stupendous column of smoke was rocketing to heaven, and as we looked an immense glow lit the column, and great cerise, orange-and-yellow fragments arched outwards towards us ... [later] the great smoke column was still thousands of feet high and mushrooming out where it met the clouds. At its base flames still flickered and the following ship was altering course to avoid them.

> One second the ship was there and the next there is a blinding flash followed by a terrific crash. Smoke towers into the sky and when it clears away not even a piece of wood can be seen.

> There was a tremendous explosion and debris showered down on us on *Daneman* like hail. Nothing and no one was left when the smoke cleared.

Captain Richard Hockey of the *William Moultrie*, steaming in the same column immediately astern of the *Luckenbach*, said when his ship passed over the spot: 'There was nothing left of her at all – not even a raft – no wreckage, not even a matchbox; hardly a ripple on the surface of the sea.' Nothing remained of the ship except a pillar of smoke when rescue craft arrived to look for survivors.

Sharpshooter was ordered to search for survivors from the incident and, after cruising around for some time in a sea covered with pieces of wreckage and oily scum, spotted a man on the edge of the debris field and pulled him on board remarkably uninjured apart from shock. It transpired he was a cook from a Liberty ship who told them he had been manning the ship's after gun when a sudden explosion blew him into the sea – apparently the only man to survive. It was later established that, though many published accounts contain the apocryphal claim he was the sole survivor of the *Mary Luckenbach* (which should have seemed extremely improbable in the circumstances), he was actually the after gunner from the *Nathanael Greene*, the crewman previously mentioned as having been blown into the water by the force of the explosion.[15] Seven I./KG 26 He.111s were lost and a further four returned damaged to base, where two crash-landed.

Many later recollections of the events that took place during this day and indeed during the previous attacks can, if not corroborated by other original sources, prove unreliable and fallible through false memory, and/or the passage of time. Details of dates and events can become confused; some untrue assertions can be sufficiently perpetuated as to be accepted as facts. In the heat of battle, with events sometimes lasting only a few minutes, plus the distractions of noise, danger and fear, records and memories can easily become confused. And so it was with PQ.18. On 15 September, Surgeon Lieutenant Commander Coulter in the *Scylla* wrote in his diary:

> Afraid that I could not possibly set down the detailed events of today with any accuracy, as the noise and activity have been so extreme most of the time, that it has been rather a 'blur'. There were certainly some heavy air attacks but I am not sure whether some of them did not take place yesterday instead of today.

> The general noise and confusion were unbelievable. At the height of the attack, the ship was near missed, and at the same time the safety valve lifted on one of the smokestacks and for about five minutes there was also the noise of steam escaping under pressure, which was itself deafening.

By 08.00 on the 16th four Russian destroyers arrived and at 15.30 the ocean escort began to depart to join QP.14. The farewell signal to the Home Fleet destroyers from the Convoy Commodore read as follows:

> Wednesday 16th September 1945 To ..... R.A.D. From Commodore.
> Before you leave us I wish to thank you and your forces very much indeed for the great efforts you have made for our protection. Do not, anyone of the screen, blame himself because a couple of Submarines got through. The scale of their attack must have been immense and that

from the air had to be seen to be believed. You had some near shaves and I hope you will all get home safely and reap the rewards you so well deserve. It is good for a 'Has Been' to see 'The Destroyer Service' still goes on as it always has done and is so ably led and commanded by yourself. Once more, my own and PQ.18's thanks to you all and I trust that the hope expressed in the Book of Proverbs, Chapter six, verse ten, will shortly come true for everyone.

Prov. 6:10: 'Yet a little sleep, a little slumber, a little folding of the hands to sleep.'

Signal timed 07.31.

The reply from Rear Admiral Burnett read:

To Commodore. From R.A.D.

We all thank you for your most appreciative signal. It is fine to have sailed with your gallant convoy. Please convey to them, in due course, my and our admiration for them. The Home Fleet destroyers and myself would have you feel it is 'the likes of you' taught 'the likes of us' and if we meet with your approbation we are proud.

'May you finish the course successfully' is our wish to you. Signal timed 08.25

At 11.30 another wave of twelve He.111s delivered an almost identical attack and *Empire Morn's* Sea Hurricane was launched to intercept. It was subsequently confirmed the pilot (Flying Officer A. H. Barr) shot down two Ju.88s, drove off other enemy aircraft by dummy attacks then finally flew 240 miles to an airfield near Archangel, where he landed with only four gallons of petrol remaining. Once again however two of the merchant ships in the convoy opened fire at the Hurricane with their close-range armament from the moment it was launched until it flew unscathed out of range. Such uncontrolled behaviour by these ships, usually American, was a source of constant irritation and concern to the Convoy Commodore.

Unlike the first attack, the second wave of torpedo bombers split into two sections and attacked from both port and starboard sides. Now the dive-bombers managed to synchronize their attacks with the torpedo bombers and, as the first wave of torpedo bombers began their run-in, began bombing through the cloud from about 2,500 feet. The port group of aircraft launched their torpedoes simultaneously at about 4,000 yards range, at heights varying between 50 and 150 feet. Those launched from the greatest height appeared to bounce back into the air after impact. The aircraft in the starboard group made a much more determined effort, closing to 1,000 yards before dropping their torpedoes, but most appeared to finish their runs amongst the rear ships and at least eight broke surface around the *Ulster Queen* who had turned stern on to the line of attack as soon as the torpedoes were seen to be dropped.

When, on 18 September, Russia proper came into view and the tip of the Kanin Peninsula was sighted it must have seemed the greatest dangers were past. Not so, as shortly before 10.00 *Ulster Queen*'s Type 279 radar plotted a large group of aircraft approaching from the west. Low flying He.111s were then spotted on the starboard quarter at 10.20. *Ulster Queen* had taken up station in the rear of the convoy formation between the fourth and fifth of the seven remaining columns when the main escort left. A turn was now made to bring all her main armament to bear, and she opened fire at 10,000 yards. In a change from previous tactics the planes now attacked from astern. Twelve spread across the rear of the convoy deploying to line abreast on the same course. The attackers met a robust barrage of anti-aircraft fire from the *Gremyaschiy*, *Sharpshooter*, and *Ulster Queen* as well as the rear merchant ships and smaller craft. The attack was so low a 'splash barrage' was put up.

Most aircraft released their torpedoes at 3–4,000 yards; these seemed to break the surface of the sea and finish their run against the rear ships. The *Kentucky* in the port wing column was hit in the no. 2 hold and dropped astern. Her fifty-five crew and fourteen armed guards promptly abandoned ship, although *Kentucky* remained afloat. *Harrier* proceeded to the rear of the escort screen, ordering *Sharpshooter* to organize rescue work with the *Cape Mariato* and Motor Minesweepers *90* and *203*, the latter picking up the crew of the *Kentucky*.

Sharpshooter was ordered by *Ulster Queen* to stand by *Kentucky* until tugs arrived, with the *Cape Mariato* retained to act as additional escort. As the *Kentucky* was in no danger of sinking and was still capable of steaming, *Sharpshooter* waited, intending to place a naval salvage party onboard and persuade the crew to return to their ship as soon as the air attack was over. Then, whilst she was turning to go alongside *Kentucky*, both ships were dive-bombed by a Ju.88. *Kentucky* was hit aft by two bombs and set on fire. *Sharpshooter* suffered a slight leak in her port oil fuel tanks from two near misses. It was now judged impossible to go alongside *Kentucky* with her stern on fire and the situation was made increasingly uncomfortable by the torpedo bombers. *Sharpshooter* fired a few rounds into the burning hull of the *Kentucky*. *Cape Mariato* was ordered to follow *Sharpshooter* to rejoin the convoy under cover of their own AA barrage (the convoy was still under torpedo attack). The trawler was bombed three times en route without injury. *Sharpshooter*, *Cape Mariato*, and MMS *90* and *203* then rejoined the convoy with the complete ship's company of the *Kentucky* joined by the *Uritsky*.

In the late afternoon of 18 September the local eastern escort of *Britomart*, *Salamander*, *Halcyon*, and *Hazard* arrived. When the convoy reached Cape Gorodetski at the entrance to the White Sea, on 19 September, it formed up in two columns and sailed south into the White Sea and the Dvina Bar at the approach to Archangel. Up until midday the sea remained dead flat calm, but the wind increased during the afternoon and by the time the ships arrived off the Bar at 16.00 the weather had begun to deteriorate, leading to a full northwesterly gale by 18.00. With darkness coming on the Commodore ordered the convoy to anchor, as the heavy weather at the time prevented the convoy from proceeding upriver.

The seas were now far too heavy for the ships to take pilots aboard and too rough to anchor. Some merchant ships tried to anchor but dragged or parted their cables and by daylight they were widely scattered. Three American merchants, the *Campfire*, *Sahale*, and *Lafayette*, and the minesweeper *Daneman* had run hard aground on Dvina Bar during the storm the previous evening.

During the afternoon of 20 September at around 15.30, as the ships were struggling to find shelter from the ongoing gale, the convoy was attacked by twelve Ju.88 dive-bombers. Fortunately, there had been advance warning of this attack. The Ju.88s conducted a series of high level bombing runs through the 8/10 cloud at 2,000 feet. Their attack was ineffective, and no damage was done. The *Ulster Queen* took up position close to the largest section of about ten merchant ships and put up a controlled and lengthy AA barrage; two aircraft were shot down and the remainder flew away after about half an hour, having achieved nothing. The Commodore's report noted the only hit to have been scored by a bomb was on the *Kentucky* after she had been abandoned. At 20.30 when it was quite dark, a Ju.88 flew at less than mast height over the bows of *Ulster Queen* and although fired on flew off unscathed.

The weather moderated during the night and at 08.45 on 21 September, twenty-four of the merchant ships of PQ.18 and escort (less *Daneman*) began going up harbour to various areas within the port to berth. *Harrier* proceeded upriver, piloted by the Master of the *Stalingrad* and landed twenty-four Russian survivors at Krasny Quay. Operations to salvage the three stranded merchant ships began on 25 September, when they began to discharge their cargo into lighters. The *Empire Bard* and *Empire Elgar* with their heavy lifting equipment were sent to speed up the unloading process. All three of the merchants were successfully refloated between 25 and 27 September and berthed up in Archangel, but the *Daneman* was not recovered until 7 October.

Twenty-seven of those forty merchant ships which sailed from Iceland on 2 September eventually reached Archangel safely, although a number arrived with varying degrees of damage. The twenty-eighth, the *Kentucky*, was bombed in the White Sea on 18 September, her cargo later salvaged by the Russians.

By comparison with PQ.17, and despite the losses, convoy PQ.18 was judged by some a success and a turning point in the fortunes of the convoys to North Russia. But others including Rear Admiral Burnett, regarded it as having been 'a close run thing'. There was certainly reasonable ground for satisfaction over the outcome and although the loss of merchant ships had been serious the escorts had hit back hard and effectively. Four U-boats had been sunk and a significant number of aircraft and crews lost from the 337 air sorties flown.

Various sources cite different numbers of Luftwaffe aircraft lost or damaged – e.g. Captain S. W. Roskill, in *The War at Sea* states 'thirty-three torpedo aircraft; six long-range Bombers and two reconnaissance aircraft were destroyed.' Post-war analysis gives thirty-one shot down and eleven damaged.

The defence of the convoy was subsequently regarded as having tipped the strategic balance in favour of the Royal Navy; moreover, it seemed clear, in Admiral Tovey's words:

> The constant [air] reconnaissance [of Altenfjord], together with the strength of the destroyer covering force, the presence of torpedo aircraft in North Russia and of our submarines off the coast, probably all contributed to the enemy's decision not to venture on a surface attack.

Rear Admiral Burnett in his official Post Convoy report stated:

> I do not know how far this operation may be visited [*sic*] to have been
> a success or failure but I am convinced that had any of a number of
> circumstances been otherwise it might have been a tragic failure.

The five determining factors relevant in his view to PQ.18 had been:

1. The weather: had conditions been bad rather than calm refuelling of the
   escorts at sea could not have been conducted as it was and the fighting
   destroyer escort would have to have been withdrawn.
2. The refuelling capability itself had one or both of the oilers been sunk,
   especially during the heavy air attacks on the 13th – the covering force
   would have had to withdraw which might have necessitated the convoy
   turning back.
3. The impact of any delay in the fighting destroyer escort refuelling before
   Scylla and the five destroyers rejoined the convoy – otherwise casualties
   during the first torpedo bomber attack might have been much higher.
4. Had the Luftwaffe followed up the first mass torpedo-bomber attack on
   the same scale, not only would very serious casualties have been incurred
   but the AA ammunition in the escorts would most likely have been
   exhausted before the convoy reached safety.
5. The most obvious point of all was that had the Germans synchronized
   the dive bomber, torpedo bomber, submarine and surface ship attacks,
   the losses would have been very heavy indeed.

Admiral Tovey remarked on the effectiveness of the air protection:

> This high scale of air support was most valuable; but a further increase
> is still required, particularly in the number of aircraft available for the
> anti-submarine escort of all forces within range of our air bases. Nor
> is one auxiliary carrier a full solution of the problem of air attack; her
> fighters are too few to deal with the great forces which the enemy brings
> against these convoys. Moreover, the weather, which on this occasion
> was exceptionally favourable to the *Avenger*, will frequently make it
> impossible to operate aircraft from her small flying deck.

QP.14 (13–26 September)

Convoy QP.14 consisting of fifteen merchant ships escorted by *Blankney*,
Middleton, Palomares, Pozarica, Dianella, Lotus, Poppy, La Malouine, Bramble

(M1), *Leda, Seagull, Lord Austin, Lord Middleton, Northern Gem* and *Ayrshire* left Archangel on 13 September for Loch Ewe, with the local eastern escort of *Halcyon, Hazard, Britomart,* and *Salamander* (13 September only). The American freighter *Ironclad* returned to harbour with defective steering gear[16] (she sailed again in QP.15). The Polish freighter *Tobruk* joined from Murmansk.

The *Scylla*, the FDE (Forces A: *Onslow, Onslaught, Opportune, Offa, Eskimo, Somali, Ashanti, Tartar;* and B: *Milne, Marne, Martin, Meteor, Faulknor, Intrepid, Fury*), the Carrier Force, *Avenger, Wheatland, Wilton;* Force Q,[17] *Grey Ranger* and *Black Ranger,* Alynbank, and submarines *P.614* and *P.615* joined the convoy from PQ.18 on 17 September.

For several days the convoy enjoyed an uneventful passage. The weather was cold. Frequent snow showers and patches of thick fog provided some protection from air attack but prevented *Avenger* from flying off any aircraft on the following day. On the morning of 19 September, the convoy continued to sail outside the range of the Luftwaffe, taking full advantage of the receding ice line and steering up the west coast of Spitzbergen. *Onslaught* was detached to escort the merchant ship *Troubadour,* which was straggling and under attack by a U-boat.

The following morning the convoy reached the Greenland Sea, now being shadowed by U-boats. The first attack came at 06.25 southwest of Spitzbergen, when *U-435* penetrated the escort screen and fired one torpedo, observing an apparent hit on a freighter after 46 seconds. Another two torpedoes were fired at 06.26 and 06.27, and two detonations heard after 4 minutes 10 seconds and 4 minutes 30 seconds respectively. A fourth torpedo fired at 06.28 also missed because it was a surface runner. *U-435* subsequently claimed one ship sunk, one damaged and one possibly damaged – in fact none were hit. At 06.31 the U-boat fired a single torpedo at a 'destroyer' and observed the ship sinking 1 minute 25 seconds after being hit. This was in fact the minesweeper *Leda,* which sank after being struck on the starboard side between the boiler rooms. *Leda* was repatriating eighteen merchant seamen from the *Navarino* and *River Afton,* sunk in PQ.17. Three of the crew of the latter were lost in the *Leda* together with one officer and forty-three ratings from the minesweeper. Of the crew of 134, the Commander, six officers, sixty-five crew, and fifteen repatriated merchant seamen were picked up by *Ayrshire, Northern Gem,* and *Seagull;* thirty-two survivors were later transferred to the rescue ship *Rathlin.*

Later at 18.15, the American freighter *Silver Sword* was hit on the port side by two torpedoes fired by *U-255*. The first struck in the bow, the explosion knocking down the forward part of the bridge. The second hit the stern, blowing off the sternpost, propeller and rudder, and blew up the after magazine. The seven officers, twenty-nine crew, twelve armed guards and sixteen passengers abandoned ship in two lifeboats and one raft. Fifty-five survivors were picked up by the *Rathlin*, and nine by *Zamalek*, one of whom later died of wounds. The wreck of the *Silver Sword* was shelled after thirty minutes by *Worcester* and sank at 19.00. The sixteen passengers were survivors from ships lost in PQ.17, fifteen from the *Honomu* and one from the *Peter Kerr*.

With the air threat receding, but increased risk of U-boat attacks, it was decided to send both *Scylla* and *Avenger*, escorted by *Fury*, *Wheatland*, and *Wilton*, back to Scapa Flow that evening to avoid exposing them to unnecessary risk and Admiral Burnett transferred his flag from *Scylla* to the *Milne*. Although the decision deprived the merchant ships of the regular anti-submarine air patrols only *Avenger* could provide (the consequences of which would soon be apparent), the Fleet Air Arm crews had reached the limits of their endurance.

This decision not to risk major warships was justified when, at 19.55, *U-703* fired a spread of three torpedoes at the destroyer *Somali*, stationed off the port wing of the convoy and observed one hit after 1 minute 32 seconds running time. Her sister ship, *Ashanti*, had unsuccessfully hunted a U-boat about 20 miles behind the convoy and rejoined at full speed, but then low on oil had changed places with *Somali* on the inner screen to await a favourable opportunity to refuel. *Ashanti* was only just ahead of *Somali* when, shortly after taking up position in the outer screen, *Somali* was hit by a torpedo on the port side abreast the engine room. The explosion flooded several compartments, blew the torpedo tubes overboard and holed the port side to a depth of about 8 feet below the waterline, killing five crew. *Somali* took a list of 15° to starboard and settled down by the stern. The leaking bulkheads on either side were promptly shored up and seemed to be holding, but there was no light or power except from an unreliable auxiliary diesel generator that powered the bilge pumps. *Zamalek* stood-by within minutes of the hit but was sent back to the convoy. *Ashanti* immediately swept round and dropped several patterns of depth charges as *Lord Middleton* came alongside *Somali* and took off about 100 merchant seamen survivors and 100 officers and ratings, leaving about 80 officers and ratings still on board as a skeleton crew, all forbidden to go below except for critical work.

The *Somali* did not sink and the CO of *Ashanti* decided to tow her to Iceland – a very long distance. Eventually, after two unsuccessful attempts, *Somali* was taken in tow at roughly 5 knots. Meanwhile the remainder of the convoy went on ahead, leaving the two sister ships alone 8 miles southwest of Jan Mayen Island. The temperature was about 25°F with an icy wind blowing and very soon snow began to fall. *Ashanti* attempted to ease the *Somali*'s passage by pumping oil over the stern to calm the sea. After an hour the tow parted again, but the ships' crews managed to rejoin the cables despite the weather conditions.

For the next three days and nights, *Ashanti* continued to tow *Somali*. At dawn on the second day, twenty ratings were sent over to *Somali* in the motor cutter to help to cut loose her deck equipment, and dump her ammunition, oil and as much top gear (easily removable equipment above the upper deck level) as possible into the sea. *Somali* was now without light and heat, her steering out of action. Her port turbine had fallen out of its mounting, making the list to starboard worse and she was by now completely waterlogged astern. During the remainder of that day *Ashanti* ran an emergency power cable to *Somali* to provide electricity for her steering motors and submersible pumps. The effort to salvage *Somali* continued; a considerable amount of top weight was jettisoned with the aid of working parties from the escorting destroyers and the degree of list reduced by pumping and bailing. Towed by *Ashanti* and escorted by *Opportune*, *Eskimo*, and *Intrepid*, *Somali* set off for Seidisfjord.

QP.14 continued to be shadowed by aircraft and U-boats throughout the day. At 05.40 on 22 September Admiral Burnett in the *Milne* parted company with the convoy, leaving it in charge of Captain Scott-Moncrieff in *Faulknor* with eleven destroyers and nine smaller ships to screen the merchant ships. After *Milne* departed, U-boats attacked again. *U-435* fired five single torpedoes at the convoy west of Jan Mayen Island and claimed five hits on three ships, the *Bellingham*, the *Ocean Voice*, and RFA *Grey Ranger*. Six of the crew from the fleet oiler RFA *Grey Ranger* were lost. The Master and thirty-two crew were picked up by the rescue ship *Rathlin* and landed at Gourock on 26 September.

The American freighter *Bellingham*, carrying a cargo of 6,100 tons of mineral ore and skins, sailing on the starboard wing in the first line of the convoy, was torpedoed in no. 4 hold on the starboard side. The engines were secured and all eight officers, thirty-one crewmen, ten armed guards and twenty-six passengers (survivors from the American merchant ships *Pan Kraft* and *Pan Atlantic*, sunk in PQ.17), abandoned ship in three lifeboats and one raft. *Bellingham* sank an hour later about 45 miles west of Jan Mayen Island. Twenty-six survivors picked up by *Rathlin* and the remainder by various escort ships were landed at Gourock on 26 September. There were no casualties.

The British merchant ship *Ocean Voice*, carrying a cargo of timber and 1,121 tons of sulphite pulp, was the ship of the Convoy Commodore, John C. K. Dowding, who had lost his ship in PQ.17. The Master, Convoy Commodore, thirty-one crew, five naval staff members, and twenty-five Russian passengers were picked up by *Seagull*, while *Zamalek* picked up sixteen crew and ten DEMS gunners; all of the crew survived. This attack came as a hard blow after so many trials and perils had been successfully surmounted, particularly for those merchant seamen who had already lost their ships in PQ.17.

Rathlin's successful rescue of 210 survivors, in addition to her own crew of 71 (plus a dog), resulted in food shortages. Permission was therefore given for *Rathlin* and *Zamalek* to leave the convoy and sail escorted by *Onslow*, *Offa*, and *Worcester* to Iceland where they would arrive at Seidisfjord late on 23 September.

During the day of the 22nd, Force P from Spitzbergen – the fleet oiler *Blue Ranger* escorted by *Oakley* and *Cowdray*, joined and oiled *Ashanti* and the other destroyers escorting *Somali*. On 23 September, after air escorts reached the convoy, a Catalina sank *U-253*. U-boat attacks then ceased. The *Onslow*, *Offa*, *Worcester*, and two rescue ships arrived at Seidisfjord that afternoon.

The remainder of the day passed without incident, but during the night of 23/24 September the weather became very heavy, the wind freshened, and *Somali*, under tow, began to yaw (swing to left and right along the direction of travel). The rate of yaw increased and north of Iceland the heavy seas caused the towing cable to part again, taking with it the power and telephone cables, after which *Somali* broke in two and sank. *Eskimo*, *Ashanti*, and *Lord Middleton* picked up the survivors. Only thirty-five men of her skeleton crew could be rescued; seventy-seven officers and ratings died, most from cold and exposure.

Events began to draw to a close on 26 September. *Rathlin* escorted by *La Malouine* was detached from QP.14 with hospital cases to the Clyde and a straggling merchant ship finally arrived in Akureyri. The main body of the convoy, ten merchant ships, with *Zamalek*, *Dianella*, *Lotus*, *Lord Austin*, *Lord Middleton*, and *Northern Gem* arrived in Loch Ewe. The last straggler arrived in Loch Ewe the following day.

Chapter 5

Suspension and Independent Sailings:
October to December 1942

Operation FB (29 October to 18 November)

The large number of ships of the Home Fleet required for Operation TORCH left too few available to provide the high level of protection needed to run convoys PQ.19 and PQ.20 and the sailings were cancelled.

The Admiralty then proposed and War Cabinet agreed, to sail ten merchant ships independently from Reykjavik to North Russia, taking advantage of the long nights and passage north of Bear Island. The Russians also agreed to sail a number of their ships independently from Beyslushaya Bay, Novaya Zemlya, to Iceland at approximately 100-mile intervals. The plan was for these independent sailings to be followed by QP.15 on about 11 November (actual date was 17 November).

On 7 October, Roosevelt agreed to add American merchant ships to the ten Churchill proposed. And so during this programme of independent sailings, code-named Operation FB, 13 merchant ships – 7 British, 5 American and 1 Russian – were sailed independently from Iceland, leaving at roughly 12-hour intervals. The original plan to sail the ships at 100-mile intervals, in order of speed, was amended to accommodate American participation, with British and American merchant ships to sail alternately. This led occasionally to one ship overtaking another along the route.

No 'through' naval escorts were provided, but four armed trawlers, *Cape Palliser*, *Northern Pride*, *Northern Spray*, and *St Elstan* were pre-positioned at intervals along the western part of the route from Iceland to act as rescue ships, whilst *Cape Argona*, *Cape Mariato*, and *St Kenan* were sailed from Murmansk to cover the eastern part of the route. In addition, two submarines, *Tuna* and the Dutch *O-15*, were deployed to provide protection between 23 October and 9 November, although their capacity to accommodate survivors was strictly limited. The eastbound ships were originally to have sailed to

Murmansk but as the ice conditions in the White Sea were better than expected, they were diverted to Archangel.

The first two eastbound merchant ships, *Richard H. Alvey* and *Empire Galliard* left Reykjavik at 12-hour intervals on 29 October. The first eastbound rescue trawler *Northern Spray* sailed early that morning. The Germans unfortunately detected the operation when on 31 October the *Northern Spray*, patrolling off Jan Mayen Island, was spotted by an FW 200, and she later detected and depth-charged a U-boat (*U-212*) in the same area. The shock from the explosion of the depth charges damaged part of the steam recycling system in the *Northern Spray*'s engine room and she had to return to Iceland on 2 November for repair, leaving a gap in the safety cover. Indications are that news of these encounters led to an increase in air reconnaissance and U-boat patrols, and later to the deployment of the *Hipper* Force of heavy cruisers.

These first two merchant ships were followed by eleven others. The *John Walker* (ship no. 3) sailed on 30 October, as did the second rescue trawler *St Elstan* and later the *Empire Gilbert* (ship no. 4). The one Russian ship, the freighter *Dekabrist*, also sailed on that day. The *John H. B. Latrobe* (ship no. 5) sailed from Reykjavik the next morning, followed later by the *Chulmleigh* (ship no. 6). The third eastbound rescue trawler *Cape Palliser* sailed for patrol the same day. The *Hugh Williamson* and *Empire Sky* (ship nos 7 and 8) left Iceland on 1 November, whilst the first westbound rescue trawler *Cape Mariato* sailed on patrol from Archangel and the fourth eastbound rescue trawler *Northern Pride* left from Reykjavik. The *Empire Scott* and *William Clark* (ship nos 9 and 10) sailed on 2 November and the second westbound rescue trawler *Cape Argona* left Archangel the same day.

After the *Northern Spray* encounter there was no further sign of enemy activity until at 01.18 on 2 November, the *Empire Gilbert* (ship no. 4 departed Reykjavik late on 30 October), sailing southwest of Jan Mayen Island was torpedoed by a U-boat (later identified as *U-586*). Two torpedoes struck the port side, and the *Empire Gilbert* sank within two minutes. The U-boat had stalked her for two hours and had missed with a first spread of two torpedoes about an hour earlier. The U-boat arrived at the sinking position thirty minutes later and rescued two survivors sitting on a beam in the ice-cold water, who were taken prisoner along with one of the six survivors on a liferaft. The U-boat crew took care of the survivors and they were landed in Norway on the 5th; however the Master, forty-six crew and seventeen DEMS gunners were lost.

The next independent, the *Daldorch* (ship no. 11) sailed at 19.45 on 3 November, and *Briarwood* (ship no. 12) at 02.45 on 4 November; the third eastbound rescue trawler, *St Kenan* left Archangel for patrol. During that day a number of ships were spotted and reported by an He.115 of KG 406A, after which a series of attacks by aircraft and U-boats developed. At 08.15 the Russian freighter *Dekabrist* reported she had come under air attack (later confirmed as Ju.88 medium-range bombers of I./KG 30). She would be attacked again on 5 November and finally sunk the following day.

Next it was the turn of the *John Walker* (ship no. 3, sailed 30 October) attacked and bombed from 11.30 by six enemy aircraft over two and a half hours. Four aircraft first appeared and began dropping bombs, but one was quickly forced to retire with smoke streaming behind. Later, two more aircraft joined. The ship underwent eight separate attacks, during six of which bombs were dropped. The *John Walker* was able to elude the attackers briefly when heavy snow began falling. When the storm cleared an aircraft approached at very close range but was driven off by anti-aircraft fire and left trailing black smoke. In all some thirty bombs were dropped near the ship.

Later the same morning the *John H. B. Latrobe* (ship no. 5, sailed 31 October) was heavily attacked, again by several He.115s, southwest of Spitzbergen. Near missed by seven torpedoes dropped at low level, her decks were strafed with machine-gun fire causing slight damage and wounding some of the crew. The attackers were again driven off by anti-aircraft fire. Shortly after, the *Empire Galliard* (ship no. 2), also reported having been attacked by aircraft and a U-boat, and SBNO North Russia believed the *Richard H. Alvey* (ship no. 1) to have been sunk.

The next casualty of the day, the *William Clark* (ship no. 10, sailed 2 November), was attacked at 11.30 by a U-boat (later identified as *U-354*) near Jan Mayen Island and hit on the port side amidships by one of three torpedoes. There are suggestions she may have been attacked earlier and damaged by bombs from a Ju.88. The torpedo struck in the engine room disabling the engine, flooding the compartment and killing the five engine room staff on watch. Eight officers, thirty-three crew and thirty USN armed guard abandoned ship in three lifeboats. The U-boat missed with another torpedo at 14.00 but struck again ten minutes later with another on the starboard side amidships. The *William Clark* broke in two and sank within a few minutes. The lifeboats kept together at first, the motor lifeboat towing the other two, but all became separated in the moderate seas. *St*

Elstan picked up twenty-six survivors in one lifeboat three days later, about 20 miles from the sinking position and landed them at Reykjavik on the 14th. Five survivors and two bodies in another boat had been picked up two days previously by *Cape Palliser* but one of them died before they were landed at Akureyri on 12 November and two of them lost legs due to exposure. The motorboat carrying the Master and twenty-two crew was never seen again after they set sail for Iceland. In total four officers, fourteen crew and thirteen USN armed guards were lost.

The same day, the Admiralty (Director Operations Division Home fleet) informed SBNO[1] North Russia by signal that *John H. B. Latrobe* and *William Clark* had been sunk. The message went on to report that enemy submarines and aircraft appeared to be active (all) along the route and recommended Russian merchant ships not already sailed be kept in harbour, and those which had not crossed 40° E, recalled. The sailing of two additional ships from Iceland had been postponed. The last two merchant ships to have sailed from Iceland, the *Daldorch* (ship no. 11, sailed 3 November) and *Briarwood* (ship no. 12, sailed 4 November) were recalled. Between the afternoons of 4 and 8 November, fog, rain, and snow shielded some, but not all, of the merchant ships along the route, from further attacks.

During 5 November the Russian freighter *Dekabrist*, and American freighter *John H. B. Latrobe* came under air attack, and the *John Walker* was located by a Russian aircraft. The first two eastbound ships to arrive in North Russia, the *Richard H. Alvey* and *Empire Galliard*, were met by Russian escorts then sighted by Russian aircraft that morning, in company with their escorts, about 100 miles north-northwest of Cape Kanin and within a few miles of each other.

The same day the British freighter *Chulmleigh* received instructions from the Admiralty to alter course to 77° N, 'before steering to pass Spitzbergen'. By this time the *Chulmleigh* had been navigating on dead reckoning for several days, with wandering compasses and in snowstorms, which meant her precise position was uncertain. Although not attacked, the *Chulmleigh* had been located during the morning in a brief break in the cloud by a BV.139 reconnaissance aircraft.

At 23.00 that evening the *Chulmleigh*, sailing on her new course in poor weather and heavy snowstorms, ran aground on a reef 10 miles south of the South Cape of Spitzbergen. (Some sources claim she was beached after having been attacked and bombed earlier in the day but this is unsubstantiated.) A distress message was sent and some of the crew took to the lifeboats. An initial attempt to restart the engines was successful but the ship could not be freed from the reef and was finally abandoned at 04.00 the following morning, when the crew took to the lifeboats again. The *Chumleigh*'s SOS was picked up by a listening station and the Admiralty sent the following signal in response, to the *Tuna* and Dutch submarine *O-15* and repeated to Operation GEARBOX:

> Following intercepted at 0315Z on 500 Kc/s. *Chulmleigh* SOS de GJGM struck reef south of south Cape Spitzbergen, making water rapidly.

The submarine *Tuna* also received the distress signal direct from the *Chulmleigh* and set off to render assistance, but was unable to locate the wreck or any survivors. Soon after daybreak on the 6th the stranded *Chulmleigh* was bombed and damaged in an attack by four Ju.88s and one He.115; two bombs hit the ship and exploded, the others missed. At around 16.00 *U-625*, homed in by the BV.139, torpedoed and shelled the stranded hulk of the *Chulmleigh* but failed to set the wreck on fire.

The Master, three crew and nine DEMS gunners landed on an isolated part of Spitzbergen. They were not rescued until 4 January 1943, by troops from the local garrison at Barentsburg; by then many had died from frostbite. The remainder eventually boarded *Bermuda* and *Cumberland* and were landed at Thurso on 16 May 1943. In total thirty-six crew and nine DEMS gunners were lost, many succumbing to frostbite. An account of the crew's subsequent deprivations appeared in the *London Gazette* of 9 November 1943[2] which announced the award of an OBE to the Master of the *Chulmleigh*, Captain Daniel Morley Williams, and an MBE to Third Officer David Firth Clark. The citation read:

> In hazy weather and difficult conditions for navigation, the ship, with a cargo of vital supplies, ran aground on a reef and had to be abandoned. The crew laid off in the boats. The next day the vessel was bombed by enemy aircraft. The survivors were then mustered in two boats, one of which was lost in the journey that followed. The Master took charge of the other and, although he fell sick on the fifth day, land was reached after seven days at sea. Almost all the occupants were suffering from frostbite, and four had died during the boat voyage. The landing was made on a desolate coast but there was nearby a number of huts, which

not only provided shelter but also contained some stores. After seven weeks of overwhelming hardships, during which fifteen men died, the nine survivors were discovered by a patrol and eventually returned to this country.

The Master displayed outstanding qualities of courage, fortitude and leadership after his ship was lost. He recovered sufficiently to resume command a few days after landing and not only helped to nurse the sick but, after three sorties had been made into the barren wastes to obtain help, he himself made a fourth.

The Third Officer also showed great courage and rendered valuable help. He took charge of the boat when the Master fell sick and was outstanding for his energetic and devoted services to his shipmates during the weeks of hardship on land. He became ill himself about a week before the survivors were rescued.

The *Richard H. Alvey* and *Empire Galliard* were by now nearing the end of their journey. Both were sighted on 6 November off Cape Kanin, close to the entrance to the Kola Inlet. The U-boat attacks continued. At 18.30 *U-625* established a contact with a steamer (later identified as the *Empire Sky)* and made visual contact one hour later. An initial attack with two spreads of two torpedoes missed the target. After a delay while the U-boat reloaded her tubes, the *Empire Sky* was attacked again. Hit by two torpedoes she settled by the bow and sent emergency radio messages. The *Hugh Williamson* received her SOS then heard a loud explosion thirty minutes later. At 22.50 a third torpedo struck the *Empire Sky*, detonating her cargo of ammunition. The ship blew up with debris falling over a wide area, some hitting the U-boat. All those aboard, the Master, forty-one crew and nine DEMS gunners were lost. Confirmation of the circumstances of the loss did not emerge until after the end of the war, following examination of the log of *U-625*. The same day the British freighters *Daldorch* and *Briarwood* were recalled to Iceland and the Russian freighter *Donbass* to the Kola inlet.

The Russian freighter *Dekabrist* was sunk the same day. She had come under air attack on the two previous days. The first onslaught had been driven off, but the crew were forced to abandon ship around midnight on 5 November after the second attack and the freighter finally sank in the early hours of 6 November, east of Spitzbergen, Norway. Nineteen survivors in small boats made their way to Hopen Island, in the southeastern part of the

Svalbard Archipelago. It was six months before the few remaining alive were spotted by a German air patrol, on 1 May 1943, and not until 24 July that *U-703*, ordered to Hopen Island, arrived to help the stranded Russian sailors. The Master was picked up and landed at Narvik the following day but it took another three months before the *U-703* returned on 7 October to collect the last two survivors, who were landed at Harstad, Norway on 9 October.

The *Richard H. Alvey* and *Empire Galliard* both finally arrived at the Kola Inlet on 7 November and were escorted to the Dvina Bar where both ships grounded (allegedly as a result of actions by the Russian pilot), with the *Empire Galliard* initially thought to be a total loss.

The Ministry of War transport report on the *Empire Galliard*'s voyage stated:

This vessel sailed from Sunderland on the 22nd Sept. loaded with a cargo of War material. 8 Matilda Tanks on deck and 48 Bren Gun carriers in cases on the hatches. On passage to Loch Ewe passing through the Pentland Firth vessel encountered very heavy weather, which caused the cases of Nos. 4 and 5 hatches to shift. Vessel was ordered to the Clyde for cargo on hatches to be restowed. Sailed from the Clyde 9th October, and arrived Loch Ewe 11th October. Sailed from Lock [sic] Ewe 18th Oct. and arrived Iceland 22nd October.

Whilst at Iceland the whole of the ship's crew were asked if they would volunteer to take the ship to Russia without escort. It was explained to them that escorts were not available at that time. All volunteered. It was then arranged that 5 American, 5 British, and 1 Russian vessel should sail at intervals of 12 hours. An American vessel sailed first and the *Empire Galliard* second. I understand that only one other British vessel reached Russia and three of the American vessels. On the passage, one enemy submarine was sighted being attacked by an Armed trawler. No attack was made upon this vessel.

Arrived Molotovsk, White Sea 8th November. Completed discharge 25th November.

The *John Walker* arrived safely outside Archangel on 8 November but also ran aground. She was refloated, reached Molotovsk five days later and finally anchored in the Kola Inlet on 16 December.

British and Russian aircraft and warships were deployed to locate and escort the remaining merchant ships into Archangel. At 15.08 on

9 November a Russian aircraft reported a merchant ship, thought to be the *Hugh Williamson*, in the vicinity of Cape Kanin. The minesweepers *Harrier* and *Gleaner* sailed at 15.45 with the Russian rescue tug *Skval*, followed later by the destroyer *Sokrushitelny*, to search for a merchant ship which had sent a distress message. The ship turned out to be the *Hugh Williamson*, located at 22.05 and escorted to Dvina Bar by the minesweeper *Gleaner*. In reply to signals the *Hugh Williamson* stated she had made no distress message but had 'reported a doubtful aircraft'. She also reported her compasses were 'in bad shape'. When located she was proceeding at slow speed to wait for daylight before making a landfall. No trace of the *Empire Sky* was ever found.

Of those thirteen merchant ships which set out from Iceland, two were recalled, one returned. Five – the *Empire Galliard, Hugh Williamson, Richard H. Alvey, Empire Scott,* and *John Walker* – reached North Russia safely. The *Empire Gilbert, Empire Sky,* and *William Clark* were all sunk by U-boats and *Dekabrist* by Ju.88s, whilst the *Chulmleigh*, taking a northern diversion route, ran onto rocks off Spitzbergen in a blizzard and was wrecked. This outcome was regarded by both the Admiralty and the Ministry of War Transport as unsuccessful and an operation not to be repeated.

A number of British merchant seamen who took part in Operation FB were subsequently decorated. The first awards, to the Master and crew of the *Empire Scott*, published in the *London Gazette* of 30 March 1943, simply stated:

> For great bravery and seamanship in taking merchantmen on the hazardous passage to North Russia.

The bare facts of this hazardous operation were summarized by the Admiralty Honours & Awards Committee in the following terms:

> These vessels sailed independently from Iceland during November 1942 for North Russian ports. Of the five vessels[3] two arrived safe – the *Empire Galliard* and the *Empire Scott*. The others were lost so far as is known with all hands.
>
> These sailings were part of special arrangements made for the maintenance of essential supplies to Russia. For this purpose it was considered necessary that in view of operations in other theatres of war, a number of British and American ships should be sailed independently

to Russia. The only means of rescue that the Navy were able to provide consisted of trawlers and some submarines.

It was fully realised that in the event of any ship becoming a casualty, the chances of being picked up were remote, and owing to the climatic conditions in the area concerned, the chances of survival were almost nil.

In view of the unusual hazards of the enterprise, it was decided that the British ships should be manned only by those who, after having been told of the proposal and of the fact that the usual protection would not be afforded, were nonetheless willing to make the endeavour to get the ships through. The Masters were informed of the proposal and in all cases they volunteered to go. They returned to their ships and the proposal was put to the officers who in nearly all cases volunteered for the voyage. The position was then explained to the crews and a response of something like 98 per cent was obtained.

As regards the two ships *Empire Galliard* and the *Empire Scott* which reached Russia, it is possible that further awards should be made and the Representative of the Ministry of War Transport in Murmansk has been requested to furnish his recommendations. They have not yet been received but the Committee may wish to consider at once the names mentioned above.

In view of the extremely hazardous nature of this undertaking the masters, officers and ratings of these five ships were given a bonus [£100 to officers and £50 to crew members, paid in advance] in addition to their normal wartime pay and also an undertaking that in the event of any of the vessels being lost by marine risk during the voyage, compensation would be paid under the Government War Compensation Schemes. It is considered that these additional benefits were fully justified having regard to the circumstances in which the voyages were undertaken and to the fact that the risks and perils to be faced were undoubtedly greater than those a fully escorted convoy would expect to meet.

Independent Russian Sailings (29 October 1942 to 20 February 1943)

After Operation FB, the Russians carried out a further series of independent sailings using their own ships in the intervals between convoys: two in late October, six in November, fourteen in December 1942, three in January, and two in February 1943. Some overlapped with the resumption of the convoy cycle in December. Between the end of October 1942 and February 1943 a total of twenty-five Russian merchant ships (some sources also include *Dekabrist*, eastbound, making twenty-six) sailed independently from North Russia to Iceland, relying for their safety primarily on the darkness of the Arctic night. All but three arrived safely. One was sunk by a German destroyer on 6 November, and two by a U-boat on 26 and 29 January 1943 respectively. The last westbound ships arrived safely on 31 January, and the eastbound on 20 February.

The last QP convoy from North Russia

QP.15 (19 November–2 December)

When the convoy programme was suspended large numbers of merchant ships from PQ.16, PQ.17 and PQ.18 remained berthed in North Russian ports, and it was decided to bring those ships into condition to make the journey home safely to the UK during the second half of November, escorted by the RN vessels still in North Russia. This was to be the last westbound convoy of the year and the last in the PQ/QP series. Those merchant ships not able to unload in time or unfit to sail through damage or defect would remain behind and suffer the challenging climate and living conditions in Archangel until the spring of 1943.

The convoy assembled at the Dvina Bar was composed of thirty merchant ships – eight British, fifteen American and seven Russian. The ocean escort from Archangel was provided by *Ulster Queen*, *Halcyon* (SO), *Salamander*, *Britomart*, *Sharpshooter*, *Hazard*, *Camellia*, *Bryony*, *Bergamot*, and *Bluebell*. *Ulster Queen* carried a special cargo of 120 tons of silver bullion. The escort joined the convoy at 18.00.

The escort was later to be reinforced by *Faulknor*, *Intrepid*, *Icarus*, *Impulsive*, and *Echo* (Captain 8th Destroyer Flotilla), which fuelled in the Kola Inlet and sailed from there at 14.00 on 19 November to join the convoy the following day. A second force of five destroyers – *Musketeer*, *Oakley*, *Orwell*, *Middleton*, and *Ledbury*, left Scapa on 17 November for Seidisfjord, Iceland, and sailed from there three days later to relieve the first force on 23 November during the passage of the convoy.

The convoy would be further protected by a cruiser cover force, comprising *Suffolk*, *London*, *Forester*, *Onslaught*, and *Obdurate*, which assembled at Seidisfjord on 17 and 18 November and sailed on the 19th to provide surface cover west of Bear Island, while four submarines patrolled off Altenfjord to discourage the *Hipper* and *Köln* from sailing.

The convoy weighed anchor in the late afternoon of 17 November, formed up in two columns, and with the help of the Russian icebreakers left the mouth of the Dvina River and sailed out into the White Sea. By this time the snow was so heavy and cloud so low the crews could not see the other ships in company. Radio silence was also imposed for fear the Germans would pick up any communications and learn the convoy was on the move.

There were two early casualties when the American merchant ships *Ironclad* and *Meanticut* ran aground in the Dvina River. The *Meanticut* refloated and set off to rejoin the convoy but failed to make contact or to reach Iceland independently and returned to Archangel on 26 November (she sailed again in convoy RA.51). *Ironclad* was badly damaged and sank in shallow water; she was salvaged and refloated by the Russians on 11 December.

The Russian destroyers *Baku* and *Sokrushitelny* joined the local eastern escort at 13.30 on 18 November. At 14.20 on arrival off Cape Gorodetski the convoy cleared the entrance to the White Sea and formed up in nine columns. The weather at the time was favourable with a light wind, and slight sea. The convoy was by now progressing at 7½ knots and for the first forty-eight hours all was relatively quiet. The weather then began to deteriorate as the southerly wind freshened from the starboard during the morning.

By 12.00 on 19 November the wind had increased to force 6 with rough seas and reached gale force at about 23.00 when visibility dropped to 2,000 yards. The deterioration in weather conditions began to expose the navigational problems that would be experienced by both merchant ships and their escorts during this passage. The convoy was no sooner out of the White Sea than it ran into a blizzard. The snow was freezing on all the boat painters. In such poor visibility ships were allowed to use navigation lights to try to keep their station in the convoy. Although the navigation lights were dimmed they proved of little value as they snowed-up and their light was completely obliterated.

Early the following day the wind shifted to south-southeast force 7, with snow squalls and continuing poor visibility. Ongoing problems with radar and communications, combined with the deteriorating weather, exacerbated the difficulties in keeping the convoy together.

As the day progressed the gale increased to force 9, leaving the merchant ships rolling heavily in high seas. By the time the convoy had reached the vicinity of Bear Island the formation was badly scattered. A number of ships found themselves on their own with no others in sight.

At 14.30, heavy seas breaking over the Russian destroyer *Sokrushitelny* tore off her stern section killing six crew. The Russian destroyers sent to assist, *Valerian Kuybyshev*, *Uritsky*, and *Razumny*, would arrive the following day to attempt a tow. They were able to rescue most of the crew but the salvage operation was reportedly abandoned the following afternoon. The hulk of the *Sokrushitelny* was never found.

The severe weather continued into Saturday, 21 November. By now the merchant ships were well scattered. The Commodore recorded at 00.10: 'Weather moderating rapidly, snow stopped falling, no ships in sight.' At 06.00 *Halcyon* recorded that the only navigational option available with the heavy sea running was to run before the gale. Aboard the *Temple Arch* the Commodore again noted at 08.00 that the weather was moderating rapidly but that it was 'very heavily overcast and dark, still no ships in sight'.

Britomart's log for 21 November noted the wind still continued to blow from the northeast at force 9. The minesweeper was rolling very heavily in high seas and the weight of the water damaged her starboard whaler and motorboat. *Britomart*'s crew complained:

> Convoy of 11 ships reported 60 miles ahead – weather putrid – snow and ice. Lost Starboard whaler – Carley float and motor boat has got a big hole in side – no abandon ship stations left – rolling like hell – afraid of turning turtle.

C-in-C Fleet's intention was to keep the convoy to the south of Bear Island to avoid potential contact with U-boats between Bear Island and Spitzbergen. The general disarray and confusion amongst the merchant ships continued.

In the late afternoon the wind strengthened again to force 10. At 18.00 the decks of the ships were being continuously covered by heavy seas breaking over them. On some this caused deck plates to open up and water to leak into the compartments below. By midnight the wind had increased to hurricane force. The ships encountered monstrous waves nearly mast-high breaking over the decks and superstructures, causing the ships to roll to 45°. In these conditions little progress could be made.

The sea conditions became a little easier on Sunday, 22 November, but by no means calm and the wind again rose to gale force during the afternoon. On *Halcyon* the starboard whaler and a mess deck scuttle were stove in and two depth charges washed overboard. *Salamander* lost touch during the evening. The wind and sea moderated but the skies remained heavily overcast. From then on, the weather improved but darkness and occasional light snow showers impaired visibility.

Then just before 01.00 the next day the *Goolistan*, now a straggler from the convoy, was torpedoed between Bear Island and Spitzbergen. The details of her fate were unknown at the time. It was later established she had been hit by one of two torpedoes fired by *U-625*. The U-boat had sighted the *Goolistan* an hour earlier and approached for what proved an unsuccessful submerged attack, frustrated by the very cold temperatures that were freezing instrument gauges and icing up the periscope head. The explosion of the torpedo warhead in this second attack reportedly set the cargo on fire and the crew began to abandon ship as *Goolistan* settled slowly in the water. At 01.45, still on fire, she finally sank thirty minutes after being hit underneath the bridge by a third torpedo. *U-625* then reportedly surfaced and her crew questioned the occupants of the lifeboats, who told them the Master had remained aboard; the U-boat then left the scene. Most of the crew had survived the attack and the *Orwell* later went to search for survivors, but none were found. The Master, forty-one crew and ten DEMS gunners were lost.

At around 07.30 on Monday, 23 November, another straggler from the convoy, the Russian cargo ship *Kuznetz Lesov* loaded with a cargo of potassium salts was also sunk. Again, the circumstances of the loss were not known at the time – she simply disappeared. It was later determined she had been attacked by *U-601* which fired a spread of three torpedoes, one of which struck and exploded forward of the bridge. The *Kuznetz Lesov* was reported to have sunk within four minutes, her Master, thirty-one crew and nine gunners all lost.

In the early hours of the next day, Captain (D8) in his signal summarizing the activity of the previous twenty-four hours, reported he had intercepted seven stragglers but not met the Commodore or any of the ocean escort minesweepers. He reported the result of his patrol over the previous twenty-four hours with *Musketeer*, *Oakley*, *Echo*, and *Middleton*, confirmed the convoy was badly scattered by the gale and *Orwell* detached to search for any survivors from the *Goolistan*. He intended to provide an escort for any ships met but considered most were now ahead of him. The *Icarus* had lost touch; the *Intrepid* was escorting *Dan-Y-Bryn*, *Bryony*, *St Olaf*, and *White Clover*, and *Camellia* was escorting *Exford*. Presuming all stragglers were now heading for Akureyri he requested a signal to this effect be sent to all ships by BAMS.

Thursday, 26 November, saw the first seven stragglers from QP.15 pass Grimsey Island at daybreak and reach the entrance to Akureyri Fjord in Iceland at 10.40. At 06.00 *Intrepid* and *Ledbury* left the convoy to go ahead to Seidisfjord, while at 08.00 the rescue ship *Copeland* joined.

At 01.00 on Friday, 27 November, the weather suddenly deteriorated and a gale blew up. Conditions in Icelandic harbours were extremely difficult, huge winds gusting and buffeting the ships, forcing them from treacherous anchor-holds in very deep water against steep rocky shores. Under such circumstances at anchorages such as Seidisfjord in winter the only sanctuary was the open sea, where most ships took refuge until the weather moderated. There were some precarious moments but the only serious incident occurred when *Sharpshooter*, as she entered Seidisfjord was involved in a collision with the *Empire Snow*, leaving the minesweeper extensively damaged above the waterline.

After following the prescribed route down the northeast coast, the Commodore's small group of ships arrived off Seidisfjord at 11.00 where the escort was relieved by *Intrepid* (SO), *Icarus*, *Landsbury*, *Middleton*, *Camellia*, and *Bluebell*. The Commodore's section did not put into Iceland but was joined at sea at 11.30 by six merchant ships from Seidisfjord – *Empire Snow*, *Exford*, *Esek Hopkins*, *Belomorcanal*, *William Moultrie*, and *Ulster Queen*. At 14.15 the convoy reformed in four columns. The Commodore's party now included the *Temple Arch* (Commodore), *Dan-Y-Bryn* (Vice Commodore), *Empire Snow*, *Empire Morn*, rescue ship *Copeland*, *Charles R. McCormick*, *Esek Hopkins*, *William Moultrie*, *Exford*, and *Belomorcanal* escorted by *Intrepid* (SO), *Icarus*, *Ledbury*, *Sharpshooter*, *Bluebell*, and *Camellia*. The Commodore reported he expected to arrive at Loch Ewe at midnight on 29/30 November. *Halcyon*, *Britomart*, *Salamander*, and *Hazard* went into Seidisfjord for damage and defects suffered during their voyage to be repaired. Seven more merchant ships arrived at Akureyri, and *Oakley* and one merchant ship at Seidisfjord, all from QP.15. Plans were then made to sail these ships from Iceland back to the UK.

Oakley and *Orwell* arrived in Akureyri on 27 November. The Masters of the ships from QP.15 attended a conference where it was decided the *Ocean Faith* would be the Commodore's ship for a new convoy designated QP.15 (M) to sail for Loch Ewe via Seidisfjord. Merchant ships at Akureyri were expected to sail in convoy the next day and to arrive in Loch Ewe on 2 December. Fifteen ships had taken refuge there: *Empire Tristram, Ocean Faith, Virginia Dare, Sahale, Patrick Henry, St Olaf, Nathanael Greene, Hollywood, Schoharie, Andre Marti, Tiblisi, Komiles, Friedrich Engels, Petrovski,* and *Empire Baffin.* In the event only thirteen of them sailed, at 11.25 on 29 November, escorted by *Musketeer, Echo, Forester, Orwell, Oakley, Britomart,* and *Hazard.* The American freighter *Hollywood* had problems with a shortage of water and diverted to Reykjavik, sailing from there on 11 December for the US. The *Schoharie* sailed for Reykjavik on 30 November, then on to Loch Ewe in convoy RU.52 arriving on 12 December.

The potential dangers were not yet over, however. *Orwell* had previously reported a suspected line of moored mines near the western edge of the swept channel. After consultation with the Resident Naval Officer (RNO), it was decided to send *Britomart* and *Hazard* to sweep the route before the convoy passed through. Sweeping was carried out off Seidisfjord during Saturday and Sunday, 28 and 29 November, in the suspected area but no mines were found.

QP.15 (M) sailed around the northeast coast of Iceland to be joined off Seidisfjord at 10.00 on 30 November by *Hazard, Britomart, Impulsive, Bergamot, Bryony,* merchant ships *Lafayette* and *White Clover* and fleet tanker *San Ambrosio* (joined for passage but not a QP.15 ship). The small convoy then set off to the south formed up into two columns, *Britomart* and *Hazard* sailing ahead until clear of the Icelandic coast. *Empire Baffin* returned to Iceland and sailed later to Loch Ewe.

On Monday, 30 November, the Commodore's section of QP.15 (nine merchant ships plus *Copeland*) finally arrived in Loch Ewe. The ships of the escort, *Intrepid, Icarus,* and *Middleton,* were then detached to Scapa where they arrived at 15.00. *Ulster Queen* and *Ledbury* headed for the Clyde, *Bluebell* and *Camellia* for the Tyne and Cardiff respectively. The speed of QP.15 (M) was governed by the rate of progress of the two minesweepers. At 00.10 on 2 December, QP.15 (M) crossed the line between the Butt of Lewis and Cape Wrath and at 05.15 (ship's log gives 07.00) arrived off Loch Ewe, where the ships cruised until daylight and entered the anchorage at 09.15. The *Empire Baffin* arrived independently on 3 December.

C-in-C Home Fleet in his post-convoy report stated that only one escort, *Salamander*, had suffered slight damage (a mooring wire carried away and wrapped itself around the port screw, stopping the engine, but then untangled itself, and the steering linkage broke so the engines had to be used to steer). In this he appears to have been slightly economical with the truth as the Reports of Proceedings by Rear Admiral 1st Cruiser Squadron and other individual ships paint a different picture. Damage was sustained by both *London* and *Suffolk* on 21 November. On *London*, most of the fuel tanks were leaking; *Suffolk* reported her upper deck fractured in an unimportant position and local leaks repaired during the previous refit were opening up. Later on, 25 November, *Suffolk* also reported four consecutive frames fractured abreast the starboard cable lockers and the ship's side 'parting' by a foot. In *London*, so much fuel was leaking into the after 6-inch magazine that it was uneconomical not to pour it back into the tank from buckets. *Hazard* had also suffered damage when, on 21 November her quarterdeck opened up in the heavy seas and water leaked below into the after compartments. *Halcyon* had three seawater leaks that affected her boilers, and suffered lost guardrails, bent stanchions and other damage above deck, whilst the *Ulster Queen* had damage to her foredeck and both her ASDIC and radar were put out of action.

In some respects this assessment reflected the experiences of PQ.17, when the convoy scattered by Admiralty signal rather than weather, and suffered serious losses.

Chapter 6

Phase Three: Winter Cycle, December 1942 to March 1943

JW.51 to RA.53

JW.51A (15–27 December)

Consisting of fifteen merchant ships and a fleet oiler, JW.51A was the first outbound convoy of the 1942/43 Winter Cycle. With the new JW/RA[1] convoy series, which replaced the old PQ/QP series suspended since September 1942, JW.51A sailed at a speed of 8 knots from Loch Ewe on 15 December with its western local escort of *Seagull*, *Honeysuckle*, *Oxlip*, *Lady Madeleine*, and *Northern Wave* (15 to 18 December).

Loch Ewe rather than Iceland was now the new convoy assembly point. With the increase in Luftwaffe reconnaissance flights over Iceland it was thought this move would reduce the early detection of sailings. JW.51A was also the first (until C-in-C Home Fleet's later policy reversal) of the smaller two-part monthly convoys sailed during the winter.

Three days after leaving Loch Ewe the ocean escort of *Faulknor*, *Echo*, *Inglefield*, *Fury*, *Eclipse*, *Beagle*, and *Boadicea* joined to protect against surface attack (18 to 27 December) and the local escort departed. A cruiser cover force comprising *Jamaica* and *Sheffield*, with *Opportune* and *Matchless*, shadowed the convoy (16 to 24 December) to guard against attack by enemy surface units. Distant cover (21 to 23 December) was provided by the *King George V* (Flag C-in-C Home Fleet) and cruiser *Berwick*, escorted by *Musketeer*, *Quadrant*, and *Raider* which sailed from Scapa Flow on 19 December and returned on Christmas Day.

The convoy enjoyed a good passage sailing south of Bear Island, undetected by reconnaissance aircraft or U-boats as it crossed the Norwegian and Barents Seas. As there had been problems with cargo handling capacity at Murmansk, five ships of the convoy were detached 5 miles north of Kildin Island on 24 December to proceed to the White Sea escorted by Russian destroyers, while the remainder continued to the Kola Inlet. The

Convoy PQ.8, HMS *Matabele*. (*IWM FL 2661*)

HMS *Edinburgh*.
(*IWM MH 23866*)

Merchant shipping, including two oil tankers, assembling at Loch Ewe, 1941. (*RMG N 38553*)

HMS *Niger*, Convoy QP.13. (*IWM FL 16786*)

HMS *King George V* at Hvalfjord after PQ.15. Extent of bow damage. (*National Maritime Museum @ Flickr Commons*)

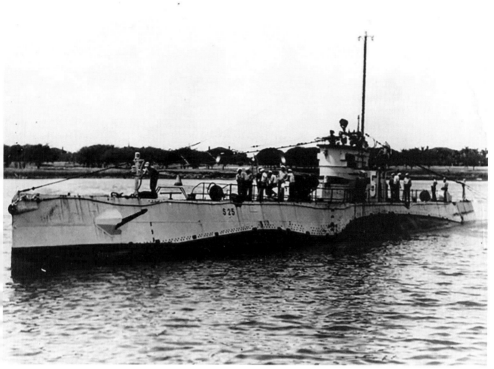

ORP *Jastrzab* (Polish). (*US Navy photo – http://www.navsource.org/archives/08/08130.htm*)

HMS *Punjabi*. (*IWM FL 25824*)

HMSs *Renown* and *Duke of York*, 2–9 March 1942. (*IWM A 7890*)

A homeward bound US freighter passing HMS *Duke of York* and USS *Washington*, PQ15/QP.11 – May 1942. (*IWM A 8962*)

PQ.16 – 21 May 1942. Merchant vessels assemble along the coastline near Hvalfjord, Iceland preparing to sail for Russia at dusk that evening. (*IWM A 9172*)

PQ.16 with the *Empire Purcell* on fire. (*WWW.WRECKSITE.EU*)

USS *Wichita* and HMS *London*, PQ.16/QP.12, May 1942. (*IWM A 9295*)

Empire Lawrence with the Hawker Hurricane 'Hurricat'. (*IWM FL 11425*)

PQ.17 assembles at
Hvalfjord, Iceland.
(*IWM A 8953*)

The cover forces
for PQ.17 at
anchor in the
harbour at
Hvalfjord, Iceland,
May 1942. (*US
Navy Photograph,
NH 61804*)

Convoy PQ.17
while forming up,
off the west coast of
Iceland. (*US Navy
Photograph Accession
80-G-24832*)

German reconnaissance photo. (*US Navy Photograph. NH 71382*)

An enemy plane, hit by anti-aircraft fire, crashes into a US merchant vessel causing her to explode. The vessel at right is turning to avoid the conflagration. (*US Navy Photograph, 80-G-40319*)

American freighter *Hoosier* under attack. (*Unknown*)

The American steamer *Carlton* sunk by a German U-boat on 5 July. Photographed from the submarine. Note lifeboats at left. (*US Naval History & Heritage Command. NH 71304*)

A German U-boat sails through floating wreckage from a sunken American steamer, in the Barents Sea. (*US Naval History & Heritage Command. NH 71307*)

Photo of survivors from the *Carlton*, taken from U-88 as she came alongside to interrogate the Master. (*US Naval History & Heritage Command NH 71305*)

Remnants of PQ.17 under escort from Novaya Zemlya to Archangel. Ships seen are (L to R): British anti-aircraft ship, SS *Silver Sword*, SS *Ironclad*, and a Russian ship. (*US Naval History & Heritage Command. NH 61805*)

HMT *Ayrshire*, seen from SS *Troubadour* during the passage of Convoy PQ.17 to Russia in July 1942. In the foreground is an M-3 Tank, whose 37mm turret gun has been improvised for anti-aircraft use. (*US Naval History & Heritage Command. NH 61806*)

Near the end of PQ.17's ill-fated passage, the SS *Troubadour* works her way into Novaya Zemlya's waterway, the Matochkin Straight, seeking suitable anchorage. The SS *Ironclad* already at anchor, is in the background. (*US Naval History & Heritage Command. NH 61808*)

Sea Hurricanes from 883 Squadron aboard HMS *Avenger* c. September 1942. (*IWM FL 1268*)

Destruction of *Mary Luckenbach*, Convoy PQ 18. (*IWM A 12273*)

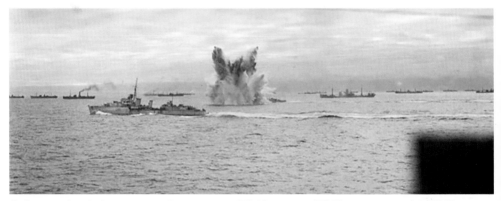

A German bomb detonating underwater near HMS *Ashanti*, HMS *Wheatland*, and HMS *Eskimo* which were escorting Allied convoy PQ 18, September 1942. (*IWM A 12022*)

Convoy JW.53 at Vaenga. (*IWM A 15419*)

Merchant ships of convoy JW.53 passing through pack ice during the voyage. Escort destroyer can be seen in the background. View from the Dido class cruiser HMS *Scylla*. (*IWM A 15360*)

Two merchant ships at anchor in Kola Inlet, north Russia. Part of HMS *Inglefield*, from which this photograph was taken, is in the foreground. (*IWM A 15421*)

HMS *Trinidad* at Iceland. (*IWM A 7683*)

RA.53 Leaving the Kola Inlet, 1 March 1943. (*Unknown*)

On board HMS *Inglefield*, 14 February to 13 March 1943. During convoy duty in Arctic waters, RA.53A. (*IWM A 15400*)

Attack on U-Boat, 3 April 1944 – JW.58. (*IWM A 22859*)

HMS *Kite* depth charge attack, 1944. (*IWM A 21989*)

Merchant ships on northern convoy duty pass through Arctic fog, which gives the impression of a boiling sea due to the difference in sea and air temperatures. (*Unknown*)

View of convoy JW.64 from HMS *Bellona*. (*IWM A 27568*)

American merchant *Henry Bacon*. (*Seafarers International Union*)

Ju.88A-17 from the 1st or 2nd Group 26th Bombardment Squadron (KG 26) at Bardufoss, before taking off to attack convoy JW.64. (*Asisbiz*)

Wildcat fighter on HMS *Campania*'s flight deck in Arctic conditions. (*IWM A 28225*)

Ice forms on a 20-inch (51 cm) signal projector on the cruiser HMS *Sheffield*, part of an escort for an Arctic convoy to Russia. (*IWM A 6872*)

Arctic convoy heading for Murmansk.

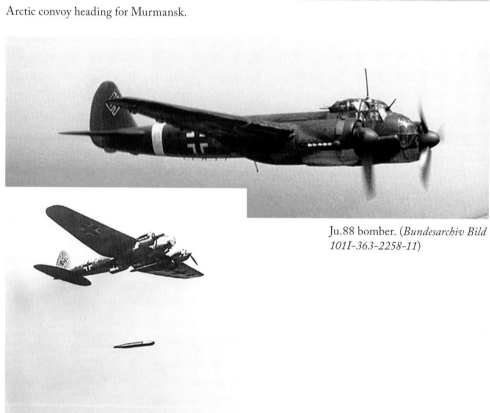

Ju.88 bomber. (*Bundesarchiv Bild 101I-363-2258-11*)

Heinkel He-111 torpedo bomber. (*Bundesarchiv Bild 183-L20414*)

Murmansk section of the convoy arrived without incident in the Kola Inlet at 08.00 on Christmas Day, and the White Sea section reached Molotovsk on 27 December

JW.51B (22 December 1942–4 January 1943)

The second part of this convoy, JW.51B, also of fifteen merchant ships,[2] sailed at 7½ knots from Loch Ewe a week after JW.51A on the afternoon of 22 December. The ships departed in single file, then formed up into four columns sailing north-northwest at about 8 knots, with the western local escort of *Bramble* (SOE), *Blankney*, *Ledbury*, *Chiddingfold*, *Rhododendron*, *Hyderabad*, *Vizalma*, and *Northern Gem*. *Bramble*, *Rhododendron*, *Hyderabad*, *Vizalma*, and *Northern Gem* would all go through with the convoy to North Russia.

Blankney, *Chiddingfold*, and *Ledbury* were to be relieved on 25 December by the 17th Destroyer Flotilla – *Onslow*, *Oribi*, *Obedient*, *Obdurate*, *Orwell*, *Achates*, and *Bulldog*, which sailed from Seidisfjord the previous day to rendezvous with the convoy at a point northeast of Iceland, to escort it to Murmansk. *Bulldog* suffered weather damage on 23 December and did not sail.

Cruiser cover (29 December to 2 January), was provided by Force R – *Sheffield* and *Jamaica*, which had escorted JW.51A all the way to Murmansk. Force R then sailed to a point southwest of Bear Island to rendezvous with JW.51B and escort it through the Barents Sea to Murmansk. Heavy cover was provided by the *Anson*, *Cumberland*, *Forester*, *Impulsive*, and *Icarus*, which would patrol in a covering position south of the convoy route (26 to 27 December). Although not part of the escort, a line of submarines was deployed off the North Cape to report any movement of German forces from Norwegian ports and attack them if possible.

The convoy ran into bad weather on 23 December when the formation became dispersed; the *Dover Hill* turned back damaged and with boiler trouble. The 17th Destroyer Flotilla joined in the afternoon of 25 December. *Blankney*, *Chiddingfold*, and *Ledbury* were then sent to round up the stragglers, after which the convoy changed course to the northeast. *Blankney*, *Chiddingfold*, and *Ledbury* left that evening. JW.51B, sailing northeast and making steady progress, crossed the Arctic Circle on the morning of 26 December and at noon was some 300 miles northeast of Seidisfjord and 200 miles south-southeast of Jan Mayen Island. By noon the following day the convoy was 200 miles east-southeast of Jan Mayen Island.

During the night of 27/28 December, the northwest wind increased to force 7, and the convoy speed fell to 7 knots. By noon the next day the convoy was midway between Jan Mayen and Bear Island. The wind strengthened and shifted to north-northwest, causing the ships to roll heavily and some experienced problems with shifting deck cargo. At noon on 29 December the convoy reached a position 180 miles west-southwest of Bear Island. That afternoon the wind eased and visibility increased to 10 miles. Only nine merchant ships could be seen; *Vizalma* and *Oribi* were missing. *Bramble* having the best radar was sent to search for them and the other missing merchant ships. The speed of the convoy was reduced to 6 knots to allow stragglers to catch up and at midnight course changed to due east.

On the morning of 30 December *Vizalma* and one merchant ship were well to the north, out of sight of the convoy, blown by the gale some 15 miles south of its scheduled course. As *Bramble* had not returned *Obdurate* was sent to round up the missing merchant ships. JW.51B had now been sighted and shadowed by *U-354*, which reported its position, course, speed, and escort strength at noon when the convoy was 100 miles south of Bear Island. The same U-boat would attempt an unsuccessful torpedo attack later that day.

At 08.00 on 31 December, twelve merchant ships were back in the convoy formation with two still missing. Around 90 minutes later the convoy was attacked by an enemy force which consisted of the heavy cruiser *Admiral Hipper*, destroyers *Richard Beitzen (Z-4)*, *Friedrich Eckholdt (Z-16)*, *Z-29*, and cruiser *Lutzow*, with destroyers *Theodor Riedel (Z-6)*, *Z-30*, and *Z-31*, which had already encountered and sunk *Bramble* with the loss of 121 officers and ratings. The destroyer escort prevented the enemy ships from breaking through to directly attack the convoy, but in the subsequent actions which included the cruiser cover force, *Achates* was badly damaged, and later sank with the loss of 112 of her crew. The *Friedrich Eckholdt* was sunk by *Sheffield* with the loss of all 325 crew. *Onslow* was badly damaged. Her CO, Captain Sherbrooke was subsequently awarded the Victoria Cross for the action. Seventeen of *Onslow*'s crew were killed. *Onslow* left the escort to land her casualties at Vaenga. *Oribi* lost touch with the convoy before the action and proceeded direct to the Kola Inlet.

At about 13.00 on 31 December the convoy, from heading southwards, turned to the southeast, resuming its course to Murmansk. During the following night the weather gradually deteriorated and by 07.30 on 1 January heavy seas and near gale-force winds slowed progress. Shortly before noon the convoy turned to the south and was joined one hour later by *Vizalma* and *Chester Valley*.

At first light on 2 January 1943 land was sighted, and at 13.00 those ships bound for the White Sea departed to follow the coast round to their destination. Despite the very foggy conditions, the eastern local escort for the White Sea section – *Harrier* and two Russian destroyers – made their rendezvous and at 13.00 the White Sea section proceeded towards Archangel.

The main body of the convoy, escorted by *Obedient*, *Orwell*, *Obdurate*, *Rhododendron*, *Hyderabad*, *Vizalma*, and *Northern Gem*, made landfall slightly to the east of Kildin Island. The weather off the Kola Inlet was very foggy and the Murmansk section of the convoy was unable to enter port until the following day. (*Seagull*, delayed by the fog, assisted some of the Murmansk ships into harbour.)

As the convoy headed towards the Kola Inlet on 3 January, *Ballot* ran aground on the northeast side of Kildin Island. The other ships were led into port safely by the escorts between 05.00 and 09.00, despite several air raid warnings and the thick fog. They included the *Calobre* with splinter damage from one of *Lutzow*'s shells, and whose steering gear had been reported as damaged. Six merchant ships docked in Murmansk that day and a further four the following day. *Honeysuckle* and *Oxlip* were despatched to stand by the *Ballot*, some of whose cargo was later removed by the Russians so as to lighten the ship for towing off, but the holds and machinery spaces were flooded, and she was written off as a total loss. The White Sea section of three merchant ships with the eastern local escort arrived at Archangel on 6 January and docked the following day.[3]

RA.51 (30 December 1942–11 January 1943)

This convoy of fourteen merchant ships escorted by *Faulknor* (Senior Officer), *Echo*, *Eclipse*, *Fury*, *Inglefield*, *Beagle*, *Gleaner*, *Cape Argona*, *Daneman*, *Cape Mariato*, and *St Kenan* left the Kola Inlet on 30 December for Loch Ewe. Following the attack by enemy surface forces on JW.51B, two cruiser cover forces were deployed in addition to the Battlefleet to provide distant cover.

The day after departure the convoy was sighted and shadowed by enemy aircraft. The same day the distant cover force, battleships *King George V* and *Howe*, and cruiser *Bermuda*, escorted by *Raider*, *Queenborough*, *Musketeer*, *Montrose*, *Worcester*, and ORP *Piorun*, sailed from Scapa and steered north to cover the passage of RA.51 until 3 January, when it left to return to Scapa Flow.

The first cruiser force (the First Cruiser Squadron) *Kent* and *Berwick*, left Scapa on 31 December, with the Battlefleet and proceeded independently to provide cover between 2 and 4 January 1943, arriving back at Scapa Flow on 6 January. The second cruiser cover force (Force R) *Sheffield* and *Jamaica* sailed on the same day. Submarines *P.216*, *P.312*, *P.49*, and *Graf* (*sic* – for ex-German U-boat renamed *Graph*) were on patrol off the north coast of Norway during the passage of the convoy.

Blankney, *Ledbury*, and *Montrose* left Seidisfjord on 5 January and rendezvoused with the convoy the following day to provide the local western escort to Loch Ewe. The destroyer escort and fleet oiler *Oligarch*, escorted by *Cape Mariato* and *St Kenan*, left the convoy for Iceland. The convoy escorted by the *Cape Argona* arrived at Loch Ewe on 11 January without loss.

No enemy air, surface, or U-boat attack materialized, although the convoy was shadowed by enemy aircraft and probably by U-boats as well during the first part of its passage.

JW.52 (17–27 January)

The fourteen merchant ships of JW.52, accompanied by the Western ocean escort, *Blankney*, *Middleton*, *Ledbury* (to 20 January), *Britomart*, *Lotus*, *Starwort*, *St Elstan*, and *Northern Pride* (to 27 January), sailed from Loch Ewe on 17 January, the ships leaving in single file ahead until out in the open sea where they formed up in two columns. At daylight on Monday, 18 January, the convoy formation expanded to a broad front, when the merchant ships took up station 5 cables apart, with each ship in each column 2 cables apart.

The escort was small, the hope being that the hours of darkness and bad weather would protect the merchant ships until *Blankney*, *Middleton*, and *Ledbury* were relieved and the escort strengthened by the seven destroyers from Seidisfjord – *Onslaught*, *Beagle*, *Musketeer*, *Offa*, *Matchless*, *Bulldog*, and ORP *Piorun* – which sailed on 20 January for a planned rendezvous that afternoon.

The convoy was also protected by a cruiser cover force which included *Kent*, *Glasgow*, and *Bermuda* (21 to 26 January). This was the first time a cruiser force shadowed a convoy all the way to Murmansk. Distant cover for both the convoy and cruiser force was provided by the Battlefleet – the battleship *Anson*, cruiser *Sheffield*, with *Faulknor*, *Inglefield*, *Eclipse*, and

Montrose (23 to 24 January). The Battlefleet was to cruise southwest of Bear Island while the convoy was passing through the area deemed most liable to surface attack. *Faulknor, Inglefield, Eclipse,* and *Montrose* were to remain with the Battlefleet until 23 January, when they would be relieved by *Queenborough, Orkan, Raider,* and *Echo.*

It had been expected the merchant ships would reach the escort rendezvous position on 20 January, but the convoy's speed was much slower than anticipated due to adverse weather conditions, with heavy seas running. Progress was also slowed by the *Empire Baffin,* which was unable to maintain the required speed of the convoy and was sent back to Akureyri the following day. The destroyer escort did not sight the convoy until a day later than planned. The wind had increased by this time, blowing 4–5 knots from the northeast, causing a head sea. Throughout the remainder of the day the weather remained stormy. During the night and into Friday, 22 January, it also became bitterly cold with heavy squalls of snow and hail.

The relief screen of *Queenborough, Raider, Orkan,* and *Echo* met up with the Battlefleet in the morning of 23 January. *Faulknor* and *Eclipse* were detached to Scapa Flow, and *Inglefield* and *Montrose* to Akureyri, while the Battlefleet set course for the covering position. The Battlefleet was sighted and reported around midday by an FW 200 reconnaissance aircraft and shortly after the convoy was detected and reported by a BV.138.

The following day radio transmissions were picked up between two or three U-boats patrolling due south of Bear Island searching for the convoy. Later U-boats were again detected in the vicinity but none found an opportunity to attack, due to the driving snow, very strong escort, and rapidly changing conditions. The convoy was located again by reconnaissance aircraft at noon, and as it approached the vicinity of Bear Island three or four He.115 torpedo bombers appeared and formed up for an attack on the port beam of the convoy (eyewitness and official accounts vary). Two were shot down – it was later established twelve He.115s had taken off to attack the convoy but in the poor weather conditions only three were able to do so.

As the day went on very heavy snow showers developed with the sea right astern, and the convoy passed the North Cape. An hour before midnight the Battlefleet left its covering position and altered course for Akureyri. Shortly after, the convoy was detected again by *U-622.* However, thanks to the increase in the number of escorts equipped with new direction-finding (D/F) equipment, it was possible to immediately pinpoint any U-boat broadcast. Those U-boats able to make contact were driven off by the escort, whilst the Convoy Commander ordered several evasive alterations of course.

On Monday, 25 January, the convoy was shadowed by enemy aircraft and there were seven air raid alarms. A bomb dropped on the *Piorun* fell wide with no damage or casualties. In the evening the escorts dropped depth charges. It began to snow heavily and quiet descended. During the night of 25/26 January the escorts detected the presence of several U-boats but again no attacks developed. Although the station-keeping of the convoy throughout the passage had been assessed as generally good the *Empire Portia* now lost contact and later arrived at Murmansk independently.

Due to the Arctic winter it was dark for the entire voyage. The weather remained extremely cold with very heavy snow and hail showers. These conditions persisted for the next forty-eight hours. The convoy spent the night of 26 January off Kildin Island waiting for dawn. It was still snowing hard when the convoy passed the island the following morning. The convoy then picked up the pilot from Murmansk and entered the Kola Inlet in the early afternoon. No eastern local escort was seen at any time and it was necessary to keep the ocean escort with the convoy until all the merchant ships had entered – by about 18.00.

JW.52 was credited with the fastest convoy passage through the Greenland and Barents Seas. When in the U-boat danger zone, it achieved a maximum speed of 10 knots and maintained an average speed of 9–9½ knots for nearly three days, making it more difficult for the pursuing U-boats to maintain contact whilst submerged. Enemy air attacks were on a small scale and the escort drove off the U-boats by energetic counteraction based largely on D/F wireless reception. A feeble torpedo attack was driven off thanks to the alertness of the escorts and, in spite of the failure of the Russian local escort to make contact, the approach to the Kola Inlet was made successfully in very low visibility; the convoy of thirteen ships arrived intact.

RA.52 (29 January–9 February)

Convoy RA.52 of eleven merchant ships escorted by *Onslaught* (Senior Officer), *Offa*, *Musketeer*, *Matchless*, *Bulldog*, *Beagle*, *Onslow* (damaged), *Forester*, *Icarus*, *Piorun*, *Harrier*, *Seagull*, *Rhododendron*, *Oxlip*, *Hyderabad*, *Honeysuckle*, *Lady Madeleine*, *Vizalma*, *Northern Gem*, and *Northern Wave*, left the Kola Inlet for Loch Ewe on 29 January 1943. The *Onslow* was detached on 2 January and arrived in Scapa Flow two days later. The same day *Forester* detached to Seidisfjord to report the convoy's position to the local escort and to fuel, arriving in the afternoon. The following day *Blankney*, *Middleton*, and *Vivacious* joined RA.52 as western local escort to Loch Ewe (to 8 February) and *Onslaught*, *Offa*, *Musketeer*, *Matchless*, *Bulldog*, *Beagle*, *Icarus*, and *Piorun* detached to Seidisfjord.

The cruiser cover force (Force 2) – *Kent* (Rear Admiral Commanding, First Cruiser Squadron), *Glasgow*, and *Bermuda* – left the Kola Inlet on 30 January to cover RA.52 until 2 February, when it left its covering position for Scapa Flow. The distant cover force, the battleship *Anson* (Vice Admiral Commanding, Second Battle Squadron) and cruiser *Sheffield*, screened by *Inglefield*, *Orkan*, *Oribi*, and *Obedient*, left Akureyri on the 30th to cover RA.52 (1 to 2 February). The local western escort was provided by *Blankney*, *Middleton*, and *Vivacious* (5 to 8 February, *Vivacious* detaching on 7th for escort of *Anson*).

The convoy was continuously shadowed by U-boats. At 14.12 and 14.13 on 3 February, about 600 miles northeast of Iceland, *U-255* fired torpedoes at them. The U-boat observed two hits on one ship after a running time of 1 minute 50 seconds, then heard a further detonation after 3 minutes 20 seconds. Lookouts on the *Greylock* observed a torpedo running towards the ship in smooth seas and broad daylight, about 300 yards off her port side. Although *Greylock* attempted to evade the torpedo it struck between the no. 5 and no. 6 holds, created a large hole below the waterline and jammed the steering gear. A second torpedo missed the bow by 75 yards. The ship immediately flooded, took on a list to starboard and settled rapidly by the stern until the decks were awash as far as the centre castle. Fifteen minutes after she was hit the ten officers, twenty-six crew, twenty-five USN armed guards and nine passengers (three survivors from the *Ballot*, bombed and sunk on 25 December) abandoned ship smartly and in good order in four lifeboats. *Harrier*, *Oxlip*, *Lady Madeleine*, and *Northern Wave* each picked up one boatload of survivors of 18, 17, 23 and 18 personnel respectively: 76 in all. At 14.43 *Harrier* fired one depth charge set to 100 feet, close to the *Greylock*'s stern and she sank a few minutes later.

Forester was detached to Seidisfjord on 4 February to report the convoy's position to the local escort and to refuel, arriving in the afternoon. The western local escort of *Blankney*, *Middleton*, and *Vivacious* then left Seidisfjord and joined RA.52 at 11.15, when *Onslaught*, *Beagle*, *Piorun*, *Musketeer*, *Matchless*, *Offa*, *Bulldog*, and *Icarus* departed for Seidisfjord to fuel, arriving in the afternoon and having left the CO of *Harrier* to assume the duties of SOE.

At 11.20 *Seagull*, with eight cracked boiler tubes, and *Honeysuckle* with less than 40 per cent fuel remaining, also detached to Seidisfjord with orders to fuel, effect boiler repairs and proceed together to rejoin the convoy the following day. On 7 February *Vivacious* was detached from RA.52 for the screen of the battleship *Anson*.

After consulting the Convoy Commodore, the SOE decided on 8 February to transfer all the survivors from the *Greylock* to ships bound for Greenock, if this could be achieved without unduly delaying them. As bad weather precluded the possibility of doing it at sea, he considered taking the ships concerned into Loch Ewe, but this would have involved considerable delay and probably proved difficult in a crowded anchorage at dark. Accordingly, after passing the Butt of Lewis at 17.00, he turned control of the convoy over to the CO of *Blankney* and ordered *Middleton*, the corvettes and trawlers, to accompany him to Broad Bay, Lewis, where he hoped to obtain sufficient shelter for *Harrier*, *Northern Wave*, and *Lady Madeleine* to transfer survivors to the *Middleton*. Too much swell was running, resulting in some damage to the *Harrier*, so it was decided to cancel the operation and, since visual signalling contact with other ships had been lost in the darkness and heavy rainstorms, the SOE then broke RT silence and ordered all ships to abandon the transfer and proceed to their final destinations.

Middleton, *Blankney*, *Harrier*, *Seagull*, *Honeysuckle*, *Oxlip*, *Rhododendron*, *Hyderabad*, *Lady Madeleine*, *Northern Wave*, *Northern Gem*, and *Vizalma* were then detached. The survivors from *Greylock* were landed at Belfast and Gourock, and four survivors were picked up by *Harrier* and taken to Scapa Flow. All the *Greylock*'s crew were reunited in Glasgow and eventually repatriated from Liverpool.

There were no further incidents and the remaining merchant ships of the convoy arrived safely at Loch Ewe on 9 February.

JW.53 (15 February to 2 March 1943): Operation FE

The convoy of twenty-five merchant ships plus an escort oiler sailed at 15.00 on 15 February with a western local escort – *Jason* (SO local escort), *Dianella*, *Bergamot*, *Poppy*, *Lord Austin*, and *Lord Middleton* (15 to 21 February).

The convoy sailed in strong winds and very heavy seas; the severe weather damaged a number of merchant ships prior to the sailing date and would continue to cause problems for four days after they left Loch Ewe. A further three merchant ships sailed from Loch Ewe on 16 February as JW.53B, escorted by *Bryony*, to catch up with the main body of the convoy and bring the total number of merchants up to twenty-eight.

The convoy was due to be joined off the coast of Iceland on 18 February by the ocean escort – the cruiser *Scylla*, carrier *Dasher* with *Impulsive*, *Blankney*, *Ledbury*, and *Milne* (SOE), with *Boadicea*, *Faulknor*, *Inglefield*, *Obdurate*, *Obedient*, *Opportune*, and *Orwell*. The *Belfast*, *Sheffield*, and *Cumberland* from Seidisfjord were to provide cruiser cover to the north of the convoy route (21 to 26 February). The battleships *King George V* and *Howe*, and cruiser *Norfolk*, screened by *Onslaught*, *Offa*, *Musketeer*, *Icarus*, *Meteor*, and ORP *Piorun*, provided distant cover (24 to 26 February). Five RN and seven Russian submarines patrolled off the Norwegian coast in case *Tirpitz* put to sea. The ocean escort was reinforced on 16 February by the arrival of the *Pytchley*, *Middleton*, and *Meynell* and later that day *Halcyon*.

Musketeer and *Matchless* from Scapa Flow rendezvoused with *Bryony* and three merchant ships of JW.53B on 17 February. In the afternoon the weather deteriorated to a force 10, westerly gale. The deck cargoes on several ships started to shift and they had to turn back. *Bryony* was detached to UK and *Lord Middleton* to Scapa Flow escorted by *Dianella* – both for weather damage repairs.

Belfast finally arrived off Seidisfjord on 18 February, but the weather prevented her from entering to refuel. *Scylla*, *Cumberland*, *Intrepid*, *Fury*, *Eclipse*, *Impulsive*, and *Orkan* were also unable to go in and all were diverted to Akureyri, arriving there on 20 February. The remaining eight destroyers of the ocean escort arrived off Seidisfjord on 15 February, but were also prevented by the bad weather from refuelling until four days later. Meantime the main body of JW.53 continued on passage. During the morning of 18 February a heavy sea was running with a swell from the northwest. Visual signalling communication between the escorts was difficult due to low visibility and height of the waves; the merchant ships became scattered and escorts unable to maintain their positions in the screen.

The poor weather continued into the next day and the convoy became badly scattered. *Scylla*, *Dasher*, *Intrepid*, *Fury*, *Eclipse*, *Orkan*, and *Impulsive* remained hove to off Seidisfjord waiting for the weather to moderate sufficiently to allow them to enter and fuel. *Blankney* and *Ledbury* refuelled, left Seidisfjord in the forenoon to rejoin *Dasher*. During the day enemy aircraft attempted an unsuccessful attack on one of the escorting destroyers. Later, warnings of the presence of U-boats were received and the escorting destroyers dropped a number of depth charges through until midnight, when it started snowing heavily again bringing a quiet night. *Sheffield* on passage from Scapa ran into severe weather during the day, and in the heavy seas part of the roof of her A turret was peeled back. On arrival at Iceland on 20 February she was replaced by *Norfolk*, whose place in the distant cover force was taken by *Berwick*.

After four days of storms the weather finally moderated on Saturday, 20 February. *Bluebell* and *Camellia* joined the escort from Seidisfjord, *Matchless* reported she was escorting a damaged merchant ship back to Scapa Flow and at noon the two remaining merchant ships of JW.53B turned back as a result of weather damage. Two hours before midnight the convoy's speed was increased to 7½ knots.

Dasher arrived in Akureyri on 20 February with serious weather damage incurred on passage. The following day it was determined she was unfit for service, could take no further part in the operation and must return to the UK for repair, leaving the convoy without air cover.[4] A total of six merchant ships had now dropped out with weather damage. The remaining twenty-two were delayed for forty-eight hours and the convoy formation was scattered, but all were rounded up northeast of Iceland and the convoy then made good progress. The ocean escort was finally reinforced by *Scylla*, *Fury*, *Orkan*, *Intrepid*, *Eclipse*, and *Impulsive*, who joined three days later than planned on Sunday, 21 February, when Captain (D), 3rd Destroyer Flotilla in *Milne*, with Captain (D) 8th Destroyer Flotilla in *Faulknor*, with *Boadicea*, *Obedient*, *Opportune*, *Orwell*, *Obdurate*, and *Inglefield*, joined and took command of the convoy. The western local escort then left for Seidisfjord. The convoy was now thirty-six hours behind schedule due to the adverse weather conditions. NCSO (Naval Chief Staff Officer) Loch Ewe reported on 22 September that five merchant ships had returned on account of the bad weather. A sixth diverted to the Faroes would arrive back in Kirkwall on 4 March.

The edge of the ice field, unusually far south for the time of the year, took the convoy within 250 miles of the Norwegian coast, the *Tirpitz* anchorage at Altenfjord and air base at Banak. On 23 February, the convoy was sighted and reported by two BV.138 reconnaissance aircraft, giving rise to concern a U-boat attack might follow, but none materialized. The convoy would be shadowed by either aircraft or U-boats almost continually from then on. BV.138s were sighted and U-boats were detected during the following two days but no attacks developed. At about midday on 26 February an estimated eleven Ju.88s attacked the convoy. No damage was done and there were no casualties. As no German surface threat had appeared the cruiser cover force left for the Kola Inlet, and the distant cover force departed for Iceland. By midnight the convoy was about 30 nautical miles north of Murmansk.

In the early hours of the following day, the seven merchant ships with orders to go to ports in the White Sea continued south along the coast with the eastern local escort, the Russian destroyers *Gromky*, *Kuybyshev* and *Uritskiy*, patrol vessels *Grozny* and *Uragan*, and *Britomart*. The Murmansk section of the convoy arrived in the Kola Inlet early that day. The following day the White Sea section was attacked by two Ju.88s, but no harm was done and the section made a fast passage through the ice, arriving off Archangel on 29 February and docking at Molotovsk on 2 March.

RA.53 (1–14 March)

Convoy RA.53, of thirty merchant ships, sailed from the Kola Inlet at 13.00 (ship's log says 10.30) on Monday, 1 March, and two merchant ships, the *Ocean Faith* and the *Oremar*, joined from Murmansk. The local escort (ex-JW.53) consisted of *Scylla*, accompanied by a destroyer escort led by Captain (D) III in *Milne* and Captain (D) VIII, in *Faulknor*, together with *Opportune*, *Obedient*, *Obdurate*, *Orwell*, *Fury*, *Eclipse*, *Inglefield*, *Intrepid*, *Impulsive*, *Orkan*, *Boadicea*, *Starwort*, *Lotus*, *Bergamot*, *Poppy*, *St Elstan* and *Northern Pride*. *Vivacious*, *Pytchley*, *Meynell*, and *Ledbury* provided a supplementary western local escort for the Icelandic passage (9 to 10 March).

Cruiser cover was provided by *Belfast*, *Cumberland*, and *Norfolk* (Force R, 9 to 10 March) which left the Kola Inlet the day after the convoy sailed. Distant or heavy cover force (4 to 5 March) was provided by the Battlefleet, comprising the battleships *King George V* and *Howe*, with cruiser *Glasgow*, and the destroyers *Forester*, *Offa*, *Onslaught*, *Icarus*, *Musketeer*, and *Piorun* sailed from Akureyri on 2 March.

When the convoy left the Kola Inlet the weather was fine and clear, with a slightly rough sea and some snow showers. Air and U-boat attacks were expected, but in the event the voyage began quietly and remained so for four days, after which the convoy ran into severe weather and came under enemy attack.

On 2 March the merchant ships were heading north; it was still snowing but the sea was calm. They were now approaching the edge of the ice shelf, having passed through small ice floes which became thicker throughout the day. It became bitterly cold, the air temperature falling to −12°F. Some pack ice was encountered and the convoy's course was altered to the west to keep clear of the ice fields.

The convoy escort received a 'Blue' warning (second stage alert to carry out emergency preparations) from SBNO indicating enemy activity was imminent, but no attacks took place. By midday, the convoy had achieved an average speed of 6 knots. In the darkness of the Arctic winter the ever-present danger and greatest risk to survival often came not from the German Navy and Air Force, but from unpredictable weather. On 3 March, the convoy altered course to the west. Conditions, described as 'thick with some snow' began to deteriorate with the onset of blizzards and even lower temperatures. There were still no obvious signs of enemy activity but the escorts, which had been dropping depth charges since the previous day, continued to do so, indicating to the merchant ships that U-boats were likely to be present, and around noon and midnight there were indications they were shadowing the convoy. Overnight on 3/4 March tension remained high. During the following day as many as three U-boats were detected and anti-submarine defence measures activated to keep them at a safe distance.

The next day the threat came from the air. At 08.00 air raid alarm bells were sounded. The convoy had been located by a BV.138. The merchant ships and escorts manned their guns. At around 09.30 a U-boat (later identified as *U-255*) appeared, dead centre in front of the convoy, sailing down between two lines of ships with just the periscope showing. She fired what was later confirmed as a spread of three torpedoes. The first missed, the second hit the second ship in the port line, the *Executive*, and the last hit the third ship in the starboard line, the *Richard Bland*. The U-boat then continued across the convoy and, as soon as she was clear, dived. The merchant ships and escorts fired their short-range weapons at tracks in the water between the columns of the convoy. *Orwell* reported a contact towards the rear of columns 1 and 2 and counter-attacked by dropping two depth charges, but subsequently failed to regain contact. It was presumed the U-boat was sunk as nothing further was seen or heard, but in fact *U-255* had successfully made her escape and survived until the end of the war.

The first merchant ship to be hit, the American freighter *Executive*, was carrying a cargo of 1,500 tons of potassium chloride. Her lookouts spotted the first of the three torpedoes crossing the bow of their ship some 25 to 30 feet away from the hull. The torpedo did not explode, but passed under the stern of the *Calobre*. The second torpedo however, struck the *Executive* on the starboard side between the no. 4 hatch and engine room. The subsequent explosion blew the covers off the hatch, and demolished the booms, engine, dynamos and all the equipment in the surrounding areas. No. 4 hold rapidly flooded and the *Executive* began to settle slowly by the stern.

Arriving on the scene *Faulknor* found the *Executive* stopped in the water, but still sitting comfortably with no list. The crew of sixty-four – five officers, twenty-five men and twenty-three armed guards – promptly abandoned ship without waiting to be instructed to do so, taking to three lifeboats and a liferaft. Fortunately, the weather at the time was clear and the sea flat calm. *St Elstan* and *Northern Pride* also arrived to assist. *St Elstan* picked up eleven survivors from one lifeboat. Another lifeboat dropped from its falls and capsized, throwing several occupants into the sea, where they died before they could be rescued. *Northern Pride* rescued forty-two. Three officers, five crewmen and one USN armed guard were lost. Although abandoned and drifting, the *Executive* did not sink so the decision was taken to scuttle her. About one hour after the torpedo attack, *Faulknor* dropped a Minol depth charge set to 50 feet under the bridge of the *Executive* then fired six 4.7-inch HE shells into the hull at the waterline. The *Executive* 'heaved' after the first explosion and was thought to have broken her back as she started settling at a faster rate. The bridge and upper works then caught fire. Finally, a Minol depth charge set to 60 feet was thrown into her after hold and the *Executive* was left sinking slowly, with her cargo of potassium chloride well alight. *Faulknor* then rejoined the convoy.

U-255's third torpedo hit the American freighter *Richard Bland* on the starboard side at the no. 1 hold. The warhead did not explode on impact but passed through the hull and exited the port side, leaving holes 8 feet in diameter on both sides. The force of the impact cracked the ship's deck, ruptured the collision bulkhead, and flooded the forepeak tank, causing a list to starboard. Although she did not sink the *Richard Bland* was left partially disabled and began to slow down, falling behind the main body of the convoy. This strike was subsequently attributed to the U-boat having penetrated the convoy's starboard escort screen, fired her torpedoes, then run on under the convoy – so only detected by *Orwell* on the port side. The Convoy Commodore in his post-voyage report wrote:

On the 5th of March 3 torpedoes were fired at the convoy from the starboard bow in broad daylight in a perfectly calm sea. How the U-boat penetrated the screen is a mystery. One hit the *Richard Bland* (2nd ship of 4th column), one hit the *Executive* (no. 51) and the other passed the stern of my ship (no. 41) and disappeared. The *Executive* dropped astern and sank. The *Richard Bland* was still able to proceed though badly damaged.

At 09.43 a number of aircraft (estimated at six BV.138s and two FW 200 Condors) were reported dropping mines or torpedoes some 5–6 miles ahead of the convoy and so within a minute an emergency turn to starboard was ordered. This was followed by a second and a third, until at 10.30 the convoy assumed its original course. Enemy air activity continued, with *Obedient* reporting (at 10.45) a sighting of aircraft dropping smoke flares on the port beam of the convoy. At 11.15 Captain (D) VIII reported:

Merchant ship in Station no. 51 on fire and sinking. Survivors in *St Elstan* and *Northern Pride*. No. 42 had been hit well forward but continued on her course, speed being reduced to enable her to keep station.

In the twenty-fours hours between noon on 4 and noon on 5 March, the convoy averaged almost 9 knots. But during the morning of 5 March, as weather conditions deteriorated, the speed fell to 7 knots. By 14.00 the sea was very much rougher. Just as the ships' crews began to think the enemy would be leaving them alone, another air raid warning came. Twelve to fourteen Ju.88 dive-bombers were sighted well ahead on the port side. About ten minutes later an air attack developed out of the cloud cover from the starboard bow, delivered by twelve Ju.88s and one or two or FW 200s. They flew in at medium level in a shallow dive, releasing salvoes of four 500lb bombs from a height of 1,500 feet. A terrific anti-aircraft barrage was thrown up, which seemed to deter the Ju.88s from pressing home their attack effectively. Each aircraft was reported to have dropped between three and six bombs. One report stated a total of forty-four dropped, and another said there were at least two mines. The attack was described as skilfully delivered, but no damage resulted. One Ju.88 left trailing smoke and it was thought some others might have been damaged. One BV.138 and one FW 200 Condor remained active ahead of the convoy but kept out of range. *Scylla* was sent ahead to deter these aircraft, which were suspected of trying to drop mines, to try to keep them at a safe distance.

The *Richard Bland*'s run of bad luck continued. She had rejoined the convoy just in time to help fight off this latest attack during which she was narrowly missed by a stick of four bombs. Although no merchant ships were hit, another stick of bombs straddled the *Ocean Faith*. One of the Russian women passengers fainted, but the convoy escaped intact. The *Ocean Faith*'s ship's log, always a source of masterful understatement records, '5/3. Attacked by enemy aircraft. Several near misses on starboard side of vessel.'

Shortly after the dive-bombers departed the wind became stronger and the sea rough. Although this weather was very uncomfortable for the convoy's crews it had the positive advantage of preventing the U-boats and dive-bombers from operating effectively. Perversely it also slowed the progress of the convoy. During the first twenty-four hours they covered about 180 miles; by the fifth day the distance covered fell to just 53 miles, but would slowly improve again. The ships' crews were left praying for the protection of the snow and darkness – now not far off. Although the *Richard Bland* had been able to rejoin the convoy that afternoon, the heavy weather during the night found her falling behind. The combination of continuing difficulties with her steering gear and the heavy seas would prevent her from catching up.

By 6 March, the wind was blowing strongly, the sea becoming rough, the sky overcast with continuous snow and sleet. The wind veered from southeast to southwest, bringing with it a heavy gale (force 7 to 8) accompanied by snowstorms and low visibility. The convoy formation became scattered, merchant ships and escorts temporarily lost contact. Fortunately, there was no evidence of air or U-boat activity in the vicinity. From midday on 5 March to midday on the 6th, the convoy maintained an average speed of 6 knots, later reduced by the gale-force winds.

Winds of up to 40 knots blew throughout the following two days. The merchant ships were all very light, with insufficient ballast (*Temple Arch* was 1,000 tons short), and the convoy remained scattered. The pitching and rolling caused by the heavy seas called for crews to continually go on deck in dangerous conditions to lash down gear as it broke loose. The convoy formation became more widely dispersed and the escort found great difficulty in steering slowly enough to maintain station or keep in contact with the merchants. The convoy's speed was reduced to a minimum for 'steerageway' (sufficient to maintain control) and the merchant ships practically hove to. *Fury* reported at 01.00 on 7 March she was now astern of all stragglers, but could not now follow a course or maintain a speed slow enough to stay with them.

By dawn the *Richard Bland* had completely lost contact but continued on course towards Iceland. Then her bridge steering gear failed. The crew struggled to keep going with emergency steering from the after steering platform, but then managed to rectify the problem and make headway again. She was now the rear ship but keeping up, still seaworthy with no list. The American freighter *John H. B. Latrobe* also experienced steering gear problems, engine trouble and a damaged propeller.

The HF/DF plot indicated the presence of two or three U-boats around the convoy. By midday, the convoy's average speed over the previous twenty-four hours had fallen to just over 3 knots. The merchant ships, unable to keep station in the convoy formation, became widely scattered. The port column of the convoy was reported to be drifting off to the southwest. *Orkan* and *Orwell* were ordered to remain with it.

Most merchant ships managed to ride out the gale but the American Liberty ship *J. L. M. Curry*, (*Curry*) developed serious structural problems and sent an SOS reporting her hull had cracked across the after deck, the crew were about to abandon ship, and requesting another ship stand by. It was subsequently reported that as the hull of the *Curry* crashed down into a heavy head sea a loud noise like gunfire was heard: the deck plates had split apart. A visual inspection revealed ominous looking fissures in the deck forward and aft of no. 3 hatch and at the after end of no. 4. The Master decided to sail on, but requested the Convoy Commodore assign an escort to stand by in case he had to abandon ship. The situation was dismal at best. The ship's log entry read: 'Thick snow squalls. Heavy westerly sea. Ship rolling and plunging.'

At 08.30 on 8 March the CO of *St Elstan* suggested the *Curry* try to put on more speed and attempt again to make a westerly course. But a new split could now be seen running through the starboard deep tank at the bottom of no. 3 hold. The Master reported he doubted his ship could put on any more speed as the hull was now cracked from the upper works down to the waterline at each end of the accommodation – the crack being over 6 inches wide at the upper deck and the *Curry* described as 'working very badly in all breaks.' The Master was prepared to abandon ship but still hoped to get his vessel to Reykjavik. In order not to risk the lives of all of those on board, he decided to send away all but a skeleton crew and signalled for assistance. *St Elstan* was ordered to stand by. The Master of the *Curry* then proposed to send some of the crew over to the trawler before attempting to increase speed.

The first lifeboat was got away at 09.15 and the occupants picked up by *St Elstan*, which then proceeded to screen the *Curry*. But by 09.30 the cracking was increasing rapidly and the oil fuel tanks had split. Two more lifeboats were picked up, at 10.00 and at 11.00; a motorboat made three trips carrying the remaining crew. The last – with the Master on board – went alongside *St Elstan* at 11.12. As the wind was by now freshening from the north the deteriorating weather conditions made salvage impossible. At 11.15, *St Elstan* opened fire on the port side of the *Curry* with her 4-inch gun, using semi-armour piercing and high-explosive shell. Three rounds were fired into the engine room on the starboard side, where holes appeared below the water line and oil spurted from the fuel tanks. A further three rounds were fired into no. 2 hold, under the forward gun and under the master's accommodation, setting fire to the bridge and midships accommodation. *St Elstan* ceased firing after dropping depth charges from the starboard thrower to a position on port side amidships. The *Curry* was last seen listing 30° to starboard and sinking. If the Master had not decided to abandon ship when he did it would have been too late, for in another twelve hours the storm grew to a full gale with violent snow squalls and high swells, conditions that might have made it impossible to get lifeboats away from the sinking ship. (This incident started the rumour that Liberty ships were unsafe in heavy seas in cold weather as the welding wouldn't hold, but in fact the inherent design fault was subsequently corrected by welding flanges at the points where the deck plating joints met the hull.)

The strong winds which scattered the convoy now backed to the south-southwest and gradually eased and the sea grew calmer.

The Icelandic escort (*Vivacious*, *Pytchley*, *Meynell*, and *Ledbury*) which left Akureyri at 23.00 on 8 March joined the convoy at daylight on 9 September. At 15.00, *Ledbury* encountered a straggler from the convoy and was detached to escort her to Seidisfjord, where both would arrive at 09.00 the next day.

Late on 9 March, *Faulknor* picked up an SOS message from the American freighter *Puerto Rican*. A straggler for two days, she was hit by a torpedo from a U-boat (later identified as *U-586*) about 33 miles astern of the main body of the convoy. There was thought to be reasonable hope of saving the crew, although the distress message said, 'boats swamped'. The torpedo struck the *Puerto Rican* on the starboard side, aft of the no. 5 hatch. Her cargo of 3,500 tons of iron ore was a dead weight and she sank on an even keel within fifteen minutes. Eight officers, thirty-two crew and twenty-five USN armed guards attempted to abandon ship in four lifeboats and life rafts in rough seas and a temperature of −30°F. In the severe weather conditions, with ice coating the ship, three of the four lifeboats were found to be frozen in their falls and useless. When the fourth hit the water the after fall could not be released due to the ice – the boat capsized and threw the occupants into the sea, where most froze to death in the icy waters. Eight eventually swam to a doughnut raft and six later transferred to a large provisioned raft, but in the following two days all except one man froze to death or were washed off the raft. *Eclipse* and *Impulsive*, immediately despatched to return to the scene, searched the area for twenty-four hours but found no sign of other survivors.

St Elstan, returning with the survivors from the *Curry* and only 12 miles from the position where the *Puerto Rican* was torpedoed, made her way to the spot. At 01.30 on 10 March, she found an extensive patch of oil floating on the surface and an empty waterlogged lifeboat, but no survivors. Their search continued until 12.00, when the wind increased to north force 9. The search was then abandoned and *St Elstan* left for Seidisfjord.

The good weather of 9 March was not to last, however. As the convoy approached Iceland during the night of 9/10 March, a northwesterly gale developed, it began to snow, and visibility fell to under a mile. Rather than attempt to navigate the east coast passage off Iceland in such conditions, the convoy was formed into two columns and turned north. The Convoy Commodore commented, 'An anxious night.'

At about 09.30, *Vivacious*, *Pytchley*, and *Meynell* were detached for Seidisfjord where they arrived later that afternoon to refuel. Soon after they left, the SOE suggested to the Commodore they wait to see if the weather improved before attempting the east coast passage off Iceland. If visibility remained poor, the convoy could then turn towards the north and wait for better weather. The precise location of the convoy at this time was in some doubt: the ships had been without 'sights' (unable to take a bearing on the stars or a navigational point on land) for two days and unable to obtain an accurate fix on their position by RDF, as the nearest beacon was only working at very reduced power due to storm damage. Fortunately, at the time, the gale blowing offshore minimized the danger. When visibility improved temporarily at 10.00 to one mile the Commodore decided to form the convoy into two columns and sent the necessary signal by radiotelephone to the merchant ships. This however had little effect, as the ships' Masters were reluctant to manoeuvre in the poor visibility.

At 10.19 on 10 March, *St Elstan* sighted the *John H. B. Latrobe* (*Latrobe*), who reported that her steering gear was disabled and propeller damaged and that she was drifting approximately south-southwest at 3 knots towards a minefield, so requested assistance – although it was not known whether the convoy was still in the vicinity at the time. Captain (D) VIII detailed *Opportune* to assist. Contact would be made at 23.20 and at daylight on 11 March *Opportune* attempted to take the *Latrobe* in tow. At 11.20 a tow was passed and the three ships set off for Seidisfjord – where *St Elstan* would also land her survivors.

By 13.30 on 10 March it was judged too dangerous to keep the convoy on a southwesterly course any longer and the Commodore radioed an alteration to the north. All the merchant ships made the turn except for the tanker *San Cipriano*, which at 17.30 reported 'land ahead' to the Commodore. This was the last heard of her until she was sighted off the Butt of Lewis by *Scylla*, at 23.00 on 12 March. She arrived independently at Loch Ewe (ahead of the convoy) the next day.

Northern Pride landed the survivors from the *Executive* at Seidisfjord in the afternoon. At 16.36 U-255 located and attacked *Richard Bland* again, this time about 35 miles off the coast of Langanes, Iceland. One torpedo hit the port side at the no. 4 hatch, but she remained afloat. Although lifeboats were lowered to their embarkation stations, the crew did not abandon ship, but a distress signal was sent (and acknowledged by a shore station) and the ship's 'confidential'[5] papers were thrown overboard. *Eclipse* and *Impulsive*, rejoining the convoy after a fruitless search for survivors from the *Puerto Rican*, were despatched to assist.

The Master of the *Richard Bland* decided to lower the lifeboats on the windward side, hoping they could be brought around to the leeward side of the ship should they be needed. However, the four men in each boat were unable to achieve this in the heavy seas. The armed guard remained at their stations. After an initial periscope sighting astern nothing more was seen of the U-boat and the Master instructed the gun crews to stand down, hoping the U-boat would now leave them alone.

At 18.30 the weather cleared and wind dropped to force 7. The convoy reassembled in two columns. It was decided to steer north until midnight, then turn east to 218° ready to attempt the east coast passage if the weather permitted. A few minutes later, at 18.35, the *Richard Bland* was hit amidships by another torpedo fired by *U-255*. The subsequent explosion caused the hull to break in two just forward of the bridge; the forward section remained afloat and the after section sank. As the ship began to break up the Master ordered the two remaining lifeboats to be lowered and liferafts launched. At the time of the attack there were heavy seas and intermittent snow. Several liferafts were lost during the attempt to launch them. The remaining crew and armed guards (around sixty in total) quickly abandoned ship in two lifeboats designed to hold twenty persons each – now so overloaded they had only a few inches of freeboard and shipped a great deal of water.

At 20.50, *Opportune* was detached to assist *St Elstan* standing by the *Latrobe*. The escort was seriously short of assets by this time (the local western escort had been unable to fuel quickly due to contaminated oil at Seidisfjord), and now comprised *Faulknor*, *Fury*, *Bergamot*, *Lotus*, *Starwort*, and *Poppy*. The SOE was content with this, assuming there were probably no U-boats nearer than the *Richard Bland*'s position some 50 miles to the north, although the escort had been informed by the Admiralty that a U-boat was probably still in contact.

By 07.00 on 11 March only the forepart of the *Richard Bland* remained afloat (the forecastle, awash, and some 100 feet of hull visible behind). There was no suitable point on the deck for a destroyer to go alongside and a signal was made to this effect. *Milne* and *Orkan* left *Impulsive* standing by and proceeded westward on the straggler's route. The requested air cooperation arrived, but no reports were received from, nor any contact made with the aircraft. The weather was fine and clear, but nothing was sighted except pack ice to the northward. Half an hour later, after a long night spent in a cramped and overloaded lifeboat in high seas, twenty-seven survivors from the *Richard Bland* in the lifeboat commanded by the third mate were picked up by *Impulsive*. She also rescued one of the windward lifeboats and its four occupants, while *Eclipse* rescued the other also with four. The second lifeboat under the command of the Master was never seen again. Of the total complement of sixty-nine, only thirty-five survived; fifteen USN armed guards and nineteen crew were lost.

That evening around 19.00, *Impulsive* reported finding wreckage, and ships were directed to the area to carry out a search and rescue operation. Later *St Elstan* found a liferaft from the *Puerto Rican* with one dead and one survivor aboard. The survivor reported no lifeboats got away from the *Puerto Rican* but thought there might be one other liferaft. *Orkan* and *Impulsive* were therefore ordered to return to the search area at daylight, then proceed to Scapa Flow looking out for possible southbound stragglers en route. It subsequently transpired that when the *Puerto Rican* was torpedoed this sole survivor managed to don one of the neck-to-toe rubber survival suits supplied to American ships on the Russian run. Although he was suffering badly from frostbite and exposure, the suit had saved his life when all his shipmates perished.

At 19.00 on Saturday, 13 March, the convoy split into two sections. The main group of sixteen merchant ships from RA.53 (the Loch Ewe section) formed up into three columns and headed towards the Butt of Lewis. The weather again deteriorated with strong winds, heavy seas running and the ships pitching and rolling, but they arrived in Loch Ewe at 15.00 (ship's log says 04.30) on Sunday, 14 March. A second group of five ships (the Clyde section) arrived there two days later.

Not all of the surviving ships arrived in Loch Ewe with the main group. The tanker *San Cipriano*, which earlier lost contact with the main body of the convoy, arrived independently on 13 March, the *El Oriente* in Liverpool on 19 March, and the *Empire Emerald* reached the Clyde on 16 March. The fleet oiler *Oligarch* sailed from Seidisfjord on 14 March escorted by *Poppy*, *St Elstan*, and *Northern Pride*, arriving in Loch Ewe on 16 March. When the remaining merchant ships anchored at Loch Ewe on the 14th their crews had the satisfaction of now knowing that, with adequate guns, they could hold their own against the most determined attacks the enemy could offer. They must have sensed the tide was slowly turning. But at that moment no doubt all that mattered to them was sleep.

The outstanding aspect of this convoy was the length of the trip, due to slow and lightly loaded ships and the bad weather encountered after passing Bear Island. The weather to the northeast of Iceland was described as the worst many had experienced, even when compared to a full Atlantic winter gale or a Chinese typhoon. The seas were exceptionally high and precipitous with a very short trough, making an occasional bump a certainty. The Convoy Commodore in his report remarked: 'This convoy has been a perfect nightmare as regards weather; my 34th convoy and the worst I have ever known.'

Suspension of Sailings: March to November 1943

By Phase Three the strengthened arrangements for convoy protection had begun to take effect and the rate of merchant shipping losses, at last, began to decrease. The continuation of this convoy cycle was however threatened, firstly by the dispute between the British and Russian governments over the Russian objections to the proposal to deploy RAF squadrons in North Russia for convoy protection (Operation GRENADINE), and secondly by British objections to the perceived ill-treatment by the Russian authorities of British Service personnel in north Russia – leading to a point where Churchill was minded in early March to stop the convoys completely. These threats were however rapidly overtaken by news of the concentration of German heavy ships in northern Norway and the refusal of the Royal Navy to run further convoys while the threat these represented remained. There was also a pressing need for all available Home Fleet escorts to be sent to the Mediterranean in June 1943 for Operation HUSKY, the invasion of Sicily. As a consequence, the convoys were suspended in March 1943.

In late August the Russians began to press for the convoys to start again and on 21 September the Soviet government made a formal peremptory demand for their immediate resumption. In an exchange of correspondence between Churchill and Stalin in early October, Churchill proposed to resume the convoy sailings subject to removal of the restrictions the Russians continued to place on British Service personnel in north Russia – otherwise he was minded to terminate the programme. After much correspondence and a series of high-level negotiations between London and Moscow, the difficulties were finally resolved and the first convoy of the new cycle, JW.54A, sailed from Loch Ewe on 15 November 1943.

Chapter 7

Phase Four: Winter Cycle
November 1943 to May 1944

RA.54A to RA.59 – Operation FS

RA.54A (1–14 November)

The first convoy of the 1943/44 cycle, run under Operation FS, was the westbound RA.54A, organized to utilize the destroyers and western approaches escorts which arrived in north Russia under Operation FR. The objective was to sail certain American-built light craft (for the Russian Navy) with the close escort for RA.54A, and to take reliefs, mails, and stores to north Russia. The convoy, consisting of thirteen merchant ships (including a fleet oiler) all capable of sailing at 10 knots or more, departed from Archangel during the forenoon of 1 November, leaving the eight slowest ships to follow later. There was an eastern local escort of *Harrier*, *Seagull*, *Gromky*, and *Kuybyshev* (to 3 November) and a through escort of *Westcott* (1 to 13 November) and *Eglantine*, *Jason* and *Britomart* (3 to 10 November).

The ocean escort (Force 3) of *Milne*, *Musketeer*, *Matchless*, *Mahratta*, *Savage*, *Saumarez*, *Scorpion*, and *Scourge* left the Kola Inlet the following day to join the convoy on 3 November. *Musketeer* and *Matchless* detached from the convoy on 8 November, followed by the *Savage* the next day. The rest of the through escort destroyers remained until 10 November, when relieved by the western local escort of *Brissenden*, *Middleton*, and *Halcyon* (10 to 13 November)

Distant cover was provided by a battle squadron (Force 2), comprising the battleship *Anson*, fleet aircraft carrier *Formidable*, cruiser *Jamaica*, with *Onslow*, *Haida*, *Venus*, *Stord*, *Capps*, and *Hobson*, which sailed from Akureyri on the 2nd to cover the convoy. The battle squadron returned to Scapa Flow on 8 November. *Belfast*, *Kent*, and *Norfolk* (Force 1) from Seidisfjord provided cruiser cover (2 to 8 November).

Thick fog delayed RA.54A but also shielded it from detection by the enemy. On 13 November the convoy split up. The western local escort relieved the through escort for the last part of the passage from off Langanes, Iceland to UK ports, and the merchant ships proceeded to east and west coast ports with local trawler escorts. All the merchant ships arrived safely on 13 and 14 November except two which suffered minor collision damage.

JW.54A/JW.54 B/RA.54B – Operation FT

JW.54A (15–26 November)

The first eastbound convoy of the cycle JW.54, sailed in two sections as C-in-C Home Fleet considered forty merchant ships too many for a single convoy, especially during the winter when bad weather could scatter them – as had happened to JW.53. The first section, JW.54A, was made up of nineteen merchant ships (including two fleet oilers and one rescue ship) and left Loch Ewe on 15 November with the close escort of *Inconstant*, *Whitehall*, *Heather*, and *Hussar* (15 to 18 November).

Three days later, the convoy was joined by the ocean escort, eight Home Fleet destroyers led by the *Onslow* with *Impulsive*, *Onslaught*, *Orwell*, and Canadian *Haida*, *Huron*, and *Iroquois* (18 to 19 November), also *Obedient* (returned early with defects), when the western local escort departed. The cruiser force and the distant cover force sailed the same day from Scapa Flow to take up their cover positions in the Norwegian Sea. The cruiser cover force comprising *Kent*, *Jamaica*, and *Bermuda*, shadowed the convoy to guard against any attack by German surface units (19 to 24 November). Distant cover was provided by the heavy cover force including the battleship *Anson*, USN cruiser *Tuscaloosa*, and USN destroyers *Forrest*, *Corry*, *Hobson*, and *Fitch* (also 19 to 24 November).

The convoy, undetected by either reconnaissance aircraft or U-boats, crossed the Norwegian and Barents Seas without incident and later separated into two groups. The eight Home Fleet destroyers from Seidisfjord with eight merchant ships arrived at the Kola Inlet at 19.00 on 24 November. The White Sea section of eleven merchant ships with *Hussar* was met at 06.00 the same day by *Seagull*, with two Russian destroyers and three Russian minesweepers in company, and arrived in the ports of Molotovsk and Ekonomia two days later. The safe arrival of the nineteen merchant ships of JW.54A and the war materiel they carried was regarded as representing a successful start to the 1943/44 convoy season.

JW.54B (22 November–3 December)

The planned sailing of JW.54B on 19 November from Loch Ewe was postponed due to a heavy gale. The convoy comprising fifteen merchant ships (including a fleet oiler and a rescue ship), with its close escort, *Beagle*, *Rhododendron*, *Poppy*, and *Dianella* (all Western Approaches), *Halcyon* and the western local escort *Saladin*, *Skate* (both Western Approaches), *Middleton*, and *Speedwell* (all to 26 November), finally sailed three days late on the afternoon of 22 November. The convoy was protected by a cruiser cover force, comprising *Kent*, *Jamaica*, and *Bermuda* (27 November to 3 December) through the danger area south of Bear Island, and a heavy cover force comprising the *Anson*, *Belfast*, *Ashanti*, *Matchless*, *Musketeer*, and *Obdurate* already on station in the Norwegian Sea covering JW.54A (27 November to 3 December).

The ocean escort of eight destroyers led by *Saumarez* (Senior Officer), with *Savage*, *Scorpion*, *Scourge*, *Stord*, *Venus*, *Vigilant*, and *Hardy* joined the convoy at 07.00 on 26 November. The western local escort of *Saladin*, *Skate*, and *Middleton* then detached to Seidisfjord, arriving at 21.00. *Speedwell* was detached to Scapa. After refuelling *Middleton* proceeded to Akureyri where she arrived at 10.00 on 27 November.

Although U-boat Wolfpack *Eisenbart* had been deployed in the Norwegian Sea the convoy was not sighted by any German reconnaissance aircraft or by any of the U-boats, and its passage through the Norwegian and Barents Seas was completed without incident.

At noon on 1 December, the White Sea section (three merchant ships) was detached for the Kola Inlet, Archangel, escorted by *Beagle*, *Rhododendron*, *Poppy*, and *Dianella*. The through escort, the destroyer *Saumarez* (Senior Officer) with *Scourge*, *Scorpion*, *Savage*, *Stord*, *Hardy*, *Venus*, and *Vigilant*, minesweeper *Halcyon*, and twelve merchant ships arrived at the Kola Inlet, Murmansk, at 13.00 on 2 December. The White Sea section arrived in Archangel on 3 December, where various merchant ships berthed in different locations between the 3rd and the 5th.[1] The same day the eight Home Fleet destroyers ex-JW.54B departed on the approaches to Archangel, to make independent passage home to Scapa Flow, where they arrived on 8 December.

RA.54B (26 November–9 December)

Convoy RA.54B of nine merchant ships and one rescue ship left Archangel on 26 November with the local eastern escort *Hussar* and *Seagull* (26 to

28 November) and *Lord Austin* (to 9 December). The ocean escort *Inconstant*, *Whitehall*, *Harrier* and *Heather*, joined on the following day and stayed with the convoy until 9 December. The convoy escort was reinforced by *Impulsive*, *Onslaught*, *Onslow*, *Orwell*, and Canadian destroyers *Haida*, *Huron* (28 November to 5 December), and *Iroquois* (to 4 December). The western local escort comprised *Brissenden*, *Middleton*, *Saladin*, and *Skate* (5 to 9 December). Cruiser cover was provided by *Bermuda*, *Jamaica*, and *Kent*, the latter carrying 54 tons of gold and silver bullion, payment for war supplies to Russia (27 November to 3 December). *Anson* and *Belfast*, screened by *Ashanti*, *Matchless*, *Musketeer*, and *Oribi* provided heavy cover from 28 November (*Matchless* left on the following day with weather damage, the other destroyers were also absent due to weather from 29 November to 1 December). There were no attacks on the convoy, which arrived in Loch Ewe on 9 December.

JW.55A/JW.55B/RA.55A/RA.55B – Operation FV

JW.55A (12–22 December)

Convoy JW.55A of nineteen merchant ships departed from Loch Ewe on 12 December 1943 with the close escort provided by *Westcott* and *Acanthus* (Western Approaches) and *Speedwell* (from 15 December), with the local western escort of *Harrier* and *Cockatrice* (to 17 December). *Wrestler* and *Scimitar* (local western escort) both from Western Approaches, were unable to sail owing to defects.

Three days later the convoy was joined by the ocean escort, comprising *Milne*, *Musketeer*, *Meteor*, *Matchless*, *Opportune*, *Ashanti*, *Athabaskan*, and *Virago* (15 to 20 December). A cruiser cover force comprising *Belfast*, *Norfolk*, and *Sheffield* sailed from Seidisfjord and followed the convoy through to the Kola Inlet, to guard against attack by surface units (16 to 19 December). Distant cover was provided by the *Duke of York*, *Jamaica*, *Savage*, *Saumarez*, *Scorpion*, and HNoMS *Stord*, which sailed from the Kola Inlet on 18 December and arrived in Akureyri three days later.

The convoy was sighted east of Bear Island by *U-386* but no attack developed. The darkness of the polar night limited action by enemy aircraft, and no reconnaissance aircraft found JW.55A during her passage. Nor did the *Scharnhorst* make any move to sortie against the convoy, though intense German radio traffic made C-in-C Home Fleet wary of the possibility, so that the heavy cover force accompanied JW.55A all the way to the Kola Inlet.

The convoy split into Murmansk and White Sea sections on 20 December. *Hussar* and *Speedwell*, three Russian destroyers and three Russian minesweepers from the Kola Inlet took over escort of the White Sea section of seven merchant ships, all of which arrived at Archangel on 22 December. The Murmansk section, twelve merchant ships, two motor minesweepers, and the eight destroyers of the ocean escort, together with *Whitehall*, *Acanthus*, and *Speedwell*, arrived in the Kola Inlet on the same day.

All nineteen merchant ships of JW.55A arrived safely, though the presence of C-in-C Home Fleet and his force caused much suspicion among the Russians. The German forces in Norway were discomfited by their lack of activity and took steps to reinforce their U-boat patrol line in the Arctic, against the next Allied convoy.

RA.55A (22 December 1943–1 January 1944)

The return convoy RA.55A, consisting of twenty-three merchant ships, departed from the Kola Inlet at 11.00 on 22 December. *Westcott*, *Beagle*, *Acanthus*, *Seagull*, *Dianella*, *Poppy*, and *Speedwell* provided the close escort. The ocean escort comprised *Milne*, *Matchless*, *Musketeer*, *Meteor*, *Ashanti*, *Athabaskan*, *Opportune*, and *Virago*. A cruiser cover force, *Belfast*, *Norfolk*, and *Sheffield* also followed the convoy from Murmansk, to guard against attack by surface units. Distant cover was provided by the heavy cover force comprising *Duke of York*, *Jamaica*, *Savage*, *Stord*, *Saumarez*, and *Scorpion*, which were at the time of RA.55A's departure shadowing the Murmansk-bound JW.55B.

RA.55A was threatened by the eight U-boats of Wolfpack *Eisenbart* in the Norwegian Sea, and the *Scharnhorst* and five destroyers stationed at Altenfjord. The Admiralty, aware of the threat of a sortie by *Scharnhorst*, placed Vice Admiral Bruce Fraser in overall command of the operation, coordinating the movements of both convoys and the various escort forces.

On 25 December, C-in-C Home Fleet received intelligence that *Scharnhorst* had sailed. RA.55A was diverted north to avoid detection, and later that day the SOE was instructed to dispatch four of the supporting destroyers to reinforce the escort of JW.55B. *Matchless*, *Musketeer*, *Opportune*, and *Virago* were sent (joined JW.55B on 26 December), later taking part in what would come to be called the 'Battle of the North Cape', and which saw the destruction of the *Scharnhorst*. This proved to be the last engagement of the war between British and German heavy ships. RA.55A itself was not sighted by any enemy forces and cleared the danger area without further incident. It was met on 30 December by the western local escort, *Hound, Hydra, Wallflower*, and *Borage*, and arrived safe at Loch Ewe on 1 January 1944.

JW.55B (20–30 December 1943)

JW.55B, made up of nineteen merchant ships escorted by *Whitehall, Wrestler, Oxlip, Honeysuckle* (all Western Approaches), and *Gleaner*, with a western local escort of *Wallflower, Borage* (Western Approaches), *Hound*, and *Hydra* left Loch Ewe on 20 December 1943. The convoy had a through escort of Home Fleet destroyers, minesweepers and Western Approaches escort vessels and was protected by a distant cover force and a cruiser cover force, while RN and Russian submarines covered the exits to Altenfjord.

The escort screen of eight Home Fleet destroyers – *Onslow* with *Onslaught, Orwell, Impulsive, Scourge, Iroquois, Haida*, and *Huron* from Skaalefjord, Faroes, joined in the afternoon of 22 December when the western local escort departed. The distant cover force (Force 2), C-in-C Home Fleet in the *Duke of York*, with *Jamaica, Savage, Saumarez, Scorpion*, and *Stord*, sailed from Akureyri at 23.00 on 23 December, to protect both JW.55B and RA.55B against surface attack. The cruiser cover force (Force 1), *Sheffield, Norfolk*, and *Belfast* left the Kola Inlet on the same day. The destroyer escort screen departed on 21 December to transfer to RA.55B. The convoy was shadowed by aircraft, who were overheard homing U-boats onto the convoy.

On Christmas Day, *Musketeer, Matchless, Opportune*, and *Virago* left the escort of RA.55A to reinforce JW.55B. C-in-C Home Fleet was concerned a German surface force would reach JW.55B before he could order the convoy to reverse course. In the event this proved too difficult, but the convoy was slowed to 8 knots in order to assist the meeting. Following a sighting by *U-601* of the *Eisenbart* Wolfpack, Admiral Bey, in the *Scharnhorst*, received permission to sortie with his force against the convoy (under Operation Ostfront).

Scharnhorst attempted to attack the convoy on the morning of 26 December, but she was detected by *Belfast*, between the cruiser force and the convoy. The cruiser cover force engaged the *Scharnhorst*, which then withdrew in an attempt to circle round the cruisers, heading off to the south with them in pursuit. Contact was lost and the cruiser cover force returned to the convoy to be joined in the forenoon by the four destroyers detached from RA.55A.

Shortly afterwards the convoy's course was altered to again position the cruisers between the convoy and the *Scharnhorst*.

The cruiser cover force reestablished contact just after midday. In the ensuing action, which lasted around twenty minutes, *Scharnhorst*, *Norfolk*, and *Saumarez* were all badly damaged, the latter two each with eleven crew killed and others injured. *Scharnhorst* was driven away from the convoy for a second time by the cruisers' determined defence and steamed off to the south for several hours, with the cruisers in pursuit. Contact was established again late afternoon, by which time the heavy cover force had joined the cruiser cover force. In the following three and a half hours *Scharnhorst* was repeatedly shelled and torpedoed, until at around 19.48 she was observed to have sunk, with the loss of almost 2,000 German sailors – only thirty-six were rescued by *Scorpion* and *Matchless*.

The convoy was met on 28 December by the local eastern escort, the minesweepers *Hussar* and *Halcyon*, together with three Russian destroyers and four Russian minesweepers which had sailed out from the Kola Inlet. The convoy then divided. The Murmansk section of ten merchant ships accompanied by the through escort, arrived in the Kola Inlet the following day. The Archangel section of nine merchant ships with local eastern escort arrived in Archangel one day later (sources disagree on dates). JW.55B arrived in North Russia without loss while the German attempt to attack the convoy led to the loss of their last serviceable capital ship in northern waters. The convoys would no longer face a serious threat from the German Navy's surface forces.

RA.55B (31 December 1943–8 January 1944)

RA.55B of just eight merchant ships, departed the Kola Inlet on 31 December, with its close escort, *Whitehall*, *Wrestler*, *Oxlip*, *Honeysuckle*, and *Rhododendron* (all to 8 January), supported by an ocean escort of eight Home Fleet destroyers led by *Onslow* with *Onslaught*, *Orwell*, *Iroquois*, *Impulsive*, *Haida*, *Huron*, *Wrestler*, *Whitehall* (to 7 January), and eastern local escort *Speedwell*, *Hussar*, and *Halcyon* (to 1 January).

Following the Battle of the North Cape on 26 December, which resulted in the sinking of the German Battleship *Scharnhorst*, the threat from German surface units was for the time being considered to have been eliminated, and RA.55B dispensed with the usual distant cover provided by heavy units of the Home Fleet. It was however threatened by the U-boat force now of some thirteen vessels of Wolfpack *Eisenbart* in the Norwegian Sea, which had operated against all the December convoys.

Air reconnaissance was however unable to find RA.55B in the gloom of the Arctic night and although several *Eisenbart* U-boats made contact, their attacks were ineffective. The convoy was able to shake off pursuit and on 7 January was met by the western local escort, *Ready* and *Orestes*, which brought the convoy into Loch Ewe the following day.

JW.56A/JW.56B/RA.56 – Operation FW

JW.56A (12–27 January)

JW.56A, with twenty merchant ships, left Loch Ewe during the afternoon of 12 January 1944, escorted by *Inconstant* (to 27 January), *Cygnet* (Western Approaches, 12 to 15 January), *Wallflower* and *Borage* (to 18 January), and western local escort *Ready* and *Orestes* (to 22 January), with *Poppy* and *Dianella* joining later the same day (also to 27 January). A cruiser cover force comprising *Kent*, *Berwick* (returned 23rd with defective dynamos), and *Bermuda* followed the convoy to guard against attack by surface units (23 to 28 January). There was no distant cover force.

On the third day out from Loch Ewe, JW.56A ran into a severe storm and the merchant ships became badly scattered. At 07.00 on 17 January, the Commodore reported: 'Convoy badly scattered, some ships damaged, and others had shifted their cargoes.' He considered all ships should be ordered to the nearest anchorage. At 22.00 Sir Bruce Austin Fraser, Vice Admiral, Second-in-Command, Home Fleet ordered the merchant ships and escorts of JW.56A to proceed to Akureyri, where they arrived the following day to seek shelter. Five merchant ships, the *Charles Bulfinch*, *Jefferson Davis*, *John A. Quitman*, *Josef N. Nicollet* and *Nathaniel Alexander*, were unable to proceed further than Iceland and returned to port.

After three days the storm abated and JW.56A, now reduced to fifteen merchant ships, was finally able to depart Akureyri at 10.00 on 21 January. The convoy formed in three columns, two of six ships, and one of three escorted by *Hardy*, *Venus*, *Vigilant*, *Virago*, *Savage*, *Stord*, *Offa*, *Obdurate*, and *Inconstant*. One merchant ship with weather damage remained at Akureyri with *Wallflower* and *Borage*.

The ocean escort, comprising *Hardy*, *Venus*, *Offa*, *Vigilant*, *Virago*, and *Obdurate* which had struggled since 14 January to join the convoy from Iceland, finally joined (26 January to 2 February).

The Germans knew from intelligence reports a PQ convoy was due to leave Iceland on 20 January and estimated it would reach the area where Wolfpack *Isegrim* was operating by the 26th. By 22 January, daily air reconnaissance missions flown by FW 200 Condor aircraft from Norway were searching a wide area all the way to the Denmark Strait, with special attention being paid to the waters near Jan Mayen Island, in an attempt to locate the convoy. Even though flights were made daily, JW.56A was not located. On the 22nd, a third merchant ship returned to Loch Ewe with weather damage. The western local escort, *Ready* and *Orestes*, detached from the convoy to Skaalefjord, arriving there on 24 January. The cruiser cover force (Force 1), *Kent*, *Berwick*, and *Bermuda*, left Akureyri on 23 January to cover the convoy. *Berwick* returned to Akureyri that afternoon with defective dynamos and a fourth merchant ship returned to Loch Ewe with weather damage.

Air reconnaissance still failed to locate the convoy but on 25 January JW.56A passed the northernmost U-boat of the patrol line, *U-739*, which broadcast an alert and commenced shadowing. Later that day the U-boat attacks began and continued throughout the day and following night. The seven U-boats in contact would carry out a total of seventeen attacks over a twelve-hour period.

Just after 18.30 *Obdurate*, pursuing a U-boat contact, was 'near missed' by a Gnat torpedo fired by *U-360*. The warhead detonated some distance from the ship's hull and the force of the explosion disabled the starboard screw and flooded the propeller shaft. Her starboard engine, now vibrating badly, was shut down and the propeller shaft stopped. As the port engine appeared undamaged the CO ordered increased speed on the remaining engine to escape from the danger area. *Obdurate*, apparently missed by a second shot from the U-boat about fifteen minutes later, then rejoined the convoy. Damage control teams successfully contained the worst effects of the flooding and damage to the hull and *Obdurate* arrived at Murmansk under her own power two days later.

The U-boats now turned their attention to the merchant ships. Shortly after 20.00 that evening *U-278* fired a spread of three FAT torpedoes[2] at the convoy, now sailing in snow squalls about 115 miles from the North Cape. The U-boat claimed the sinking of two ships of 7,000 tons each after hearing two detonations and sinking noises. In fact, both torpedoes hit the *Penelope Barker* (carrying 8,000 tons of steel, vehicles, aircraft, tanks, food, four locomotives, four flat cars and containers of acid, and sailing in station no. 12 of the convoy formation), in the port side. One struck in the no. 5 hold, blew off the hatch cover and beams, destroyed the port lifeboats and knocked the port AA gun out of its mounting. The second hit in the engine room, toppled the funnel, and damaged the bridge area and engine compartment.

Shortly before the *Penelope Barker* was torpedoed, *Obdurate* had been detached from the screen to provide medical assistance, transferring a Royal Navy medical officer across to treat one of her armed guards for appendicitis. After the missile strike the armed guard commander and the medical officer had gone below to assist trapped seamen; both were drowned when the ship sank. Eight officers, thirty-five crew, and twenty-eight USN armed guards began to abandon ship in two lifeboats, but she sank by the stern within ten minutes and some were forced to jump into the sea. In all one officer, nine crew, five USN armed guards and the RN medical officer were lost. The survivors were picked up forty minutes later by *Savage* and taken to Murmansk.

A few minutes after midnight on the night of 25/26 January, the convoy was attacked by two U-boats. First *U-716* fired a spread of three FAT torpedoes, heard two hits and reported one ship of 7,000 GRT sunk and another of 7,000 GRT damaged. The target was the American freighter *Andrew G. Curtin*, which was hit by a single torpedo on the starboard side between the no. 2 and no. 3 holds. As the ship settled by the head and listed to starboard the engine room duty watch secured the engines. The force of the explosion cracked the deck forward of the no. 3 hold. This crack extended right across the deck, and as it widened the bow arced upwards by about 25°. The complement of eight officers, thirty-five crew and twenty-eight USN armed guards abandoned ship in some confusion, in one liferaft and four lifeboats, aft of the damaged deck. Two crewmen were drowned and one armed guard died in the explosion. The survivors observed the *Andrew G. Curtin* break in two before sinking in less than thirty minutes. *Inconstant* picked up the survivors and landed them later in Murmansk. The ship had been carrying 9,000 tons of cargo and steel in her holds and two locomotives, two tenders and two US-built PT boats as deck cargo, at least one of which broke free and floated away.

The victim of the second attack, the British merchant ship *Fort Bellingham*, was the ship of the Convoy Commodore. She was struck by one of three torpedoes fired by *U-360*. The Master reported he was in the chartroom at about midnight when he heard an explosion he believed was from a torpedo striking the *Andrew G. Curtin.* Almost immediately a torpedo struck his own ship. The sea was moderate with a heavy swell and a west wind, force 3, the weather fine and clear with good visibility.

The Master's report vividly describes subsequent events:

No one saw the track of the torpedo, which struck on the port side, in the after end of no. 3 hold, forward of the engine room. There was a dull explosion and a fair amount of water thrown up on the port side. No flash was seen. The ship rolled to starboard, then to port, but quickly righted herself, settling bodily. The engine room bulkhead was pierced, both boilers collapsed, and the main steam pipe was fractured filling the compartment with live steam. A spray of oil and steam was thrown high into the air, which obscured the view from the bridge. The engines and dynamos stopped immediately, the ship lost all power and all the lights went out. Ventilators were blown off, some of which landed on the after deck. Nos 2 and 4 lifeboats were destroyed. The deck did not appear to be torn or buckled. The ship began taking on water but although she settled several feet in the water, seemed to be in no immediate danger of sinking. After the signal for emergency stations was rung, the third officer went to the upper bridge to fire the rockets, but the portfire failed, the cap being lost in the darkness. The Confidential Books were collected up and the Chief and second officers sent to the boat deck to clear away the lifeboats. They found no. 1 lifeboat hanging by the after fall and submerged, apparently it had been lowered by the DEMS ratings assisted by a number of seamen and engineers; when it capsized they went to no. 3 lifeboat, lowered it, cast off and drifted astern. The ship at this time was still underway at about four knots. The Master had given no orders to abandon ship, so obviously these men had panicked under the impression the cargo contained ammunition and feared a second torpedo. No deck officer was present when these men, numbering about twenty, abandoned ship.

The Chief Officer went round the decks and reported all life rafts, except one on the port side of the lower bridge and one in the after rigging, had been slipped and were floating astern. One raft with a few men on it was seen near the lifeboat, whilst two others appeared to be empty. The Master gathered the remaining men together (about thirty-five in all) and finally freed the raft from the lower bridge, giving instructions it was to remain alongside, but as it became waterborne about eighteen men jumped on to it, cut the painter and it quickly drifted away from the ship's side.

The Chief Officer then took a party of men and attempted to release the raft from the after rigging. Meanwhile, the Master with the first officer and fourth engineer, searched the accommodation, then tried to enter the engine room, but found it completely flooded and filled with smoke and steam. As the raft on the port side aft was proving very difficult to free, the Chief and second officers went over the side to the waterlogged lifeboat in an attempt to make it serviceable. They were soon soaked in cold water and covered with oil fuel.

The damage to the *Fort Bellingham* could have been far worse: the ship's manifest shows she was carrying 50 tons of cordite among her 4,900 tons of stores. About an hour and a half after the explosion *Offa* attempted to go alongside, but in the heavy swell her bows crashed against the side of *Fort Bellingham*. *Offa* then lowered her whaler (a small wooden seaboat, pointed at both ends), which managed to get alongside the stricken vessel and take off all those on board. She showed no signs of sinking but in her Master's opinion it would have been impossible to tow her into Murmansk and she could not be saved. The Commander of *Offa* attempted to sink her with torpedoes and gunfire, partially succeeding at 03.30 after two torpedoes and eighteen rounds of HE shell had been fired into her hull. Although red lights were seen from the no. 3 lifeboat and a liferaft believed to hold two or three men, the CO of *Offa* decided to rejoin the convoy, under the impression another vessel would pick up these other survivors. Unfortunately, they were not heard of again and were presumed missing, although there was some hope the motor lifeboat might reach land 130 miles away as it held sufficient fuel for 200 miles, plus the usual modern equipment, blankets, food, and water. Also, though the survivors were mainly DEMS gunners and engine room ratings, they were not entirely without leadership or knowledge of navigation, as the chief engineer and one deckhand (a Newfoundlander) were on board. The weather was fine during the first night but deteriorated later, lessening their chances of survival.

The Master, the Commodore, four naval staff members, twenty-three crew and seven gunners picked up by *Offa* were landed at Murmansk. Twenty-one crew, fourteen DEMS gunners and two naval staff members were lost. The abandoned hulk of the *Fort Bellingham* was finally sunk some hours later by *U-957*.

The Wolfpack continued its search but by 07.00 most U-boats had lost touch. The last contact was made by *U-957* which came across a debris field in which were liferafts, a cutter and a PT boat. *U-957* fired on the PT boat and cutter with her deck gun. Two men found on the PT boat, apparently survivors from the *Fort Bellingham*, were taken prisoner and interrogated, and the boat itself sunk.

The same day, the eastern local escort, *Gremyaschiy*, *Grozny* and *Razumny* from Murmansk, joined the convoy and took over the White Sea section of nine merchant ships. At 23.00 on 28 January, the Murmansk section of JW.56A (three merchant ships) arrived in the Kola Inlet (*Obdurate* with action damage). The ocean escort detached, to head back through the Wolfpack *Isegrim* patrol area, to meet and reinforce JW.56B. The White Sea section went on to the Dvina Bar with the eastern local escort and arrived there the following day. One merchant ship from Akureyri arrived back at Loch Ewe with *Wallflower*.

JW.56B (22 January–2 February)

The planned departure of JW.56B of seventeen merchant ships was delayed until 22 January, when it sailed with its western local escort, *Wrestler*, *Westcott*, *Whitehall*, *Rhododendron*, *Honeysuckle*, *Onyx*, and *Hydra* (all to 26 January). One merchant ship, the *Henry Lomb* returned. A cruiser cover force comprising *Kent*, *Berwick*, and *Bermuda* was also at sea (23 to 28 January) to guard the convoy against attack by German surface units. The destroyer escort of *Milne*, *Musketeer*, *Mahratta*, *Opportune*, *Scourge*, and *Huron* left Seidisfjord and joined the convoy on 26 January when the western local escort departed. On 27 January *Meteor* left Skaalefjord to join JW.56B the following day, to replace *Matchless*. The destroyer escort of JW.56A was ordered on 24 January to reinforce JW.56B in the vicinity of Bear Island, while *Hardy*, *Venus*, *Vigilant*, *Virago*, *Savage*, *Stord*, and *Offa* left the Kola Inlet on 28 January and joined JW.56B the following day.

On 29 January, JW.56B entered the area where JW.56A had been attacked, where ten U-boats of Wolfpack *Isengrim*, reinforced with five newcomers and reorganized as Wolfpack *Werewolf* was waiting. Six made contact the next day, mounting a total of thirteen attacks during the day, when the convoy was about 50 miles south of Bear Island. They were unable to penetrate the escort screen to reach the merchant ships, but *U-278* hit the destroyer *Hardy* with an acoustic torpedo. *Hardy* was crippled, abandoned and sunk later by *Venus*. Thirty-five of her crew were killed. *U-314* was detected, attacked and sunk by *Whitehall* and *Meteor*, after which the Wolfpack abandoned its assault.

On 1 February the convoy divided. The Murmansk section of ten merchant ships, with the through escort and destroyers *Milne*, *Musketeer*, *Meteor*, *Mahratta*, *Opportune*, *Scourge*, *Huron*, *Venus*, *Vigilant*, *Virago*, *Offa*, *Savage*, and *Stord* arrived at the Kola Inlet later that day. The White Sea section of six merchant ships proceeded with the eastern local escort from the Kola Inlet to Archangel, where it arrived the following day.

RA.56 (3–10 February)

The second part of Operation FW now began: RA.56 of thirty-nine merchant ships sailed from the Kola Inlet on 3 February, at a speed of 9½ knots, escorted by *Gleaner* and *Seagull* (3 to 5 February). Those merchant ships unable maintain the speed were excluded from the convoy. The *Empire Pickwick* and *Philip Livingstone*, two stragglers who could not keep up, were sent back with the eastern local escort.

The convoy was strongly escorted by all the fleet destroyer and Western Approaches escorts which accompanied JW.56A and JW.56B, together with three fleet minesweepers returning from North Russia. The close escort comprised *Westcott*, *Whitehall*, *Cygnet*, *Dianella*, *Oxlip*, *Poppy*, *Rhododendron*, *Halcyon*, *Hussar*, and *Speedwell* (the last three until 10 February), and *Offa*, *Opportune*, *Savage*, *Venus*, and *Vigilant* (to 7 February), *Inconstant*, *Mahratta*, *Meteor*, *Milne*, *Musketeer*, and *Scourge*, as well as the Canadian destroyer *Huron* and the Norwegian *Stord* (all to 9 February) and *Obedient*, *Swift*, and *Verulam* (6 to 9 February). *Bermuda*, *Berwick*, and *Kent* provided cruiser cover (5 to 7 February).

A last-minute diversion of the convoy to the east, ordered by the Admiralty, evidently achieved its objective of avoiding the U-boats patrolling about 100 miles north of Kola Inlet near the original route. RA.56 was not detected or attacked, and arrived off Cape Wrath on 10 February with the western local escort of *Wrestler*, *Borage*, *Honeysuckle*, *Wallflower*, *Cockatrice*, *Loyalty*,

Rattlesnake, and *Ready*. The merchant ships then proceeded direct to their destinations, arriving safely the following day. *Speedwell*, *Halcyon*, and *Hussar* detached from the convoy to proceed to Scapa Flow, their tour of service in North Russia having come to an end.

JW.57/RA.57 – Operation FX

JW.57 (20–29 February)

JW.57, a single large convoy of forty-two merchant ships plus two fleet oilers, a rescue ship and six Russian light craft, left Loch Ewe for North Russia on 20 February, accompanied by the western local escort comprising *Burdock*, *Dianella* (Western Approaches), *Rattlesnake*, *Orestes*, *Loyalty*, and *Hydra*.

Keppel, *Boadicea*, *Beagle*, *Walker*, *Bluebell*, *Camellia*, *Lotus*, and *Rhododendron* (Western Approaches) provided the close escort. The ocean escort, the cruiser *Black Prince* (Vice Admiral (Destroyers)) and escort carrier *Chaser* escorted by *Verulam* and *Vigilant* joined on 22 February. A Western Approaches support group (B1) remained with the convoy as far as the Bear Island area. Also on 22 February, the convoy was joined by the ocean escort, Captain (D) 23rd Destroyer Flotilla in *Serapis*, in company with *Matchless*, *Impulsive*, *Obedient*, *Offa*, *Swift*, *Meteor*, *Mahratta*, *Onslaught*, *Oribi*, *Savage*, and support group B1, *Strule* (Senior Officer), *Byron*, *Watchman*, and *Wanderer* (to 26 February). *Berwick*, *Jamaica*, and ORP *Dragon* (detached 25 February, arrived Scapa Flow 26th but took no further part) were deployed to cover the convoy from 26 to 27 February, to guard against attack by smaller surface units, but no battle squadron took part as the surface threat was confined to enemy destroyers. Five Russian submarines were on patrol off the north coast of Norway.

The JW.57 convoy was sighted and reported by reconnaissance aircraft on 23 February. These planes were attacked several times and seen off by *Chaser*'s Martlet fighters (also known as 'Wildcats') but none were shot down. The fourteen U-boats deployed in two patrol lines made a determined attempt to intercept and destroy the ships. They made contact on 24 February but were unsuccessful in their attacks, and *U-713* was sunk in a counterattack by *Keppel*, assisted by a Swordfish from *Chaser*. (*U-713* sent her last radio message on 24 February and was posted as missing after repeatedly failing to report her position on 26 February.) Fifty of *U-713*'s crew were killed.

Enemy aircraft shadowed the convoy from 25 February onwards. One U-boat, *U-601*, was detected and sunk that day with depth charges by the anti-submarine air escort, a Catalina of 210 Squadron flying at extreme range from Sullom Voe in the Shetlands; there were no survivors.

At 20.55 on 25 February the destroyer *Mahratta* was hit by a Gnat torpedo from *U-990*, about 280 miles from the North Cape while escorting the rear section of the convoy formation – she blew up and sank within minutes. *Impulsive* and *Wanderer* were quickly on the scene to pick up survivors but only sixteen from her crew of 236 could be rescued.

On 28 February, despite the very bad weather, Swordfish aircraft from the carrier *Chaser* carried out a number of anti-submarine patrols without result. Early the same day the U-boat operation was suspended and there were no further attacks.

As the minesweepers normally stationed in North Russia had returned to the UK with RA.57, the eastern local escort for the White Sea section of JW.57 was for the first time an all-Russian one, composed of *Gromky*, *Gremyaschiy*, *Razumny*, and *Razyaronnyi*, four minesweepers and four submarine chasers. After the convoy entered the comparative safety of the Kola Inlet, still being shadowed by reconnaissance aircraft, it split into two sections. The Murmansk section of thirty-two merchant ships and the six Soviet light craft arrived in the Kola Inlet with all the through escorts (less the *Mahratta)* on 28 February. The White Sea section of ten merchant ships proceeded with the eastern local escort and arrived off the Dvina Bar the following day. The convoy suffered no loss or damage.

RA.57 (2–10 March)

The RA.57 convoy of thirty-two merchant ships, including a rescue ship and three fleet oilers (*San Adolfo*, *San Ambrosia*, and *San Cirilo*), sailed from the Kola Inlet on 2 March, strongly guarded by the escorts of JW.57, *Black Prince* (Flag), *Impulsive*, *Meteor*, *Obedient*, *Swift*, *Verulam* (2 to 7 March), *Gleaner*, and *Seagull* (Home Fleet), all of whom stayed with the convoy until 8 March. The close escort comprised *Keppel*, *Boadicea*, and *Beagle* (2 to 9 March), *Walker*, *Bluebell*, *Camellia*, *Lotus*, and *Rhododendron* (Western Approaches – to 10 March). The escort carrier *Chaser*, with *Matchless*, *Milne*, *Offa*, *Onslaught*, *Oribi*, *Savage*, *Serapis*, and *Vigilant*, accompanied them (2 to 8 March). No battle squadron or cruiser force took part as the surface threat was confined to enemy destroyers. Five Russian submarines were on patrol off the north coast of Norway.

During 3 March aircraft shadowed the convoy, homing U-boats onto it. The U-boats made contact the following day near the Kola Inlet. At 15.45, *U-703* fired a spread of FAT torpedoes and sank the British freighter *Empire Tourist*, carrying 400 standards of timber and 600 tons of coal. *Milne*, nearby, attacked the U-boat with depth charges for several hours. The *Empire Tourist*'s Master, forty-one crew, twenty-three gunners, and three naval personnel were picked up by *Gleaner* and later landed at Loch Ewe. The destroyer *Swift* was then attacked by *U-739*, which fired an acoustic torpedo but missed. Another U-boat, *U-472*, was then counterattacked and damaged by rocket projectiles fired from a Swordfish of 816 Squadron from the carrier *Chaser* and later scuttled with gunfire by *Onslaught*. Twenty-five survivors were rescued from the U-boat.

A number of U-boats had assembled to attack the previous incoming convoy (JW.57), but RA.57 avoided them, partly thanks to the efforts of Russian aircraft and partly by making a wide diversion to the east after leaving the Kola Inlet.

On 5 March a Swordfish of 816 Squadron from *Chaser* attacked and sank *U-366*. The following day two more U-boats were damaged and *U-973* was sunk by a Swordfish from the *Chaser*; three survivors were picked up.

The western local escort, *Hydra*, *Loyalty*, *Onyx*, *Orestes*, and *Ready* joined on 8 March and the following day *Beagle* and *Seagull* departed. The close escort remained with the convoy until 10 March when it dispersed, the merchant ships sailing to their respective west coast ports, where they arrived in the afternoon. *Gleaner* detached to Loch Ewe, arriving in the morning to land the survivors from the merchant ship and U-boats.

JW.58/RA.58 – Operation FY

JW.58 (27 March–4 April)

Convoy JW.58, of forty-four merchant ships with the USN cruiser *Milwaukee*, being transferred to the Russian Navy, departed Loch Ewe on 27 March. The western local escort (to 29 March) included *Rhododendron*, *Stalwart*, *Onyx*, *Orestes*, and *Rattlesnake*. The close escort (to 4 April), was provided by *Westcott*, *Whitehall*, *Wrestler*, *Bluebell*, *Honeysuckle* and *Lotus*. The convoy was joined from Iceland by three more merchant ships (one of which returned with defects), together with frigate *Fitzroy* and minesweepers *Chamois* and *Chance*.

The ocean escort, *Impulsive, Inconstant, Obedient, Offa, Onslow, Opportune, Oribi, Orwell, Saumarez, Serapis, Scorpion, Venus*, and the Free Norwegian *Stord* joined on 2 March. The escort also included *Beagle, Boadicea, Keppel, Walker, Starling, Magpie, Wild Goose, Wren*, and *Whimbrel* (to 4 April). Late on 29 March *U-961* on passage to the North Atlantic was detected as it crossed the path of the escort, then was depth charged and destroyed by *Starling* and *Magpie*.

Distant cover was provided by elements of the Home Fleet, already at sea having sailed from Scapa Flow on 30 March for Operation TUNGSTEN. They included battleships *Anson*, and *Duke of York*, fleet carriers *Furious* and *Victorious*, escort carriers *Emperor, Fencer, Pursuer* and *Searcher*, cruisers *Belfast, Jamaica*, and *Sheffield*, anti-aircraft cruiser *Royalist*, and destroyers *Milne, Meteor, Onslaught, Undaunted, Ursa, Verulam, Vigilant, Virago, Wakeful*, and Canadian destroyers *Algonquin* and *Sioux*.

Three days after the convoy's departure, aircraft located and reported the convoy and there then followed a succession of actions between 'shadowers' and fighters from the carriers. The latter did notably well, shooting down no fewer than six of the long-range aircraft during the convoy's passage. When the convoy was located the *Blitz, Hammer*, and *Thor* Wolfpacks were moved to a patrol line southwest of Bear Island, with orders to commence their attack on the night of 31 March, by which time sixteen U-boats were to be in position.

JW.58 crossed the first U-boat patrol line on 31 March and over the next forty-eight hours the Wolfpacks mounted eighteen attacks. No merchant ships were hit, but three U-boats were destroyed in counterattacks. The first, *U-355*, was sunk by *Beagle* and aircraft from *Tracker* on the 31 March. On 2 April, *Keppel* destroyed *U-360* in a Hedgehog attack.[3] The next day a Swordfish from *Activity* attacked and sank *U-288*, with help from a Martlet and an Avenger from the *Tracker*. There were no survivors. The same day JW.58 was joined by the eastern local escort of *Gremyaschiy, Kuibyshev, Razumny*, and *Razyaronnyi*, and arrived at the Kola Inlet on 4 April without further incident.

RA.58 (7–15 April)

The second part of Operation FY, convoy RA.58, consisted of thirty-eight merchant ships (including one escort oiler and two rescue ships). It left the Kola Inlet on 7 April escorted by *Beagle, Boadicea, Inconstant, Keppel, Venus, Walker, Westcott, Whitehall, Wrestler, Activity* (7 to 12 April), *Diadem, Offa*,

Onslow, Opportune, Orwell, Saumarez, Serapis and Norwegian *Stord* (7 to 13 April), *Tracker, Impulsive, Obedient, Oribi,* Scorpion, *Bluebell, Honeysuckle, Starling, Magpie, Whimbrel, Wild Goose,* and *Wren* (7 to 14 April).

The passage was uneventful; none of the sixteen U-boats on patrol made contact. The convoy split up on 14 April, the merchant ships then proceeding to east and west coast UK ports where they arrived the following day. The operation was completed without loss to the merchant ships of the convoy or the escorts.

Operation FZ

RA.59 (28 April–7 May)

Operation FZ, the passage of convoy RA.59, began on 28 April 1944. As there was no corresponding eastbound convoy, the escorts sailed direct from Scapa Flow on 19 April to the Kola Inlet where they arrived on 23 April and returned with the convoy after a five-day turnaround.

The convoy of 45 merchant ships, (including an escort oiler) sailed from the Kola Inlet (at a speed of 9½ knots) on 28 April escorted by *Diadem, Activity, Fencer, Beagle, Boadicea, Inconstant, Keppel, Marne, Matchless, Meteor, Milne, Musketeer, Ulysses, Verulam, Virago, Walker, Westcott, Whitehall,* and *Wrestler,* and Canadian frigates *Cape Breton, Grou, Outremont,* and *Waskesiu.*

The escorts took on board 346 officers and men of the USS *Milwaukee* (turned over to the Russians) and four senior Russian officers. The convoy was to have included a personnel ship *Nea Hellas,* but unfortunately she broke down and returned to Scapa Flow. The escort therefore arrived in the Kola Inlet without means to transport 2,348 Russian Navy personnel who were supposed to man the Royal Navy warships to be handed over in the UK. In order to accommodate the numbers involved, arrangements were made for the USN personnel to return in the RN warships and for the empty merchant ships to embark the Russian officers and ratings as passengers. No battle squadron or cruiser force covered the convoy, since the surface threat was confined to destroyers.

On 1 May, fighters from the carrier *Activity* shot down a BV.138 reconnaissance aircraft. The escorting destroyers and carrier aircraft continued to attack U-boat contacts and succeeded in sinking three U-boats over a two-day period – *U-277* on 1 April and two the following day, *U-654* and *U-959*; there were no survivors. Four destroyers left the convoy on the

3rd to land their US and Russian naval passengers in the Clyde on the 5th. Another four with US naval personnel left on 3 May for Scapa, and the following day a further six destroyers left to land their US naval passengers on 6 May. The convoy dispersed and the merchant ships reached Loch Ewe and the Clyde on 6 and 7 May respectively, having lost one merchant ship sunk by a U-boat. The arrival of RA.59 brought this particular convoy cycle to a close.

Chapter 8

Phase Five: The Final Cycle,
August 1944 to May 1945

JW.59/RA.59A – Operation VICTUAL

JW.59 (15–25 August)

The convoy cycle resumed in August 1944 with what was to be its final phase, Operation VICTUAL, the passages of JW.59 and RA.59A.

JW.59, of thirty-three merchant ships (including one rescue ship and one replenishment oiler), sailed from Loch Ewe on 15 August 1944 and included a number of warships being delivered to the Russian Navy. The western local escort (15 to 25 August) comprised *Cygnet, Loch Dunvegan, Bluebell, Camellia, Charlock, Honeysuckle, Oxlip, Kite, Mermaid, Peacock, Keppel* and *Whitehall*. The ocean escort (17 to 25 August) included the cruiser *Jamaica*, escort carriers *Striker* and *Vindex*, all of whom went through with the body of the main convoy and destroyers *Caprice, Marne, Meteor, Milne,* and *Musketeer*.

Heavy cover for JW.59 and RA.59A was provided by the main strength of the Home Fleet under Operation GOODWOOD (18 August to 3 September). It sailed in two task groups designated Force 1 and Force 2. Force 1 comprised Commander-in-Chief Home Fleet, in the battleship *Duke of York*, together with Rear Admiral Commanding, First Cruiser Squadron in the fleet carrier *Indefatigable*, with carriers *Formidable* and *Furious*, heavy cruisers *Berwick* and *Devonshire* of the 1st Cruiser Squadron, destroyers *Cambrian, Myngs, Vigilant, Sioux*, and Free Norwegian *Stord* of the 26th Destroyer Division. Force 2 consisted of the escort carriers *Trumpeter* and the Canadian-manned *Nabob* (on loan from Admiral Sir Max Horton's Western Approaches command). Forces 1 and 2 were supported by an underway replenishment group, the fleet oilers RFA *Black Ranger* and RFA *Blue Ranger*, escorted by the destroyer *Nubian* and corvettes *Poppy, Dianella,* and *Starwort* – designated Force 9. All three task forces sailed from Scapa

Flow on 18 August, their course set northerly to pass to the east of the Faroe Islands.

Early on 21 August the sloop *Kite* stopped to recover equipment from overnight anti-U-boat operations and was hit by two torpedoes on the starboard side. She immediately heeled over, the stern broke off, the sloop floated for a few seconds then sank. *Keppel* stopped to pick up survivors, while *Peacock* and *Mermaid* screened the rescue operation. Only fourteen of sixty were rescued alive from the ice-cold water, five more later died on board the rescue ships and were buried at sea; a total of 217 officers and ratings were lost.

Although not part of the convoy escort, the carrier *Nabob*, sailing as part of the distant cover force, and frigate *Bickerton* part of the escort screen for the *Nabob*, were detected and attacked by *U-354* in the early hours of 22 August, as she searched for JW.59 northwest of the North Cape in the Barents Sea. *U-354* hit *Nabob* with one torpedo in the starboard side aft, resulting in a hole about 32 feet square, located aft of the engine room and below the waterline. Two minutes later, the U-boat fired a Gnat to finish off the carrier but struck the frigate *Bickerton* in the stern, killing thirty-eight of her crew and leaving many seriously injured. Disabled by the loss of her propeller shafts, the *Bickerton* was abandoned and the order given for her to be sunk in view of the threat of further U-boat attacks during any attempt to establish a tow. The survivors were taken aboard *Bligh* and *Aylmer*, and *Bickerton* was torpedoed and sunk by *Vigilant*. *Nabob* had sustained serious damage, including a bent propeller shaft, with twenty-one crew killed, but was able to steam and continue to operate aircraft. She returned to Scapa Flow on 27 August, was subsequently declared a constructive loss and taken out of service.

The next day aircraft from *Striker* shot down a shadowing BV.138 flying boat. Two days later *U-344*, attempting to approach the convoy to the north of the North Cape, was detected, attacked and sunk in a combined action by *Keppel*, *Loch Dunvegan*, *Mermaid*, and *Peacock* (the latter two both sister-ships of *Kite*). Whilst waiting in the Bear Island area for the arrival of convoy RA.59A, *U-354* was detected, attacked and destroyed by a Swordfish aircraft of 825 Squadron FAA from *Vindex*. There were no survivors from either U-boat.

All thirty-three merchant ships of JW.59 arrived safely in the Kola Inlet at 06.00 on 25 August. During the passage, U-boats were sighted on twenty-three occasions, but the effective anti-submarine patrols meant none was allowed closer than 40 miles from the convoy. Aircraft from the two carriers flew for 444 hours in the U-boat area and made fourteen attacks on U-boats at distances of between 50 and 75 miles from the convoy, without incurring any losses.

RA.59A (28 August–5 September 1944)

The nine merchant ships of westbound convoy RA.59A left the Kola Inlet at 11.00 on 28 August. The through escort comprised *Jamaica, Striker, Vindex, Caprice, Marne, Meteor, Milne, Musketeer Keppel, Whitehall, Loch Dunvegan, Mermaid, Peacock, Cygnet, Bluebell, Camellia, Charlock, Honeysuckle,* and *Oxlip.* The Commander-in-Chief Home Fleet, in *Duke of York,* and units of the Home Fleet provided distant cover (18 August to 3 September). At 19.56 on 30 August *U-307* fired a spread of three FAT torpedoes at the convoy, by then about 50 miles south of Bear Island. The U-boat heard three detonations and sinking noises and reported two ships sunk and one ship damaged. However, only the American freighter *William S. Thayer* in station no. 33, carrying 950 tons of sand as ballast, was hit by two torpedoes on the starboard side between the no. 1 and no. 2 hatches and in the no. 4 hold. The explosions destroyed the shaft and engines and broke the ship in three in the areas of no. 1 and no. 4 holds. The forward part listed to starboard and sank in about 30 seconds, followed by the midships section two minutes later. The eight officers, thirty-three crew, twenty-eight armed guards and 175 passengers (Russian naval personnel) did not have time to launch the lifeboats and abandoned ship on six small square floats. The survivors were picked up by the American Liberty ship *Robert Eden* and landed in Glasgow. Most of the Russians stayed on the stern section and were taken off by *Whitehall* which then scuttled the wreck by gunfire. Six officers, seventeen crew, seven armed guards and thirteen passengers were lost.

On 1 September, aircraft from *Striker* sighted a U-boat on the surface in a snow shower and there were further indications of U-boat deployments in the vicinity of the convoy. The merchant ships had no contact with the enemy, but the following day a patrol of three Swordfish aircraft of 825 Squadron from *Vindex* sighted a surfaced U-boat southeast of Jan Mayen Island and, under fire from the U-boat, carried out rocket attacks, followed by depth charges that failed to explode. *Keppel, Whitehall, Mermaid,* and *Peacock* then carried out sustained anti-submarine attacks over a period of six hours resulting in the sinking of *U-394*[1] with the loss of all hands. There were no U-boat attacks on 3 September but air search operations continued. Ju.88 German reconnaissance aircraft were sighted by a Hurricane interception flight but escaped.

The convoy arrived at Loch Ewe on 5 September. *Vindex, Striker, Jamaica,* and fleet destroyers arrived at Scapa Flow the following day.

JW.60/RA.60 – Operation RIGMAROLE

JW.60 (15–23 September)

JW.60, a convoy of thirty-one merchant ships (the majority American), a fleet oiler and a rescue ship, sailed from Loch Ewe on 15 September with a close escort consisting of *Bulldog, Keppel, Whitehall, Allington Castle, Bamborough Castle,* and *Cygnet.*

The ocean escort sailed from Scapa Flow at 13.00 on 16 September and joined at 05.00 the following day. Led by Rear Admiral Commanding First Cruiser Squadron in the battleship *Rodney* the escort comprised *Diadem, Campania, Striker, Marne, Meteor, Milne, Musketeer, Saumarez, Scorpion, Venus, Verulam, Virago, Volage,* and Canadian destroyers *Algonquin* and *Sioux.* At 06.00 *Rodney* took up station in the centre of the convoy with a screen of *Milne, Marne, Meteor,* and *Musketeer. Campania* and *Striker* took up position astern of the convoy, which then proceeded at a speed of 9½ knots. The ocean escort accompanied the convoy all the way to the Kola Inlet. The convoy was not detected and arrived safely at its destination on 23 September.

RA.60 (28 September–4 October)

The next convoy was RA.60, comprising thirty merchant ships and one rescue ship, with the close escort provided by the 7th Escort Group, comprising *Bulldog, Keppel, Whitehall, Cygnet, Allington Castle,* and *Bamborough Castle,* which sailed from Kola Inlet on 28 September. The ocean escort off the Kola Inlet was the same as for JW.60.

At first the convoy avoided the twelve U-boats of Wolfpacks *Grimm* and *Zorn* awaiting its departure, but at around 16.30 the next day it was intercepted off the North Cape by *U-310*, which fired FAT torpedoes and hit the American freighter *Edward H. Crockett* and British freighter *Samsuva.*

The *Edward H. Crockett,* carrying 1,659 tons of chrome ore as ballast, was struck by one torpedo on the starboard side forward of the no. 4 hatch.

The explosion broke the propeller shaft, wrecked the engine, damaged the forward bulkhead of the hold and killed the first assistant engineer. The eight officers, thirty-three crew and twenty-seven armed guards abandoned ship in four lifeboats and were picked up an hour later by *Zamalek* and landed at the Clyde on 5 October. The wreck was later shelled and sunk by *Milne*.

Another torpedo struck the *Samsuva* in the engine room, killing the three members of the watch on duty at the time. The chief engineer and the chief officer tried to go below but the ladders had been blown away. In the meantime the motor lifeboat was launched and most of the crew abandoned ship, leaving a few on board since there appeared to be no immediate danger of the *Samsuva* sinking due to her cargo of pit props. The lifeboat made its way to the rescue ship *Rathlin* where most of the crew scrambled up the rescue nets slung over the side. A few stayed in the lifeboat and returned to *Samsuva* to collect the Master and rest of the crew and bring them back to *Rathlin*. The *Samsuva*, although still afloat with her 3,000 tons of pit props, could not be salvaged and was then shelled and sunk by *Bulldog* and *Musketeer*. Three of the crew were lost. The Master, thirty-six crew and twenty DEMS gunners picked up by *Rathlin* were landed at Clyde on 5 October.

The next day, Swordfish of 813 Squadron from the *Campania* sank *U-921*. All fifty-one crew were lost. *U-921* sent its last radio message on 24 September, from approximately 74.45N, 13.50E, saying that it had to return to port due to unspecified damage. The U-boat was ordered to postpone its return and to operate against convoy RA.60, but posted as missing on 2 October when it failed to arrive at Narvik following the convoy battle. The *Edward H. Crockett* and *Samsuva* were the only losses suffered by the convoy, which arrived in Loch Ewe on 5 October.

JW.61/RA.61 – Operation TRIAL

JW.61 (20–28 October)

Convoy JW.61 of twenty-nine merchant ships (including two escort oilers and one rescue ship) sailed from Loch Ewe on 20 October.[2] With the risk from *Tirpitz* now neutralized after the serious damage inflicted by the RAF on 15 September (Operation PARAVANE, carried out by RAF bombers from an airfield in north Russia – and *Tirpitz* could not be repaired as it was no longer possible for the Germans to sail her to a major port) and the air threat reduced, there were concerns the Germans would increase U-boat operations. The close escort was therefore heavily reinforced with two escort groups and a third escort carrier.

The close escort comprised *Walker, Lapwing,* and *Lark, Camellia, Oxlip,* and *Rhododendron* of the 8th Escort Group. On 22 October the ocean escort, *Dido, Obedient, Offa, Onslow, Opportune, Oribi,* and *Orwell* of the 17th Destroyer Flotilla joined. Distant cover was provided by the escort carriers *Nairana, Tracker,* and *Vindex,* escorted by the frigates *Byron, Conn, Deane, Fitzroy, Inglis, Lawson, Loring, Louis, Mounsey, Narborough, Redmill,* and *Rupert* of the 15th and 21st Escort Groups to provide additional anti-submarine patrols and fighter protection against air attacks.

Very heavy weather almost stopped the convoy in the first two days but conditions improved, good progress was made, and on reaching the 73rd Parallel the 3rd Escort Group and *Vindex* began operating 30 miles ahead of the convoy.

U-boats were first encountered on 26 October as the convoy rounded Bear Island, when the HF/DF sets started detecting transmissions between the U-boats of what was later confirmed to have been the nineteen-strong *Panther* Wolfpack. The escorts eventually made contact with the Wolfpack, but difficult ASDIC conditions caused by variations in the water temperature and density, which can deflect sonar transmissions, made maintaining contact a challenge for the operators. A number of T5 torpedoes were fired by the U-boats, but successful counter measures were taken and the convoy sailed safely into the Kola Inlet on 28 October without loss.

In the month of October 1944, for the first time since September 1939, no merchant ships were lost throughout the length and breadth of the North and South Atlantic, including the Arctic.

RA.61 (2–9 November)

The return convoy RA.61 left the Kola Inlet at daybreak on 2 November with thirty-three merchant ships (some had started the voyage in the White Sea on 30 October), including two fleet oilers and one rescue ship. Also stationed within the formation of the convoy were *Dido, Nairana, Tracker,* and *Vindex.* The convoy was escorted by *Lapwing, Lark, Walker, Camellia, Oxlip,* and *Rhododendron* (2 to 9 November), with *Obedient, Offa, Onslow, Opportune, Oribi, Orwell, Byron, Conn, Deane, Fitzroy, Redmill,* and *Rupert* (2 to 7 November), and *Inglis, Lawson, Loring, Louis,* and *Narborough* (2 to 6 November).

The 3rd, 15th and 21st Escort Groups sailed from the Kola Inlet on 31 October in an operation to clear U-boats from the convoy's route. During this operation, on 2 November the frigate *Mounsey* of the 15th Escort Group, was hit by a torpedo fired by *U-295*. Some of the frigate's deck plates were buckled but she remained afloat and *Narborough* towed her back into the Kola Inlet for temporary repairs; the attack unfortunately resulted in eleven members of the crew losing their lives. The convoy itself had an uninterrupted passage and arrived safely at Loch Ewe on 9 November.

JW.61A/RA.61A – Operation GOLDEN

JW.61A (31 October–6 November)

The subsequent operation, GOLDEN, was not for the shipment of supplies to North Russia but for the transfer of Russian prisoners of war, together with a Norwegian military contingent and relief stores destined for liberated northern Norway. JW.61A sailed from Liverpool on 31 October and arrived in the Kola Inlet on 6 November. It consisted of two liners, *Empress of Australia*, and *Scythia*, escorted by *Berwick*, *Campania*, *Saumarez* (Captain (D) 23rd Destroyer Flotilla), with *Scourge*, *Serapis*, *Caprice*, *Cambrian*, and *Cassandra*. The liners were carrying 11,000 ex-Russian servicemen captured in France while fighting for the Germans (under duress), now being repatriated at the insistence of Stalin, together with other Russian nationals including women and children.

RA.61A (10–16 November)

On 10 November, the 3rd Escort Group sailed out of the Kola Inlet four hours ahead of the return convoy RA.61A, to sweep the area ready for it to proceed at a fast speed as the weather had become more settled. On the afternoon of 13 November two fighters from *Campania* shot down a shadowing aircraft. The following day, the cruiser, carrier and the 23rd Destroyer Flotilla left the convoy to return to Scapa Flow and the 3rd Escort Group took over close escort of the two liners which arrived back in the UK on 16 November.

JW.62/RA.62 – Operation ACUMEN

JW.62 and RA.62, the last pair of convoys of 1944 were the first to sail with no danger of intervention from the *Tirpitz*, but now faced an increased threat of air attack from the strengthened force of Ju.88 torpedo bombers which had reappeared in Norway after an absence of over two years; there was also now a heavy concentration of U-boats in the approaches to the Kola Inlet.

JW.62 (29 November–7 December)

By the time JW.62 sailed, two *Gruppen* – equivalent to an air wing, made up of three squadrons totalling 30–40 aircraft – of Ju.88s had been transferred to Norway for the specific purpose of resuming the campaign against the convoys. KG 26 was now well established as a fully-fledged torpedo-bomber *Geschwader* (wing). After service in the Mediterranean and operations against the Allied landings in both Normandy and southern France, KG 26 had been withdrawn to Germany to rest and refit and it was from here that I./KG 26 was deployed to Bardufoss, and II./KG 26 to Trondheim, although the latter was temporarily redeployed to Bardufoss for the attack on JW.64. II./KG 26 relocated to Banak, Norway on 25 October 1944.

JW.62, of thirty-one merchant ships including three fleet oilers and one rescue ship, sailed from Loch Ewe at 17.30 on 29 November, strongly escorted by *Bellona*, *Campania*, and *Narnia*, the 17th Destroyer Flotilla – *Onslow*, *Offa*, *Oribi*, *Orwell*, *Onslaught*, *Obedient*, *Beagle*, and *Bulldog*, the 1st Division of the 7th Destroyer Flotilla – *Caesar*, *Caprice*, *Cambrian*, *Cassandra*, *Keppel*, and *Westcott*, *Cygnet*, *Lapwing*, and *Lark*, *Allington Castle*, *Bamborough Castle*, *Tavy*, *Bahamas*, *Tortola*, *Somaliland*, and Canadian 9th Escort Group – *Monnow*, *Nene*, *Port Colborne*, *St John*, and *Stormont*, with *Loch Alvie*. There was no heavy cover force, reflecting the success of Operation CATECHISM in finally eliminating *Tirpitz* as a threat (she was sunk on 12 November).

The *Stier* Wolfpack of eighteen U-boats[3] initially deployed in the area to the west of Bjørnøya and to the north of the Kola Inlet, was relocated on 1 December to the Kola Coast, on the false premise that the convoy had already transited the Bjørnøya Passage. The convoy had in fact detoured to the north as its support groups made an unsuccessful foray against the suspected U-boat concentration.

The following day *U-318* attacked both the merchant ships and the escorts. The strength of the latter had been increased by the arrival of the Russian destroyers *Baku*, *Gremyaschiy*, *Razumnyi*, *Uritskyi*, *Deyatelnyi*, *Derzkiy*,

Doblestnyi, *Zhivuchiy* and four submarine chasers. One of *U-293*'s torpedoes exploded in the wake of the *Deyatelnyi* but no ships were actually hit.

Despite the concentration of U-boats operating off the Kola Inlet, JW.62 passed unchallenged, apart from a shadower shot down on 27 November. The convoy had a safe passage and arrived intact on 7 December.

RA.62 (10–19 December)

Before RA.62 sailed, British and Russian warships carried out a sweep in the Kola Inlet in an attempt to drive the waiting U-boats away from the entrance. During this operation east of the Rybachy Peninsula, *Bamborough Castle*, serving with the 8th and 20th Escort Groups, sank *U-387* with a depth charge. All fifty-one crew were lost.

RA.62, of twenty-eight merchant ships including three fleet oilers and one rescue ship, left the Kola Inlet on 10 November with the escort of JW.62. The cruiser and the escort carriers once again sailed within the main body of the convoy, along with the damaged *Mounsey* returning to UK for repairs. The same day *U-365* made an unsuccessful attack on one of the fleet oilers. Then at 08.00 on 11 November, as she searched for the U-boat to prevent any further attack on the convoy, the destroyer *Cassandra* was hit by a Gnat torpedo fired by *U-365*. The whole of the destroyer's bow section was blown off. *Bahamas* took *Cassandra* in tow stern first, then passed the tow to a Russian tug which took the *Cassandra* to the Kola Inlet for temporary repairs. Sixty-two of the crew of 186 officers and ratings were killed.

The next day the Norwegian corvette *Tunsberg Castle* was lost with five of her crew, sunk after she reportedly struck a mine, though the precise circumstances remain unclear. It has recently emerged she was on a mission to Batsfjord, to take relief supplies to the local population, 'show the flag' and engage any enemy shipping encountered en route. The same day also saw an unsuccessful air attack by Ju.88 torpedo bombers of I./KG 26 from Bardufoss.[4] The rescue ship *Rathlin*, attacked twice, shot down the second attacker and may also have fatally damaged the first, though it was not seen to crash. Luftwaffe records indicate the attack was to be undertaken by about fifteen Ju.88s but the aircraft became separated in bad weather. One by one the crews managed to locate the convoy, but their individual uncoordinated torpedo strikes promised little hope of success. No merchant ships were hit. Two Ju.88s were lost, one going down on fire, the other being seen to ditch. Two Fleet Air Arm aircraft were also lost.

A further air attack, this time by ten Ju.88s, was attempted the following day, but again no merchant ships were hit. This was to be I./KG 26's last major action of the war. The same day as the convoy passed Jan Mayen, *U-365* which had been stalking the convoy was attacked and sunk by depth charges dropped by two Swordfish aircraft of 813 Squadron, flying from the escort carrier *Campania*. All fifty U-boat crew were killed. The convoy continued without further disruption and arrived safely in Loch Ewe on 19 December.

JW.63/RA.63 – Operation GREYSTOKE

JW.63 (30 December 1944–8 January 1945)

JW.63, of thirty-seven merchant ships including two fleet oilers, sailed on 30 December 1944. One ship returned to Loch Ewe. *Keppel, Walker, Westcott, Cygnet, Lark, Alnwick Castle, Bamborough Castle, Bluebell,* and *Rhododendron* formed the close escort. The convoy was joined on 1 January 1945 by *Diadem* and *Vindex* to reinforce the anti-submarine defence. *Myngs, Savage, Scourge, Serapis, Zambesi, Zebra,* the Canadian destroyers *Sioux* and *Algonquin,* and Norwegian destroyer *Stord,* were deployed as the fighting destroyer escort. The convoy was not detected, there was no contact with German forces, and JW.63 entered the Kola Inlet in fog and heavy snowstorms on 8 January.

RA.63 (11–23 January)

The return convoy RA.63, of thirty-one merchant ships including three escort oilers, sailed on 11 January 1945. The escort was the same as for JW.63 plus *Scorpion*. There was no contact with the enemy, however the convoy ran into a series of three severe gales in eight days. A gale northeast of the Faroe Islands scattered the convoy and caused superficial damage to a number of ships. There were minor mishaps and some weather damage, but no losses, although the *Andrew Turnbull* and *Fort Highfield* had to shelter in the Faroes on 17 January for seven days, arriving in Loch Ewe on 26 January.

The main body of the convoy took refuge at Tórshavn in the Faroe Islands on 18 January to re-form, while the escorts hove to and reassembled offshore. The main body sailed again two days later to complete its passage. Three ships arrived at Kirkwall on 20 January. The convoy finally arrived in Loch Ewe on 21 January and the Clyde-bound ships two days later.

JW.64/RA.64 – Operation HOTBED

JW.64 (3–15 February)

JW.64, of twenty-six merchant ships plus two escort oilers and a number of ex-RN ships transferring to the Russian Navy, departed from Greenock on the Clyde on 3 February 1945. The convoy sailed directly from the Clyde because the Loch Ewe anchorage had been closed as a convoy assembly point to save naval manpower, although it would remain in use as a Royal Naval support base.

The close escort from 3 February comprised *Cygnet*, *Lark*, *Whitehall*, *Alnwick Castle*, *Bamborough Castle*, *Bluebell*, and *Rhododendron* (3 to 15 February).

The fuelling force, the fleet oiler *Black Ranger* escorted by *Serapis* and *Denbigh Castle*, joined the convoy on 5 February. The ocean escort sailed from Scapa Flow the same day and included the *Bellona*, *Campania*, *Nairana*, *Lapwing*, and Norwegian trawler *Oksøy*. The escort screen of nine destroyers, *Onslaught*, *Onslow*, *Opportune*, *Orwell*, *Serapis*, *Zambesi*, *Zealous*, *Zest*, and the Canadian *Sioux* of the 2nd and 17th Destroyer Flotillas, joined on the morning of 6 February northeast of the Faroes to provide anti-submarine cover.

An area of low pressure lay over the Arctic Ocean that day, bringing with it strong winds, clouds and showers. Despite these adverse weather conditions, about an hour after the escort joined, the convoy was sighted and reported by a Ju.88, on a routine meteorological flight. The plane was intercepted and shot down by two fighters from *Campania*, but by now the location and course of the convoy were known and it would be shadowed by enemy aircraft at intervals, day and night, until the day before it reached the Kola Inlet. Between 7 and 10 February, II./KG 26 and III./KG 26 would conduct a series of attacks with the express orders to target the aircraft carrier reported to be sailing in the middle of the convoy.

The shadowers returned early in the morning of 7 February, when III./KG 26 and the *Geschwader* headquarters, both stationed at Trondheim-Vaernes, and II./KG 26 based at Bardufoss, 50 miles north of Narvik, received orders to carry out a torpedo mission against the convoy. At the same time Wolfpack *Rasmus* (6 to 18 February) of eight U-boats, was deployed to intercept the convoy in the area of the Bear Island passage, the narrows between Bear Island and the North Cape.

The aircraft of the *Geschwader* Headquarters and III./KG 26 took off from Trondheim between 05.20 and 05.36 and after forming up took a northerly heading for JW.64. A little later, at 05.50, II./KG 26 took off from Bardufoss. According to the evening report by the Luftwaffe operations staff, a total of forty-eight aircraft of KG 26 took part in the mission.

At 07.45, a number of torpedo bombers were detected approaching the convoy in two groups, to the northwest and southwest. The SOE having anticipated an early morning attack had ordered a 90° change of course to starboard to place the approaching aircraft astern. The expected mass air attack did not however materialize. The two formations operated independently of one another, but because of the bad weather neither was able to locate the convoy. After almost five hours in the air and more than 1,200 miles flown, the bulk of III./KG 26 landed back at Trondheim-Vaernes at about 10.50. The II. *Gruppe* had already arrived back at Bardufoss at about 10.35. Inexplicably four of II./KG 26's aircraft were found to be missing.

The Luftwaffe operations staff's evening report mentions an attack on a convoy by a single aircraft between 08.00 and 08.45, but the aircraft involved must have been a Ju.88 from I.(F)/120. The bomb hits on a destroyer claimed in the evening report were not confirmed by convoy records, nor was the reported sighting of a burning cargo vessel.

Luftwaffe records subsequently revealed that their 'shadower' aircraft failed them at a critical moment, causing the main body of the attack force to miss its target. Those torpedo bombers who found the convoy were driven off by the fighters and anti-aircraft fire from the escort. This abortive sortie cost the Luftwaffe seven aircraft – six shot down by fighters from the carrier and a seventh by anti-aircraft fire from the *Denbigh Castle*. (German records admit three aircraft shot down and many more damaged.)

Throughout 8 and 9 February, U-boats and aircraft continued to search for the convoy. Reconnaissance aircraft located the convoy periodically and appeared to be sending homing signals to U-boats, but were unable to maintain continuous contact in the prevailing weather conditions. In the early hours of 8 February, reconnaissance aircraft located the ships again. One Ju.188, four Ju.88s (probably from I.(F)/120) and three BV.138s (from Marine Reconnaissance Group 130) took part in the search, but again continuous contact with the convoy was not maintained. The same day the Ju.188s of III./KG 26 flew in to Bardufoss from Trondheim-Vaernes.

Air patrols flown from the carriers to attempt to locate the U-boats, found none. The escort carriers however, with no night-fighters embarked, lacked any means to deal effectively with shadowing aircraft during the long hours of darkness. Fortunately, KG 26 aircraft were not committed on 9 February, bad weather having suspended all flying. Later in the day the convoy was located again south of Bear Island and plans were immediately made for a strike by the two *Gruppen* the next morning, when the convoy would only be about 250 miles from Bardufoss and easily within striking range.

The two *Gruppen* were to mount a combined assault to attack the convoy and sink the carrier. Take-off was timed for 08.30 on 10 February. The first wave comprised the fourteen remaining serviceable Ju.88s of II./KG 26, followed thirty minutes later by the sixteen Ju.188s of III./KG 26. It was to prove no easy task to coordinate an attack by two different types of aircraft, approaching a target over 300 miles away from two different directions, and in poor flying conditions, with solid cloud cover down to around 200 feet, rough seas and light snow. The aircraft were unable to maintain formation due to the lack of visibility and had difficulty locating the convoy.

Thirty torpedo bombers launched the first attacks on the convoy at around 10.30. They emerged from the cloud cover and flew over the centre of the convoy formation. The cargo vessels were clearly visible from the air, thick ice covering their superstructures and hawsers in the heavy seas. In attempting to break through the fighter and anti-aircraft defences the torpedo bombers ran into intense anti-aircraft fire and splash barrages from the escorts, followed by attacks from the carrier-borne Martlet fighters. Perhaps not surprisingly the attack did not go according to plan, with the two waves coming separately one hour apart, rather than as a combined group. The repeated torpedo-bomber assaults were driven off, some aircraft jettisoning their torpedoes to increase manoeuvrability and escape the Martlets – which themselves were fortunate to escape the 'friendly fire' of the merchant ships and some of the escorts in the convoy.

Having failed to break through the convoy's defences the torpedo bombers withdrew and returned to Bardufoss. In the event not one vessel of JW.64 was sunk or damaged by their attacks. The aircrew claimed major successes – eight torpedo hits on merchant ships and destroyers – but in reality, they did not harm a single ship let alone an aircraft carrier. A total of six aircraft failed to return and were later reported missing. The remainder of the passage was fairly uneventful, as poor weather conditions restricted aircraft operations for both sides.

The Russian eastern local escort, *Karl Libknekht*, *Uritskyi*, *Zhivuchiy*, *Zhosktiy*, *Groza*, two minesweepers and six BO-type submarine chasers arrived on 12 February and the Archangel section then departed for the White Sea with *Lark*, *Lapwing*, and *Alnwick Castle*. The remainder of the convoy arrived at the entrance to the Kola Inlet that night and proceeded up harbour in darkness, snow squalls and poor visibility. Two merchant ships, the *Fort Crevecoeur* and *Arunah S. Abel* managed to collide at the entrance to the Inlet.

Eleven U-boats were encountered the following day. At five past midnight, as the convoy was entering the Inlet, *U-992* detected propeller cavitations, fired a single torpedo on the bearing of the sound and reported a steamer damaged. The actual target was the corvette *Denbigh Castle*, hit on the port side. Although damaged she remained afloat and was towed first by *Bluebell* and then by the Russian salvage vessel *Burevestnika* into the Kola Inlet, where she was to be beached at Bolshaya Volokovaya Bay near Vaenga. However, before reaching the anchorage *Denbigh Castle* ran aground, capsized and was written off as a total loss. Eleven of her crew of 120 officers and ratings were killed.

After JW.64's arrival in Murmansk, news was received the Germans were attacking the Norwegian population on Sørøya, a large island at the entrance to the Altafjord. C-in-C Home Fleet then ordered *Zambezi*, *Sioux*, *Zealous*, and *Zest* to sail from the Kola Inlet on 14 February to evacuate the Norwegian population without delay. A total of 525 Norwegian civilians, men women and children, were successfully evacuated in Operation OPEN DOOR on 15 February and the destroyers returned to Murmansk the next day, where the Norwegians were distributed among the unladen ships of RA.64 for passage back to the UK (see below).

RA.64 (17 February–1 March)

The U-boats continued to search for targets. On 14 February the American freighter *Horace Gray* and Norwegian motor tanker *Norfjell*, sailing in convoy BK-3 from the White Sea to Murmansk to join RA.64, were attacked by *U-968* off the Kola Inlet. The *Norfjell* was hit by a torpedo in the engine room, killing two men on watch below and opening a large gaping hole in her side. The tanker remained afloat, was taken in tow by the escort and beached near Tree Roochia in the Kola Inlet. The damage was temporarily repaired later at Murmansk and she left under tow on 20 October 1945 on her way to Stavanger for permanent repairs, arriving there on 15 November. The *Horace Gray* was hit also by a torpedo, on the port side at the bulkhead between the no. 4 and no. 5 holds, minutes later. The resulting explosion blew the hatch covers off, opened a hole 20ft by 60ft in the port side and another 20ft by 20ft on the starboard side. The *Horace Gray* settled rapidly by the stern until water reached the after deck. Twenty minutes after the torpedo struck, the eight officers, thirty-three crewmen and twenty-eight armed guards abandoned ship in the four lifeboats and were picked up by two Russian escort vessels. An hour later, the Master and some crewmen returned to the ship and, after raising steam, a small Russian tug began towing her to Kola Inlet. While she was underway a crack appeared on the starboard side and the *Horace Gray* began to sink. Eight hours after being torpedoed she was beached at Tyuva Bay and two days later declared a total loss, with all holds completely flooded.

RA.64, of thirty-three merchant ships including one escort oiler, sailed from the Kola Inlet on the morning of 17 February. As there was known to be a strong concentration of U-boats operating in the approaches to the Kola Inlet, the close escort was deployed in the afternoon of the 16th to conduct an anti-submarine sweep prior to sailing.

During the anti-submarine operation, *U-425* was detected, depth-charged and sunk by *Lark* and *Alnwick Castle*; there was only one survivor. Later at 10.24 *Lark*, sweeping the channel ahead of the convoy for U-boats, was torpedoed by *U-968*. The U-boat fired one LUT torpedo at a warship initially identified as a Russian destroyer of the *Grozny* class and observed a hit after 6 minutes and 20 seconds. The target was in fact the *Lark*. Her stern was blown off, but she remained afloat. Later that day she was towed into the Kola Inlet and beached near Rosta, where she was subsequently declared a total loss, stripped, and abandoned to the Russians as a hulk. Three of her crew had been killed.

The close escort (to 1 March), was the same as for JW.64, (*Whitehall*, part of the close escort detached on 21 February). The ocean escort comprised *Bellona, Campania, Nairana, Onslaught, Onslow, Opportune, Orwell, Serapis, Zambesi, Zealous, Zest,* and Canadian destroyer *Sioux* (17 to 27 February). The escort was reinforced by *Savage* and *Scourge* (21 to 26 February), *Zebra* (26 to 27 February) and *Cavalier, Myngs,* and *Scorpion* (25 to 27 February).

The leading ships passed Toros Island at 07.45 on 16 February but the convoy was very slow in departing and two hours later the last eight merchant ships were still inside the Kola Inlet. This provided an excellent opportunity for the strong concentration of U-boats loitering off the Kola Peninsula.

Around midday *U-968* attacked the American freighter *Thomas Scott* about 13 miles southwest of Kildin Island, as the freighter was attempting to manoeuvre into her assigned station in the convoy formation. The torpedo struck at the no. 3 hatch and the damage caused an immediate 25° list to starboard. The *Thomas Scott* went out of control and almost broke in two, the hull only held together by deck plates on the well deck. Ten minutes after the torpedo struck eight officers, thirty-four crew, twenty-seven USN armed guards and forty Norwegian refugees abandoned ship in four lifeboats and a liferaft. They were picked up after about forty minutes by *Onslaught* (some sources incorrectly say the carrier *Fencer*) which transferred the Americans (eight injured) two hours later to the Russian destroyer *Zhestokiy* and tug *M-12*. *Onslaught* took the Norwegians to Britain, where they were landed in Greenock on 25 February. The Russian ships took the badly damaged *Thomas Scott* in tow, stern first, but she broke in two at 19.37. The stern sank immediately followed by the bow at 21.00 despite a salvage attempt by the *Zhestokiy*. The survivors were landed at Vaenga at 16.00 on 18 February.

Five and half hours after *Lark* was torpedoed, as the close escort was shepherding the merchant ships back into the convoy formation, the corvette *Bluebell*, part of the anti-submarine force searching for U-boats off the Kola Inlet ahead of the convoy, was torpedoed about 30 miles east-northeast of Kildin Island. Increasing speed after having apparently detected a U-boat, she was struck in the stern by a Gnat torpedo fired by *U-711* and sank in less than thirty seconds, 8 miles northeast of the Kola Inlet, after her ready-use depth charges detonated. When *Zest* arrived at the sinking position within about ten minutes her lookouts heard cries from a dozen or so men swimming in the ice-cold water, but she could not stop due to the danger of being torpedoed. *Zest* searched for the attacker until relieved by *Opportune*. Only one of the three unconscious survivors recovered could be revived; eighty-nine officers and ratings were killed.

On the afternoon of 18 February, the weather deteriorated, the wind increased to force 8 on the Beaufort scale, and the escort carriers were forced to suspend air operations. During the night the storm intensified with winds gusting up to 60 knots, bringing a heavy sea and swell. The convoy formation split up and the ships became scattered.

The U-boat force had now been divided. Some pursued the convoy while others continued to loiter off the entrance to the Kola Inlet. In fact, the greater danger was from the violent weather which scattered the convoy. The storm continued throughout 19 February, only moderating at about 23.00 that evening. It finally abated the next morning when the task of reforming the convoy began, and the escort vessels started to round up the scattered merchant ships. A task now the more urgent, since enemy aircraft had detected the convoy at 04.00, and a torpedo-bomber attack was expected to follow. By 09.00 twenty-nine of the merchant ships were back on station, with just four still straggling.

One hour later, about 185 miles northwest of the North Cape, groups of aircraft were detected coming from the port bow and crossing ahead of the convoy. The sea remained rough with a strong swell, but *Nairana* flew off fighters in an attempt to intercept the approaching aircraft. The convoy now came under attack by more than twenty-five Ju.88 torpedo bombers (thirty-five according to German records). A large number of torpedoes were dropped but most exploded prematurely, the warheads apparently detonating as the torpedoes broke the surface of the troughs in the rough seas. The attack was unsuccessful and by 11.40 *Nairana*'s fighters had driven off the last of the attackers. The by now well-coordinated air defences proved extremely effective. It was estimated six Ju.88s were shot down and four damaged. Actual losses were two Ju.88s. No ships in the convoy were hit.

On the basis of wildly extravagant claims of success made by the German aircrews, *U-286*, *U-307*, and *U-716* were despatched to finish off the many ships reported as damaged. That afternoon *Savage*, *Scourge*, and *Zebra*, sent by C-in-C Home Fleet to replace the casualties suffered off the Kola Inlet, joined the convoy.

Reconnaissance aircraft continued to shadow the convoy on 21 and 22 February but no further attacks came. Then, just as most of the stragglers had rejoined, the convoy encountered one of the worst storms ever recorded in the Barents Sea. Once again the formation broke up in the extreme conditions. The winds increased to force 12, with speeds of 70 to 90 knots and temperatures falling to $-40°F$. One of the mainsprings on the American freighter *Henry Bacon*'s steering gear broke and the retaining pin sheared, causing her to drop out of the convoy to make repairs.

The poor weather persisted for the remainder of the passage with heavy seas and gale force winds. Some merchant ships hove to with engine and steering gear defects, shifting cargoes, and splitting hull seams. One of the *Bellona*'s bulkheads cracked, and the escort carriers again suspended air operations.

Mid-afternoon on 23 February the *Henry Bacon*, now struggling some 50 to 60 nautical miles astern of the main convoy, was attacked by twenty-three Ju.88 and Ju.188 torpedo bombers of KG 26, operating out of Bardufoss, 250 miles away. The Ju.88s were on their way to attack the main convoy and apparently thought they could finish off this lone straggler with little effort. The *Henry Bacon* was however armed with eight 20mm anti-aircraft guns, a 5-inch (127mm) gun aft and a 3-inch (76mm) gun forward. The ship's USN armed guard fought off the attacking aircraft for over an hour, shot down five, damaged at least four others and claimed to have managed to defend against several torpedoes by detonating them with shellfire before they reached the ship.

Despite their best efforts, a torpedo struck the starboard side at the no. 5 hold and detonated the aft ammunition magazine, tearing a large hole in the hull. The rudder, propeller and steering engine were destroyed. The *Henry Bacon* settled by the stern and was abandoned about forty minutes later. Lifeboats 1 and 2 were launched safely but no. 3 lifeboat capsized while being lowered, and no. 4 lifeboat was lost as the davits had been damaged during the storm. Three of the four liferafts released prematurely drifted away. The two surviving lifeboats were filled to capacity with all of the Norwegian passengers and some members of the crew. This left a number of crew stranded aboard. When he became aware of the situation the Chief Engineer, Donald Haviland, insisted on giving his place in the lifeboat to a younger member of the crew and returned aboard. For his sacrifice, Chief Engineer Haviland was posthumously awarded the Distinguished Service Medal, the highest award for the men of the US Merchant Marine. *Opportune* and *Orwell*, detached from the convoy to search for survivors, found the ship's lifeboats on 23 February. All the Norwegian civilians survived but the Master, fifteen crew, nine armed guard and two Navy signalmen were lost.

On the evening of 23 February a force of eight Staffel III./KG 26's Ju.88 torpedo bombers, searching for the convoy, came across and sank the hulk of the *Henry Bacon*, which achieved the doubtful distinction of being the last Allied merchant ship sunk by German aircraft in World War II. The *Henry*

Bacon's heroic action was judged to have helped save the main convoy from attack, as most of the torpedo bombers were forced to return to Bardufoss as a result of battle damage, or the need to refuel and reload with ammunition.

The gales continued to blow during 23 and 24 February, reducing the speed of the convoy to about 3½ knots. Little progress was made. The escorts now running short of fuel were detached to the Faroe Islands, as refuelling at sea was impossible. The convoy was now greatly scattered due to the severe weather. Several merchant ships and escorts suffered damage (twelve destroyers were docked with weather damage on return to Britain). C-in-C Home Fleet despatched three more destroyers *Cavalier*, *Myngs*, and *Scorpion*, which joined the convoy on the evening of 25 February. As the battered convoy struggled slowly past the Faroe Islands conditions at last began to improve.

Fortunately, the bad weather had offered protection from further U-boat and Luftwaffe attacks, and RA.64 reached the Clyde on 1 March. One straggler, missing since the first gale struck the convoy, finally made harbour safely after nothing had been heard of her for a week.

This was to be the final involvement of the Luftwaffe in the war on the Arctic convoys, as a result of the critical fuel situation and lack of confirmed ship sightings.

JW.65/RA.65 – Operation SCOTTISH

JW.65 (11–21 March)

JW.65, of twenty-six merchant ships including two fleet oilers, sailed from the Clyde on 11 March. *Allington Castle*, *Alnwick Castle*, *Bamborough Castle*, *Lancaster Castle*, *Camellia*, *Honeysuckle*, *Oxlip*, *Myngs*, the Norwegian destroyer *Stord*, and *Lapwing* provided the close escort. The ocean escort, *Diadem*, *Campania*, *Onslaught*, *Opportune*, *Orwell*, *Scorpion*, *Zambesi*, and the Canadian *Sioux*, with *Farnham Castle*, joined the next day, reinforced by *Trumpeter* with *Savage* and *Scourge* on 15 March. During the passage *Onslaught* was damaged in a collision with the fleet oiler *Black Ranger* and had to return to the Clyde for repairs.

The threat of attack increased as JW.65 approached the Bear Island passage. RA.64 had already come under air attack north of Norway, and several ships were sunk or damaged beyond repair by U-boats. The Admiralty, who had been reading coded command radio communications to and from U-boats since December 1942, were well aware of German intentions and U-boat deployments. In fact on 5 March they had intercepted and decoded a radio message from Captain (U/B) Northern Waters, informing his forces of the intent to attack JW.65 off Murmansk.

The convoy did not cross 60°N until 13.00 on 14 March in order to avoid reconnaissance aircraft from Trondheim. The following day a Luftwaffe plane passed south of the force, and although FW 200 reconnaissance aircraft flew missions on both 14 and 15 March north of Scotland and west of Norway across the suspected course of JW.65 nothing was sighted. It was not until the morning of 17 March that the Germans obtained firm information from intercepted radio traffic that a force had passed through the Bear Island passage. The U-boats off the Kola Inlet were ordered to report any signs of the approach of JW.65 as well as any increase in air activity.

JW.65 passed Bear Island on 17 March, then turned southeast towards the Kola Inlet. There was no contact with the enemy except for a 'doubtful' sighting of a U-boat by a carrier-based aircraft. Knowing its entrance into Murmansk would be contested by U-boats, the SOE suspended flight operations by the two escort carriers to 'conserve' resources.

The fact that the convoy enjoyed unusually good weather until just before reaching its destination makes the failure of the air reconnaissance undertaken on a daily basis between 14 and 17 March all the more inexplicable, as the convoy passed through the U-boats' initial patrol line without being detected.

The favourable conditions did not last, however – as the convoy approached the entrance to the Kola Inlet, a snowstorm disrupted all air operations from the escort carriers. The U-boats of the *Hagen* Wolfpack lying in wait were now able to seize their limited opportunity after the convoy had passed through the first patrol line at about 09.00.

At 09.10 *U-995* fired torpedoes at the convoy about 25 miles east of North Kildin Light and reported one ship sunk and two others damaged. One ship, the American freighter *Horace Bushnell*, was hit by a torpedo on the port side in the engine room. The blast created a hole 33ft by 26ft, cracked the main deck and completely destroyed both engines, killing the second engineer and three members of crew on watch below. The explosion also blew the engine room skylight over the side, cut off the power, destroyed one lifeboat and filled another with oil. The *Horace Bushnell* settled with a slight list by the stern until the water level reached 34 feet, then steadied. The survivors among the eight officers, thirty-four crew and twenty-seven USN armed guards on board made preparations to abandon ship, while *Orwell* took the *Horace Bushnell* in tow. Heavy seas however prevented the destroyer from making any headway and the crew were advised to abandon ship. At 11.50 the survivors went directly on board *Orwell*, which took them on to Murmansk. The *Horace Bushnell* was taken in tow by two Russian salvage tugs and later beached at Teriberski, where the Russians salvaged the cargo and the ship was declared a total loss. In 1949 the wreck was salvaged and repaired by the Russians.

As the convoy passed through the second U-boat patrol line around midday, *U-716* attacked but missed an escort, and *U-313* and *U-968* carried out attacks in which the American freighter *Thomas Donaldson* and sloop *Lapwing* were sunk. The *Thomas Donaldson*, the twentieth ship in line as the convoy formed into one column to enter the Kola Inlet, was torpedoed by *U-968* at about 13.15. The torpedo struck in the engine room, killing the one officer and two crew on watch below and destroying the engines. The Master ordered the survivors, eight officers, thirty-four crew and twenty-seven USN armed guards to abandon ship after ten minutes, being concerned the dangerous cargo might explode. Some survivors took to the two port lifeboats and a liferaft and were picked up by *Bamborough Castle*. Others jumped overboard and were picked up by *Oxlip*. One died after being rescued. The Master and eight of the crew remained onboard and were later taken off by *Honeysuckle*, which took the *Thomas Donaldson* in tow towards the Kola Inlet. At 16.30 a Russian tug took over the tow, but the *Thomas Donaldson* sank stern first about fifteen minutes later, just half a mile from Kildin Island.

At about 13.25, shortly after the attack on the *Thomas Donaldson*, *U-968* torpedoed the sloop *Lapwing* of the 7th Escort Group. She was hit amidships by a T5 acoustic torpedo and broke in two. Her stern section remained afloat for twenty minutes, enabling some survivors to be rescued by *Savage*, but 168 out of the crew of 229 officers and ratings were lost. That afternoon, *U-968* reported a destroyer and a Liberty ship sunk and another Liberty ship damaged – in fact, this was *Lapwing* and the *Thomas Donaldson*.

The Russian Navy had carried out an Admiralty request for a channel to be swept through the German minefield to the north of the Kola Inlet, to make it possible for convoys to come and go from Murmansk by a shorter, more direct route. At the same time, *U-997* was damaged by depth charges and forced to return to Norway. In the confusion the U-boats apparently did not notice the escort carriers had succeeded in entering the port – they were ordered at 00.45 on 21 March to search for the carriers to the north. This was the day the remaining ships of JW.65 reached Murmansk.

RA.65 (23 March–1 April)

Also on 21 March, a group of twelve unladen merchant ships and three empty fleet tankers made the first movement by elements of RA.65 from Archangel to Murmansk (which they reached on 24 March), escorted by *Karl Libknekht*, *Zhivuchiy*, *Zhostkiy*, *Derzkiy*, *Uritskiy*, *Smerch* and three submarine chasers.

The problem now confronting C-in-C Home Fleet was how to safely sail RA.65 out of Murmansk past the waiting U-boats, even as Group North sought to inflict maximum casualties. Fortunately, the order to the *Hagen* Wolfpack to take up stations by 24.00 on 21 March at the entrance to the Kola Inlet was intercepted and decoded at 16.29 that day.

The first use of the newly swept channel was made by RA.65 when twenty-six unladen merchant ships, including the escort oilers *Blue Ranger* and *Lacklan*, departed from Murmansk on 23 March. The escort carriers *Campania* and *Trumpeter* departed in advance of the convoy to provide air cover.

RA.65 sailed with the same escort as had accompanied JW.65. Although the weather prevented carrier air operations until after 07.35, no U-boats were encountered and only a few HF/DF bearings were obtained from some to the west. The convoy's dedicated anti-submarine escorts went ahead to break up the concentration of U-boats, nine of which were lying in wait, while four destroyers put up a pyrotechnic display on the old, abandoned route to divert attention. This scheme was clearly successful, as no U-boat reported the sailing of the convoy until it was well on its way west. Although several U-boats were despatched in pursuit and air searches flown, they failed to locate the convoy.

At 12.14 on 24 March, after RA.65 had evaded them off the entrance to the Kola Inlet, the U-boats were ordered to proceed 'at once' for the Bear Island passage in another attempt to intercept the convoy. In the event RA.65 most likely avoided detection because the U-boats were ineffectively positioned, too far to the west. *U-313* did obtain some hydrophone bearings and reported that the convoy had sailed. As a result, at 00.05 on 25 March,

Captain (U/B) Northern Waters directed nine U-boats of the *Hagen* Wolfpack to proceed at 'maximum speed' to set up a patrol line in the Bear Island passage, again attempting to intercept the convoy.

Between 25 and 27 March, BV.138 reconnaissance aircraft searched the sea in the vicinity of the Bear Island passage as Group North still believed the convoy might be found there, but because of the convoy's 'remarkable radio silence', its passage west of 25° E. could not be clearly established. The Wolfpack was then ordered to 'move west unobserved.' Although radar on the ships in RA.65 picked up enemy aircraft, none of the planes sent sighting reports. The CO of *Campania* concluded the aircraft were flying parallel track searches with one passing first in front, and then just astern, of the convoy. 'It is incredible,' he concluded, 'that this aircraft at least did not sight the outer screen.' Enemy aircraft again appeared on the ships' radar on 28 March but their radio transmissions indicated they were still failing to sight RA.65. Nonetheless, carrier air patrols were flown to prevent U-boats from getting ahead of the convoy.

By 29 March RA.65 had made good its escape. That afternoon Captain (U/B) Northern Waters abandoned the search and ordered six U-boats to return to Norway for refuelling and re-arming. Several hours later U-boats off the Faroe Islands were warned of RA.65's approach. In a later report Captain (U/B) Northern Waters concluded that even though his U-boats had travelled 300 miles a day against moderate seas, they failed to intercept the convoy because the departure from Murmansk was not promptly detected. Moreover, RA.65's precaution of maintaining radio silence had denied the Germans a timely source of intelligence. The convoy arrived safely in the Clyde on 1 April.

JW.66/RA.66 – Operation ROUNDEL

JW.66 (16–25 April)
JW.66 was the last eastbound supply convoy to run to North Russia before the German surrender. The convoy of twenty-seven merchant ships, including three fleet oilers and one rescue ship, sailed from the Clyde late on 16 April 1945 under the overall command of Rear Admiral A. E. M. B. Cunninghame-Graham, in the carrier *Vindex*. The close escort included *Cygnet, Alnwick Castle, Bamborough Castle, Farnham Castle, Honeysuckle, Lotus, Oxlip, Rhododendron, Loch Insh, Loch Shin, Cotton, Goodall,* and

Anguilla (19th Escort Group). The ocean escort comprising *Bellona*, *Premier*, *Vindex*, *Offa*, *Zealous*, *Zephyr*, *Zest*, *Zodiac*, Canadian destroyers *Haida*, *Huron*, and *Iroquois*, and Norwegian destroyer *Stord*, joined on 18 April.

The B-Dienst radio intercept and decryption service detected the sailing of JW.66 and Flag Officer U-boats deployed *U-286*, *U-295*, *U-307*, *U-313*, *U-363* and *U-481* to a planned ambush position to the west of Bear Island as the *Faust* Wolfpack on 16 April.

At 13.00 on 19 April the main body of the convoy was joined from the Faroes, by the Canadian destroyers *Haida*, *Huron*, and *Iroquois*,[5] the Norwegian destroyer *Stord*, corvettes *Alnwick Castle*, *Bamborough Castle*, *Farnham Castle*, and sloop *Cygnet* of the 7th Escort Group, together with sixteen Russian submarine chasers being delivered to North Russia.

Air reconnaissance and the U-boats of the *Faust* Wolfpack west of Bear Island were unable to locate the convoy until 21 April. The U-boats then moved to positions off the Kola Inlet where they were reinforced by another ten, *U-278*, *U-294*, *U-312*, *U-318*, *U-427*, *U-711*, *U-716*, *U-968*, *U-992*, and *U-997*, bringing the total available for action against the convoy to sixteen.

Throughout 22 April, aircraft from *Premier* and *Vindex* flew around the convoy. At 19.55 a Swordfish 'ditched' when its rocket-assisted take-off gear failed. The escort rescued the aircrew. The day ended with *Oxlip* depth-charging a sonar contact, which was subsequently lost.

By 12.00 the next day, the convoy had reached the Bear Island passage north of Norway. During the night the convoy changed course and steamed southeast towards the Kola Inlet. At 00.26 the following day, *Zodiac* obtained an HD/DF bearing at 126° on a U-boat radio transmission. An aircraft was dispatched but found nothing. Throughout the day, visibility remained poor. The Russian anti-submarine aircraft arrived to escort the convoy. Between 16.00 and 17.00, HF/DF bearings indicated the presence of a number of U-boats, about 25 miles ahead. From previous experience, as well as from decrypted intelligence and radio traffic analysis, it was known a number of U-boats would be lying in wait off the entrance to Kola Inlet, and it was expected the convoy would most likely have to fight its way into Murmansk. The anti-submarine frigates *Anguilla*, *Cotton*, *Goodall*, *Loch Insh*, and *Loch Shin* of the 19th Escort Group were sent ahead of the convoy to clear a way through the expected U-boat concentration.

As an aside, the convoy included two Norwegian ships, the *Kron Prinsen* and the *Kong Haakon* carrying relief supplies (these vessels are counted in the overall numbers that sailed but did not proceed to the Kola Inlet). Before the convoy's arrival at Murmansk they were detached to sail independently to Kirkenes, where they berthed on 24 April. Following the discharge of her cargo the *Kron Prinsen* sailed for Murmansk where she would join the final convoy back to the Clyde.

At 11.30 the day after completing their sonar sweep of the approaches to the Kola Inlet, the destroyers of the 9th Escort Group met JW.66 and patrolled to the eastward until it had passed. The convoy entered Murmansk screened by aircraft patrolling its flanks and dropping sonar buoys in front, while the escorts continued to attack sonar contacts and drop depth charges at random. Altogether, 26 sonar contacts were attacked and more than 400 depth charges dropped. Significantly, there were no assaults on JW.66 during this operation although *U-711* had reported a sighting as the convoy approached. *U-363* was attacked by escort vessels and reported encountering strong anti-submarine patrols but 'saw no evidence' of an Allied convoy.

Operation TRAMMEL

As a prelude to the arrival of JW.66 in North Russia, the Royal Navy initiated Operation TRAMMEL: to lay a deep minefield off the mouth of the Kola Inlet in an effort to destroy and deter U-boats operating in this chokepoint on the approach to Murmansk. The mines were to be laid at sufficient depth to allow ships to pass safely over, but to damage any U-boats 'driven down' by the escort. The cruiser minelayer *Apollo* and mine-laying destroyers *Obedient*, *Opportune*, and *Orwell*, escorted by the *Dido*, departed Scapa Flow on 17 April and reached the Kola Inlet four days later to refuel. The following day, with fuelling completed, the force proceeded to lay a field of 276 mines prior to the arrival of JW.66. The 19th Escort Group was deployed to deter any U-boats from approaching the mine-laying vessels, which returned to Scapa Flow on 26 April.

On 25 April, Russian destroyers *Uritskiy*, *Karl Libknekht*, *Kuybyshev*, *Zharkiy*, *Zhestokiy*, *Derzkiy*, and *Dostoinyi*, minesweeper *T-113* and five submarine chasers joined the escort of JW.66. Only *U-711*, which had penetrated the farthest into the Kola Inlet, was able to launch torpedoes at the convoy's merchant vessels, and no ships were hit. JW.66 reached the Kola Inlet later that day without loss.

RA.66 (26 April–8 May) The last convoy battle of the War

RA.66, the penultimate westbound convoy, experienced the last convoy battle of the War. The convoy was due to sail on 26 April and there were fourteen U-boats waiting off the Kola Inlet for its departure. At 18.17, Captain (U-boats) Northern Waters ordered *U-711* and *U-295* to proceed 'immediately at maximum speed' to a point southwest of Bear Island to be prepared to intercept the convoy, and directed the other U-boats to report the convoy's departure at once. The next day the *Faust* Wolfpack was informed there was a 'delay in the return convoy' and the Luftwaffe planned to send a reconnaissance aircraft over Murmansk.

The problem now for the Admiralty was how to extricate the return convoy safely out of the Kola Inlet past the U-boats. In order to deceive them into thinking RA.66 was going to depart on the night of 27/28 April, the Russians were requested to turn on a number of navigational lights and deploy anti-submarine vessels in the Kola Inlet to drop depth charges between 00.01 and 01.00, while British warships transmitted dummy radio messages as if they were sailing. SBNO also sent false radio signals; but at this point the ruse seemed unsuccessful as at 2.55 on 28 April, Captain (U/B) Northern Waters warned the *Faust* Wolfpack there were 'signs of departure of convoy' but *Faust* was to remain unobserved until there was a 'worthwhile shot'. The next day, at 19.55, however, the U-boats were informed RA.66 had apparently sailed, a conclusion based on the significant amount of wireless transmissions from Polyarnoe in the morning of 29 April. The U-boats were therefore directed, to proceed 'at top speed' to attempt to intercept the convoy southwest of Bear Island. The deception had worked.

Before the convoy sailed, the 19th Escort Group, supported by Russian destroyers *Zharkiy*, *Zhestokiy*, *Derzkiy* and four submarine chasers, had been deployed to sweep the waters off the Kola Inlet in an attempt to drive off the estimated fourteen U-boats lying in wait for the convoy. The frigates proceeded in line abreast formation 3,000 yards apart, searching for U-boats. At 18.56, *Loch Insh* obtained a sonar contact at a range of 780 yards at 65°, turned towards the target and at 19.00 attacked with an A/S projectile called a Squid mortar round. Thirty seconds later *U-307* surfaced and was attacked with gunfire by *Loch Insh*, *Loch Shin*, and *Cygnet*. A few minutes later, *U-307* sank stern first. Thirty-seven of the crew were killed. After fourteen survivors had been picked up the frigates continued their sweep.

At 21.00 that evening, *U-968* fired Gnat torpedoes at the convoy escort and claimed two destroyers sunk. No ships had been hit but the corvette *Alnwick Castle* observed two end-of-run detonations and a Gnat torpedo was seen to have near-missed the frigate *Goodall*. Shortly after, at about 22.00 and about seven miles from Murmansk, *U-286* attacked *Goodall* again with a Gnat torpedo. This detonated causing a huge explosion under the bridge. The frigate's ammunition magazine blew up, blowing away the forward section and killing the CO. The *Goodall* did not sink immediately and *Honeysuckle* and *Farnham Castle* were able to rescue seventeen survivors, but 112 officers and ratings from a crew of 156 were lost. The abandoned hulk of the *Goodall* was sunk the next day with gunfire by *Anguilla*.

Just before she was torpedoed the *Goodall* obtained and was preparing to attack a sonar contact. At about the same time the *Loch Shin* made sonar contact with the same target and attacked with an anti-submarine projectile. *Anguilla* then followed up with depth charges. After a third attack, cotton, oil and wreckage were seen on the surface, marking the end of *U-286*; all fifty-one of the crew were killed.

Goodall thus acquired the dubious distinction of being the last major warship of the Royal and Dominion Navies lost in the war against Germany, in what was the last confirmed U-boat success in the northern theatre. On 29 April *Anguilla*, *Cotton*, *Loch Insh*, and *Loch Shin* of the 19th Escort Group detected, tracked down and sank *U-307* and *U-286*, and this was the last encounter between U-boats and warships of the Royal Navy during the Second World War.

Of the other U-boats, *U-427* just missed *Haida* and *Iroquois* with torpedoes, then had to survive a long and determined counterattack during which no fewer than 678 depth-charge explosions were counted. *U-313* was attacked by Russian submarine chasers but managed to escape unharmed. As a result of these actions the U-boats were successfully driven off, and unable to approach the convoy. RA.66 of twenty-seven merchant ships, including three fleet oilers and one rescue ship, was able to set out from the Kola Inlet on the night of 29 April with the escorts that had accompanied JW.66.

The convoy, followed by *Premier*, *Vindex*, and *Bellona*, finally cleared the Kola Inlet at 02.00 the next morning. After departure a number of HF/DF bearings to the southward were obtained, but there was no indication the convoy was being shadowed by U-boats.

With the departure of RA.66, Captain (U/B) Northern Waters cancelled the orders to pursue the convoy and ordered his U-boats to move offshore at economical speed. The next day those in need of repairs and rearmament returned to base.

On 1 May Luftwaffe reconnaissance aircraft shadowed the convoy but were unable to maintain contact. III./KG 26 had been ordered up to Bardufoss, but the planned strike by II./KG 26 and III./KG 26 against RA.66 (the penultimate homebound Allied convoy of the campaign) was called off at the very last moment, the Ju.188s promptly flew back to Trondheim, and efforts to attack the convoy were terminated. The next day the U-boats were informed of the death of Hitler and at 13.50 on 5 May, ordered to end operations against the Allies.

The merchant ships of convoy RA.66 all arrived safely in the Clyde on 8 May, three days after the War in Europe ended.

JW 67/RA 67 – Operation TIMELESS

The last operation to escort convoys to and from North Russia, Operation TIMELESS took place soon after the German surrender.

JW.67 (12–20 May)

Convoy JW.67 left the Clyde on 12 May with twenty-six merchant ships, including one escort oiler and a rescue ship. The two Norwegian cargo ships in the convoy, the *Roald Amundsen* and *Ivaran*, carrying relief supplies to Norway, did not go all the way to Murmansk but left the convoy for Kirkenes and later Tromsø.

JW.67 was escorted from the Clyde by *Onslow*, *Obdurate*, *Bazeley*, *Bentinck*, *Byard*, *Drury*, and *Pasley* of the 4th Escort Group, joined by *Queen*, *Offa*, and *Oribi*, which left Scapa Flow on 14 May (the two destroyers returned to Scapa on 16 May) and the 9th (Canadian) Escort Group, (E.G.9) *Matane*, *Loch Alvie*, *St Pierre*, *Monnow*, and *Nene*. JW.67 arrived at the Kola Inlet on 20 May without incident.

RA.67 (23–30 May)

Three days later, the return convoy, RA.67, of twenty-five merchant ships, eighteen of them American and five British (including one escort oiler and one rescue ship), plus two Norwegian (one an escort oiler) departed the Kola Inlet with the same escort as had accompanied JW.67. They arrived safely in the Clyde on 30 May 1945, having sailed throughout with full navigation lights.

Chapter 9

Summary and Conclusions

The first (eastbound), supply convoy from Britain to North Russia, code named Dervish, sailed from Liverpool for North Russia on 18 August 1941 and the last, JW.67, from the Clyde on 12 May 1945. The first (westbound) return convoy from North Russia, QP.1, sailed from Archangel on 28 September 1941, and the last, RA.67, on 23 May 1945. After Dervish each convoy, eastbound and westbound, was assigned an individual alpha-numeric identification code: PQ/QP up to September 1942, and JW/RA from December 1942 until the end of the war.

As mentioned at the start of this book, the convoy programme did not run continuously or at regular intervals, the frequency and size of the convoys being determined by wider political and military constraints, including competing strategic military objectives and the strength of the German opposition at the time.

The first continuous convoy cycle ran from August 1941 to September 1942 in two phases. Distinct variations in the pattern of enemy activity resulted in higher casualty rates during certain months than others. During Phase One, between 12 August 1941 and 22 February 1942 (Dervish to PQ.11), 12 convoys containing 93 merchant ships sailed to North Russian ports and 6 convoys of 67 merchant ships returned. Of the 93 eastbound, one returned to port and one sank, whilst of the 67 westbound, 3 returned to North Russian ports. The only merchant ship lost was a straggler sunk by a U-boat. The RN destroyer *Matabele* was sunk in convoy PQ.8, while the German Navy suffered no losses.

The Germans made little serious attempt to interfere with the passage of the convoys during this period, largely due to the lack of sufficient military resources in northern waters and competing military priorities elsewhere.

During the first part of Phase Two, between 23 February and 20 March 1942, only two convoys, one eastbound (PQ.12), and one westbound (QP.8), of 17 and 15 merchant ships respectively, were at sea in the two weeks between 1 and 12 March. Only one merchant ship, the Russian *Ijora* from

QP.8, was sunk, but events during these four weeks marked a watershed in what had come before and what would follow, with the changes in tactics and operations adopted by both the British and German Navies and a subsequent shift in the direction and intensity of German efforts to disrupt the sea-line of communications to North Russia. From then on, between 13 March and 26 September 1942, the convoys come under increased, sustained, and intense air and U-boat attack, and the threat of potential attack by surface forces following the deployment of German heavy surface ships and destroyers to northern Norway. PQ.12 was the first convoy to North Russia to be targeted in this way, with a planned, though unsuccessful, attack by heavy surface forces.

Up until PQ.18 in September 1942, the Royal Navy's ability to protect convoys remained very limited. The ongoing shortage of naval escort vessels, and limitations on the endurance of the destroyers due to difficulties in refuelling at sea, restricted the capacity of the escorts both to protect the convoys and to pro-actively hunt and destroy U-boats. The deployment of the German heavy surface warships, particularly *Tirpitz*, against the convoys, whilst perceived by the Admiralty as a major ever-present threat from a 'fleet in being' was constrained by shortages of fuel and severe operational restrictions placed by the German High Command on their use.

The six eastbound convoys of the second part of Phase Two, from April onwards, contained 179 merchant ships, of which 21 returned to port, primarily due to weather conditions, and 158 went on to North Russian ports, while 51 merchants and 2 naval auxiliaries were sunk. Two-thirds of those lost were American and Panamanian. PQ.17 and PQ.18 together accounted for two-thirds of all the losses incurred during this period – the highest rate for the whole of the convoy programme.

Initially German attention focused on the eastbound convoys, but in late April instructions were issued for the westbound ships to be targeted. These attacks fared little better: of 143 merchant ships, 5 turned back to North Russia. Of the 138 that went on, 15 (11 per cent of the total) were sunk or wrecked, 5 in QP.13 when the convoy ran into a British minefield off Iceland. In addition, a single naval auxiliary was sunk, while 8 Royal Navy warships and a Polish submarine were also lost. The German Navy lost 2 destroyers and 6 U-boats.

After the severe losses sustained in PQ.17 and PQ.18, and in the face of the competing demand for RN resources to support the invasion of North Africa

(Operation TORCH), the convoys were suspended between September and December 1942, although one return convoy (QP.15) was run in November to bring back a number of merchant ships stranded in North Russia.

During the suspension between 29 October and 18 November, 13 merchant ships sailed independently from Iceland to North Russia under Operation FB. Of these only 5 arrived safely, 3 turned back, one was wrecked on the coast of Spitzbergen and 4 sunk either by aircraft or U-boat attack – an attrition rate of 39 per cent. This Allied operation was judged a failure and not to be repeated. The Russians sailed a further 8 merchant ships independently for Iceland, of which 7 arrived safely with one intercepted and sunk by a German destroyer. They also organized a further programme of independent sailings by 27 merchant ships to Iceland between 29 October 1942 and 20 February 1943, relying for their safety primarily on the darkness of the Arctic night. All but three of these arrived safely.

The third phase of the programme began on 15 December 1942, with sufficient RN escort forces found to provide the level of protection thought necessary. After some debate on the risks involved, it was decided to sail each convoy in two sections, each of about 16 merchant ships, with an interval of seven days between the sailing dates of each section. This phase turned out to be a short cycle with only four eastbound and three westbound convoys, before operations were again suspended following the redeployment of the German heavy ships to northern Norway. The four eastbound convoys included 73 merchant ships, of which 8 were forced by weather to return to port and one wrecked on arrival in the Kola Inlet; none were sunk by enemy action. The three eastbound convoys of 52 merchant ships suffered greater losses, with four of them sunk by U-boats and one foundered. As all the torpedo and heavy bombers of the German Air Force had been withdrawn to the Mediterranean in October 1942, it had been left to the U-boats and surface forces to mount most of the attacks, but on New Year's Eve convoy JW.51B was attacked by the pocket battleship *Admiral Lutzow*, heavy cruiser *Admiral Hipper*, and five destroyers deployed under Operation Regenbogen. In the action that followed the German destroyer *Friedrich Eckholdt* and RN destroyer *Achates* were sunk. This engagement came to be known as the Battle of the Barents Sea. The RN minesweeper *Bramble* was also lost in a separate action during JW.51B and one Russian destroyer was lost.

By this time strengthened arrangements for convoy protection had begun to take effect and the rate of merchant shipping losses finally to decrease.

The continuation of this convoy cycle was however threatened in early 1943, firstly by the ongoing dispute between the British and Russian governments over Russian objections to the proposal to deploy RAF squadrons in North Russia for convoy protection (Operation GRENADINE), and secondly by British objections to the perceived continued ill-treatment by the Russian authorities of British Service personnel in North Russia – to the point where Churchill was minded in early March to stop the convoys completely. These threats were however rapidly overtaken by news on 11 March of the concentration of German heavy ships in northern Norway and on 16 March the War Cabinet decided to cancel the next convoy, planned for May. As it happened, it would in any case have been necessary to discontinue further convoys until August, owing to the pressing need for all available Home Fleet escorts to be sent to the Mediterranean in June 1943 for Operation HUSKY, the invasion of Sicily.

After some lengthy political manoeuvring, the difficulties over the treatment of British personnel in North Russia were largely resolved. By 15 November the convoy cycle was able to be resumed and it ran through until 7 May 1944. The convoys were by now much larger, of up to 40 merchant ships each, the maximum deemed manageable on the route. During this phase of the programme 197 merchant ships sailed for North Russia in eight convoys. Seven returned to port, and of the remaining 190 only 3 were lost, a significant reduction over previous sailings. The seven return convoys again included 197 merchants. Although 4 returned to port for various reasons, only 2 of the remaining 193 were lost, both to U-boats. The Royal Navy lost 2 destroyers, both sunk by U-boats during convoy operations in January and February 1944, but as the measures to counter the submarine threat gained traction, the Royal Navy and RAF sank a total of 16 U-boats between January and May, before the return of RA.59 on 7 May 1944 brought this particular convoy cycle to a close.

The convoy programme then remained suspended during the summer of 1944 while all available naval resources were committed to Operation OVERLORD – the D-Day Landings – but Phase Five resumed on 15 August with JW.59 and continued until 26 May 1945. The convoys now took between 30 and 35 merchant ships. As the sinking of *Scharnhorst* during JW.55B left the Germans with no effective heavy ships in north Norway, heavy cover for the convoys was no longer required and the protection effort now focused on countering the U-boats.

At the start of this phase there was less threat to the convoys from enemy air attack, but a strong concentration of U-boats remained in Arctic waters, and five German destroyers remained at Altenfjord. Once the risk from *Tirpitz* had been neutralized by the RAF bombing on 15 September, and given the reduced air threat, there was concern the Germans would increase U-boat operations. In fact, reinforcement of the German 5th Air Force following the return of torpedo bombers to northern Norway in December 1944, and the strengthening of the U-boat force following redeployments from the Atlantic after the loss of bases in western France now combined to intensify both the air and underwater threat. This was accompanied by the adoption of new U-boat tactics and increased efforts to disrupt the convoys, in particular by concentrating U-boat wolfpacks off the entrance to the Kola Inlet, where the restricted waters and poor ASDIC conditions made anti-submarine operations difficult and presented the Royal Navy with a significantly greater challenge.

The changes in convoy defence tactics now adopted by the Allies, focusing on countering the U-boats and Luftwaffe, significantly reduced losses. Of the 249 merchant ships in the nine convoys to North Russia during this phase (excluding four Norwegian ships that did not go right through), none returned to port and only two were lost. A total of 223 merchant ships sailed in the nine westbound convoys; none returned to port but six were sunk, one by aircraft and four by U-boats, one on the way to join the departing convoy.

Despite the reduction in losses of merchant ships, the cost to the Allied Navies, particularly the Royal Navy, in countering these more determined attacks was high. As a result of the intensified efforts by the U-boats to disrupt the convoy traffic, 6 Allied warships were sunk for the cost of 12 U-boats.

When the programme of sailings came to an end, 40 convoys had carried supplies to North Russian ports and 35 convoys had returned. Convoy Identification Codes had been allocated, 42 for shipments to North Russia and 36 for the return, a total of 78 – but of these, PQ.9 and PQ.10 were combined into a single sailing, and JW.61A/RA.61A involving the repatriation of Russian prisoners of war and Russian civilians, carried no supplies.

As the Admiralty foreword to the C-in-C Home Fleet's 'Despatches on Convoys to North Russia', published in the *London Gazette* on 13 October 1950[1] noted:

The Russian convoy routes, in contrast to the complete freedom of movement of the Atlantic routes, were restricted to the east and south by an enemy-occupied coastline of Norway and to the west and north by ice fields. The convoys themselves were subject to attack by surface forces over a large part of their 2,000-mile passage, to air attack for 1,400 miles, and to U-boat attack throughout their entire run. The severe Arctic weather added to their navigational difficulties during winter months, but they ran a greater risk of attack between March and September owing to the continuous daylight of the Far Northern summer. Nevertheless, in spite of these very adverse conditions, under British command, and almost entirely under British naval and air escort, forty outward and thirty-five homeward bound Russian convoys made the passage during a period of nearly four years.

Most published sources quantify the convoy programme by number of sailings, rather than number of merchant ships, where there are varying degrees of inconsistency in analysis and presentation of data. The figure of 811 most commonly quoted represents individual sailings by merchant ships in all 40 convoys. However not all those which sailed from UK ports went on to Russian ports; some left at Iceland, where others joined, some returned to Iceland or UK ports due to bad weather, damage, or mechanical problems, some sailed again in later convoys, others did not, and a small number sailed more than once. We can say with certainty there were 806 sailings,[2] 38 ships returned, 58 were sunk, 4 (Norwegian relief ships) were diverted, and 706 arrived.

A figure of 717 is quoted for the number of return sailings. Again, we can demonstrate there were 697 sailings. Of these, 12 ships returned to port, 28 were sunk or sank (2 foundered) and 657 arrived. The difference between the number of sailings to and from Archangel and Murmansk is accounted for by Russian ships that sailed only one way, ships lost in Russian ports, ships that returned after RA.67 and ships that did not return at all, for example Norwegian vessels that remained in Norway or transferred to the Russian merchant fleet. This gives a total of 1,503 sailings, with 50 ships returned, 4 diverted, 86 sunk by enemy action on passage, 2 foundered and 1,363 arrived. In addition, 3 naval auxiliaries were sunk, 7 merchant ships were lost in north Russian ports, and 5 sunk during Operation FB, for a total loss of 103.

The losses have historically been presented as a percentage of the number of sailings rather than number of participating merchant ships, and the officially published loss rates are also based on the former rather than the latter. The *London Gazette* of 13 October 1950 quoted 1,531 sailings, stating:

> During the next two years [December 1942 – May 1944] the Russian convoys ran only during the long dark months of winter and lost only three ships, all in January 1944. No further losses were sustained until March 1945, when one ship was sunk. This proved to be the final casualty and brought the total losses in outward bound Russian Convoys to sixty-two, or 7.8 per cent, of the 792 ships sailed in them during the war. In the homeward bound Convoys, twenty-eight, or 3.8 per cent of the 739 ships sailed were lost.

A total of 527 merchant ships participated in the sailing programmes (including Operation FB). Of these, a total of 100 (excluding naval auxiliaries) were sunk, wrecked, or damaged beyond repair, giving a loss rate of circa 1/5, or just under 19 per cent. Official Government statements based on 1,503 sailings and the 94 per cent of shipments arrived safely, have thus arguably sadly and significantly understated the true human and material cost.

Although the convoys might be regarded as primarily a British enterprise the majority of ships involved were American owned, some of Panamanian or Honduran registry. The first American ship sailed in convoy PQ.8 and by 1945 American merchants formed the majority of those in the convoys. Although some Russian merchant ships participated in the early convoys they sailed mainly westbound from Russia, very few sailed to North Russia, none after late 1942. The American merchant marine sustained the bulk of the losses with 52 ships sunk or wrecked on passage, a further 3 sunk in North Russian ports and one in Operation FB, for a 64 per cent lost rate on passage and 56 per cent of overall losses. Over 1,500 merchant seamen, the largest percentage of them American, lost their lives. An untold number were injured or died later of wounds.

Royal Navy and Allied naval losses were significant particularly in the later years. No RN warship was sunk during 1941. During 1942, 12 Royal Navy warships and one Polish submarine were sunk, damaged or declared a total loss, 6 of these between May and July 1942. There were no losses during 1943. Four warships were sunk during 1944, and 5 more between February and April 1945, when U-boat attacks on convoys in the approaches to the

Kola Inlet intensified. The Russian Navy lost one destroyer in November 1942. No American or other Allied warships were lost. A total of 21 Royal Naval vessels were sunk and 5 badly damaged in action, with more than 2,000 personnel killed. Fleet Air Arm and Royal Air Force losses in aircraft and crew are not readily available.[3]

The first German naval losses occurred during 1942 with 3 destroyers and 6 U-boats sunk. During 1943 one U-boat and a battle cruiser were lost. The increasingly pro-active anti-U-boat campaign from 1944 onwards carried out by the escort groups and aircraft from the escort carriers brought a steep increase in the rate of losses with 22 U-boats sunk – 12 in the space of six weeks during attacks on JW/RA.57 and JW/RA.58, most accounted for by Swordfish aircraft. A further 3 were sunk in the early months of 1945, bringing the total lost to 31. An estimated 5,250 personnel were killed. German air force losses in aircraft and crews are not known.

The psychological impact of the German heavy ships as a 'fleet in being' had a profound deterrent effect on British naval strategy, which was not in the event reflected in reality. The Kriegsmarine were cautious in their deployment of their surface forces, being unwilling to confront convoy escorts of superior strength or containing an aircraft carrier. Much of the effort to disrupt the convoys fell on the U-boats, whose numbers in the early years were disproportionately small in relation to the challenge they faced and the comparatively greater strength and fire power of the German surface fleet. Strength in numbers and firepower coupled with the political constraints placed on the use of the surface ships did not however guarantee success. The nine surface operations conducted between December 1941 and December 1943 against west- and eastbound convoys and independent sailings resulted in the sinking of only three merchant ships – all stragglers from the main convoys. Of the 86 merchant ships lost on passage, 35 were sunk by U-boats, 30 by aircraft, 16 were 'joint kills', 3 sunk by destroyers and 2 lost to other causes (foundered).

The 40 outward-bound convoys delivered to Russia £428,000,000 worth of materiel, including 5,000 tanks and over 7,000 aircraft. Churchill's Russian convoys thus delivered on his promise to Stalin to aid the Russians in their fight against Germany, although the frequency of the sailing programme over a period of four years of war was at times interrupted by competing operational priorities, unacceptable levels of threat presented by German forces in Norway and, on occasion, the intransigence and demands of the Russian authorities, who seemed to regard the assistance as an absolute right and whose behaviour provoked Churchill on more than one occasion to consider abandoning the venture. They represented a significant operational burden on the Royal Navy and Home Fleet. Theirs is a tale of bravery and heroism in the face of adversity and at times seemingly impossible odds. But as time went on the balance of advantage over the enemy was won, albeit at great human and material cost.

On a final note, Winston Churchill has often been quoted as having described this sea passage as 'the worst journey in the world'. Though the quote itself has proved after detailed investigation to be apocryphal, yet the weather conditions alone on the route to Russia in winter undoubtedly made it one of the most hazardous as well as one of the most courageous undertakings of the war.

Appendix

Tables of Convoy Sailings

1. Convoy Sailing Programme
2. Analysis of Sailings and Losses by Convoy
3. Summary of Convoy Departures, Returns, Losses and Arrivals Phase
4. American and Panamanian Ships in Convoys
5. British Merchant Ships in Convoys
6. Russian Merchant Ships in Convoys and Independent Sailings to and from North Russia
7. Other Allied Merchant Ships in Convoys to and from North Russia
8. American and Panamanian Merchant Ship Losses
9. British Merchant Ship Losses
10. Other Allied Merchant Ship Losses
11. Total Merchant Ship Losses by Convoy and Nationality
12. Total Merchant Ship Losses by Convoy Cycle and Nationality
13. Cause of Merchant Ship Losses by Convoy
14. Merchant Ships Lost in North Russia (or not Included in Return Convoys)
15. Royal Navy, Naval Auxiliary, and Allied Naval Losses
16. German Naval Losses
17. Operation FB: Independent Sailings Iceland to North Russia
18. Russian Independent Sailings, North Russia to Iceland

Table 1. Convoy Sailing Programme
1941

CONVOY SERIAL	EAST BOUND	CONVOY SERIAL	WEST BOUND
Dervish	D. Hvalfjord August 21[1] A. Archangel August 31		
PQ.1	D. Hvalfjord September 29 A. Archangel October 11	QP.1	D. Archangel September 28 A. Scapa Flow October 10
PQ.2	D. Liverpool October 13 A. Archangel October 30		
PQ.3	D. Hvalfjord November 9 A. Archangel November 22	QP.2	D. Archangel November 3 A. Kirkwall November 17
PQ.4	D. Hvalfjord November 17 A. Archangel November 28		
PQ.5	D. Hvalfjord November 27 A. Archangel December 13	QP.3	D. Archangel November 27 Dispersed, A. December 3
PQ.6	D. Hvalfjord December 8 A. Murmansk, December 20		
PQ.7a	D. Hvalfjord December 26 A. Murmansk January 12, 1942	QP.4	D. Archangel December 29 Dispersed, A. January 9, 1942
PQ.7b	D. Hvalfjord December 31 A. Murmansk January 11, 1942		

Notes
1. Originated Liverpool 12 August

CONVOY SERIAL	EAST BOUND	CONVOY SERIAL	WEST BOUND
PQ.8	D. Hvalfjord January 8 A. Archangel January 17	QP.5	D. Murmansk January 13 Dispersed, A. January 19
Combined PQ.9 and PQ.10	D. Reykjavik February 1 A. Murmansk February 10	QP.6	D. Murmansk January 24 Dispersed, A. January 28
PQ.11	D. Loch Ewe February 7 D. Kirkwall February 14 A. Murmansk February 22	QP.7	D. Murmansk February 12 Dispersed, A. February 15
PQ.12	D. Reykjavik March 1 A. Murmansk March 12	QP.8	D. Murmansk March 1 A. Reykjavik March 11
PQ.13	D. Reykjavik March 20 A. Murmansk March 31	QP.9	D. Kola Inlet March 21 A. Reykjavik April 3
PQ.14	D. Oban March 26 A. Murmansk April 19	QP.10	D. Kola Inlet April 10 A. Reykjavik April 21
PQ.15	D. Oban April 10 A. Murmansk May 5	QP.11	D. Murmansk April 28 A. Reykjavik May 7
PQ.16	D. Reykjavik May 21 A. Murmansk May 30	QP.12	D. Kola Inlet May 21 A. Reykjavik May 29
PQ.17	D. Reykjavik June 27 Dispersed, A. July 4	QP.13	D. Archangel June 26 A. Reykjavik July 7
	(August sailing postponed)		(August sailing postponed)
PQ.18	D. Loch Ewe September 2 A. Archangel September 21	QP.14	D. Archangel September 13 A. Loch Ewe September 26
	(PQ Cycle ended)	QP.15	D. Kola Inlet November 17 A. Loch Ewe November 30
Operation FB	Sailings by independent unescorted ships		(QP Cycle ended)
JW.51A	D. Loch Ewe December 15 A. Kola Inlet December 25		
JW.51B	D. Loch Ewe December 22 A. Kola Inlet January 4, 1943	RA.51	D. Kola Inlet December 30 A. Loch Ewe January 11, 1943

CONVOY SERIAL	EAST BOUND	CONVOY SERIAL	WEST BOUND
JW.52	D. Loch Ewe January 17 A. Kola Inlet January 27	RA.52	D. Kola Inlet January 29 A. Loch Ewe February 9
JW.53	D. Loch Ewe February 15 A. Kola Inlet February 27	RA.53	D. Kola Inlet March 1 A. Loch Ewe March 14
	(Convoys suspended through summer)		(Convoys suspended through summer)
JW.54A	D. Loch Ewe November 15 A. Kola Inlet November 24	RA.54A	D. Kola Inlet November 1 A. Loch Ewe November 14
JW.54B	D. Loch Ewe November 22 A. Archangel December 3	RA.54B	D. Archangel November 26 A. Loch Ewe December 9
JW.55A	D. Loch Ewe December 12 A. Archangel December 22	RA.55A	D. Kola Inlet December 22 A. Loch Ewe January 1, 1944
JW.55B	D. Loch Ewe December 20 A. Archangel December 30 (*See* Battle of the North Cape)	RA.55B	D. Kola Inlet December 31 A. Loch Ewe January 8, 1944

CONVOY SERIAL	EAST BOUND	CONVOY SERIAL	WEST BOUND
JW.56A	D. Loch Ewe January 12 A. Archangel January 28		
JW.56B	D. Loch Ewe January 22 A. Kola Inlet February 1	RA.56	D. Kola Inlet February 3 A. Loch Ewe February 11
JW.57	D. Loch Ewe February 20 A. Kola Inlet February 28	RA.57	D. Kola Inlet March 2 A. Loch Ewe March 10
JW.58	D. Loch Ewe March 27 A. Kola Inlet April 4	RA.58	D. Kola Inlet April 7 A. Loch Ewe April 14
		RA.59	D. Kola Inlet April 28 A. Loch Ewe May 6
	(Convoys suspended through summer)		(Convoys suspended through summer)
JW.59	D. Loch Ewe August 15 A. Kola Inlet August 25	RA.59A	D. Kola Inlet August 28 A. Loch Ewe September 5
JW.60	D. Loch Ewe September 15 A. Kola Inlet September 23	RA.60	D. Kola Inlet September 28 A. Clyde October 5
JW.61	D. Loch Ewe October 20 A. Kola Inlet October 28	RA.61	D. Kola Inlet November 2 A. Loch Ewe November 9, Clyde Nov. 10
JW.61A[2]	D. Loch Ewe October 31 A. Murmansk November 6	RA.61A	D. Kola Inlet November 11 A. Clyde November 17
JW.62	D. Loch Ewe November 29 A. Kola Inlet December 7	RA.62	D. Kola Inlet December 10 A. Loch Ewe December 19, Clyde Dec. 20
JW.63	D. Loch Ewe December 30 A. Kola Inlet January 8, 1945	RA.63	D. Kola Inlet January 11, 1945 A. Loch Ewe January 21, Clyde Jan. 23

2. Not a supply convoy. Repatriation of Russian POWs. Excluded from statistics

Cont.

1945

CONVOY SERIAL	EAST BOUND	CONVOY SERIAL	WEST BOUND
JW.64	D. Clyde February 3 A. Kola Inlet February 15	RA.64	D. Kola Inlet February 17 A. Loch Ewe February 28, Clyde March 1
JW.65	D. Clyde March 11 A. Kola Inlet March 21	RA.65	D. Kola Inlet March 23 A. Clyde April 1
JW.66	D. Clyde April 16 A. Kola Inlet April 25	RA.66	D. Kola Inlet April 29 A. Clyde May 8
JW.67	D. Clyde May 12 A. Kola Inlet May 20	RA.67	D. Kola Inlet May 23 A. Clyde May 30

PHASE ONE: AUGUST 1941 to FEBRUARY 1942

Convoy	RN Battle Summary 22	Current Analysis	Ships Turned Back	Ships Sunk	Ships Arrived
	No. of Ships (Fleet Oilers + Rescue Ships)				
Dervish	7	6 +(1)¹	–	–	6 + (1)
PQ.1	10	10	–	–	10
PQ.2	6	6	–	–	6
PQ.3	8	8	1	–	7
PQ.4	8	8	–	–	8
PQ.5	7	7		–	7
PQ.6	7	7 + (1)		–	7 + (1)
PQ.7a	2	2	–	1²	1
PQ.7b	9	9	–	–	9
PQ.8	8	8	–	–	8
PQ.9	7³	8 + (1)	–	–	8 + (1)
PQ.10	3	1	–	–	1
PQ.11	13	13	–	–	13
PQ.12	16⁴	17	1	–	16
TOTAL C/F	111	110 + (3)	2	1	107 + (3)

PHASE TWO (PART 1): 1–11 MARCH 1942

Convoy	Battle Summary 22	No. of Ships	Ships Turned Back	Ships Sunk	Ships Arrived
QP.1	14	14	–	–	14
QP.2	12	12	–	–	12
QP.3	10	10	2	–	8
QP.4	13	13 + (1)	1 + (1)	–	12
QP.5	4	4	–	–	4
QP.6	6	6	–	–	6
QP.7	8	8	–	–	8
QP.8	15	15	–	1	14
TOTAL	82	82 + (2)	3 + (1)	1	78

Notes
1. Convoy included RFA *Aldersdale*
2. *Waziristan* see Admiralty Despatches
3. Included *Noreg* escort oiler
4. *Bateau* was originally included, to give 17 ships, but returned; sailed in PQ.13. Also Battle Summary 22 main text quotes 15 merchant ships plus one escort oiler

PHASE TWO (PART 2): 26 MARCH to 30 NOVEMBER 1942

Cont.

Convoy	RN Battle Summary 22	Current Analysis	Ships Turned Back	Ships Sunk	Ships Arrived
	No. of Ships (Fleet Oilers + Rescue Ships)				
TOTAL B/F	111	110 + (3)	2	1	107 + (3)
PQ.13	18[5]	18 + (1)		5	13 + (1)
PQ.14	24[6]	24	16	1	7
PQ.15	25[8]	25	–	3	22
PQ.16	35[9]	35	1	7	27
PQ.17	36[11]	36 + (2) (3)[12]	3	22 + (2)[13]	11 + (1) + (2)
August Sailing Postponed					
PQ.18	40[14]	41 + (2)[15]	1	13	27 + (2)
PHASE TWO TOTAL	178	179	21	51	107
TOTAL	289	289 + (11)	23	52 + 2	214 + (8)

Convoy	Battle Summary 22	No. of Ships	Ships Turned Back	Ships Sunk	Ships Arrived
TOTAL B/F	82	82 + (2)	3 + (1)	1	78
QP.9	19	19	–	–	19
QP.10[7]	16	16	1	4	11
QP.11	13	13	–	1	12
QP.12	15	15 + (1)	2[10]	–	13 (1)
QP.13	35	35	–	5	30
QP.14	15[16]	15 + (2) + (2)	–	3 + (1)	12 + (1) + (2)
QP.15	28[17]	30 + 1	2	2	26 + 1
PHASE TWO TOTAL	141	143	5	15 + (1)	123
TOTAL	223	225 + (6)	8	16 + (1)	201

CONVOYS SUSPENDED OCTOBER–DECEMBER 1942

5. Three ships left at Iceland. Two merchant ships and escort oiler Scottish American joined. Column 1 should read 18 6. Originally 26 ships but *Winona* and *Cape Corso* did not sail 7 *London Gazette* gives 16, 1, 4 8. Includes two ice breakers, Montcalm and Krassin – carried no cargo 9. Convoy-web and other sources quote 36 including CAM ship *Empire Lawrence*. *Black Ranger* was Force Q 10. Battle Summary 22 gives one only returned. *Hegira* and *Kuzbass* returned and sailed again QP.13 11. Battle Summary 22 Main text quotes 35. Admiralty Dispatches give 34 merchants, 1 escort oiler and 3 rescue ships. So 36 in Battle Summary Appendix presumably includes oiler 12. One escort oiler, three rescue ships 13. RFA *Aldersdale*, rescue ship *Zaafaran* 14. 41 merchant ships sailed but *Richard Basset* was sent back, unable to maintain speed of convoy 15. Hague includes *Oligarch* and *Blue Ranger* (Force P) which did not sail in convoy. *Gray Ranger* sailed in convoy as escort oiler. Plus one rescue ship 16. Plus two rescue ships 17. Battle Summary 22 Main text says 22 put to sea, plus one grounded, and one did not sail. *Meanticut* returned, sailed in RA.51. *Ironclad*

PHASE THREE: 15 DECEMBER 1942 to 14 MARCH 1943

Convoy	Battle Summary 22	No. of Ships (Fleet Oilers + Rescue Ships)	Ships Turned Back	Ships Sunk[18]	Ships Arrived	Convoy	Battle Summary 22	No. of Ships	Ships Turned Back	Ships Sunk	Ships Arrived
TOTAL B/F	289	289 + (11)	23	52 + 2	214 + (8)		223	225 + (6)	8	16 + (1)	201
JW.51A	16[19]	16	-		16	RA.51	14	13 + (1)			13 + (1)
JW.51B	15[20]	15	1[21]	1[22]	13	RA.52	11	10[24]		1	9
JW.52	14	14[23]	1	-	13	RA.53	30	29 + (1)		4	25 + (1)
JW.53	28	28 + (1)	6	-	22 + (1)	TOTAL	55	52 + (2)	-	5	47
TOTAL	73	73	8	1	64	TOTAL C/F	280	277 + (8)	8	21	248
TOTAL C/F	362	362	31	53 + 2	278						

CONVOYS SUSPENDED MARCH – NOVEMBER 1943

18. Auxiliaries shown as +
19. Battle Summary 22 Main text quotes 15 + 1 escort oiler.
20. Battle Summary 22 Main text gives 14 merchant ships. Presumably excludes *Dover Hill*?
21. *Dover Hill*. Engine trouble. Sailed JW.53
22. *Ballot* wrecked on arrival
23. *Atlantic* did not sail
24. Convoy.web gives 10

PHASE FOUR: 15 NOVEMBER 1943 to 6 MAY 1944

Convoy	Battle Summary 22	No. of Ships (Fleet Oilers + Rescue Ships)	Ships Turned Back	Ships Sunk[25]	Ships Arrived	Convoy	Battle Summary 22	No. of Ships	Ships Turned Back	Ships Sunk	Ships Arrived
TOTAL B/F	362	362	31	53 + 2	278		280	277 + (8)	8	21	248
JW.54A	18	18	–	–	18	RA.54A	13	13			13
JW.54B	14	14	–	–	14	RA.54B	9	8 + (1)			8 + (1)
JW.55A	19	18 + (1)[26]	–	–	18 + (1)	RA.55A	22	22 + (1)	1		21 + (1)
JW.55B	19	19	–	–	19	RA.55B	8[27]	7 + (1)	–	–	7 + (1)
JW.56A	20	20 + (2)	5	3	12 + (2)						
JW.56B	16[28]	17	1[29]	–	16	RA.56	37[30]	39[31] + (2)	2		37
JW.57	42	42 + (2) (1)	–	–	42 + (2) + (1)	RA.57	31[32]	28[33] + (3)	1[34]	1	26 + (3)
JW.58	49	49	1	–	48	RA.58	36[35]	35[36] + (1) (2)	–	–	35
						RA.59	45	45 + (1)	–	1	44 + (1)
TOTAL	197	197 (4) + (1)	7	3	187	TOTAL	201	197 + (21)	4	2	191
TOTAL C/F	559	559 (19)	38	56 + 2	465	TOTAL C/F	481	474 + (21)	12	23 + (1)	439

25. Auxiliaries shown as +
26. RFA *San Ambrosio*
27. Includes RFA *San Ambrosio*
28. Excludes *Henry Lomb*
29. *Henry Lomb* returned
30. 39 sailed but 2 returned
31. *Empire Pickwick* and the American *Philip Livingston* were also in convoy but returned
32. Battle Summary 22 figures include 3 escort oilers
33. *Empire Bard* returned
34. *Empire Bard*

PHASE FIVE: 15 AUGUST 1944 to 30 MAY 1945

JW Convoys

Convoy	Battle Summary 22	No. of Ships (Fleet Oilers + Rescue Ships)	Ships Turned Back	Ships Arrived	Ships Sunk[37]
TOTAL B/F	559	559 (19)	38	465	56 + 2
JW.59	33[38]	32 + (2)[39]	–	32 + (2)	–
JW.60	30	30 + (1)	–	30 + (1)	–
JW.61	29[40]	26 + (2) + (1)	–	26 + (3)	–
JW.62	30[41]	30 + (1)	–	30 + (1)	–
JW.63	35[43]	35[44] + (2)		35 + (2)	–
JW.64	26	26 + (2)	–	26 + (2)	–
JW.65	24	24 + (2)	–	22 + (2)	2

RA Convoys

Convoy	Battle Summary 22	No. of Ships (Fleet Oilers + Rescue Ships)	Ships Turned Back	Ships Sunk	Ships Arrived
TOTAL	481	474 + (21)	12	23 + (1)	439
RA.59A	9	9	–	–	9
RA.60	30	30 + (3)	–	2	28 + (3)
RA.61	33	29 + (3) + (1)	–	–	29 + (3) + (1)
RA.62	28[42]	25 + (3) + (1)	–	–	25 + (3) + (1)
RA.63	30[45]	27 + (3)	–	–	27 + (3)
RA.64	34[46]	32 + (1)	(1[47])	2	30 + (1)
RA.65	25[49]?	24 + (2)	–	1[48]	–

37. Auxiliaries shown as +
38. Includes 2 escort oilers and 1 crane ship
39. Includes 2 escort oilers, 1 rescue ship and 1 crane ship *Empire Buttress*
40. Includes 2 escort oilers and 1 rescue ship
41. Includes 3 fleet tankers. Other sources give 31 sailed, including 1 rescue ship
42. Include 2 escort oilers
43. Assumes *Adolph S. Ochs* did not sail
44. *Blue Ranger* sailed in convoy as escort oiler. Also RFA *Lacklan*
45. Included 3 RFAs
46. Includes 2 merchant ships that did not join – one sunk, one badly damaged beforehand
47. Convoy records show 33 merchants sailed, 2 sunk, 31 arrived. Reference may be to *Empire Celia*, diverted to Faroes 27 February, but arrived Loch Ewe 4 March, or to *Alanson B. Houghton*, not shown
48. Sunk before joined – included in Battle Summary 22 numbers
49. Includes RFA *Blue Ranger* – escort oiler?

Cont.

Convoy	Battle Summary 22	No. of Ships (Fleet Oilers + Rescue Ships)	Ships Turned Back	Ships Sunk[50]	Ships Arrived	Convoy	Battle Summary 22	No. of Ships	Ships Turned Back	Ships Sunk	Ships Arrived
JW.66	22[51]	23[52] + (2) + (1)		-	21 + (3)	RA.66	24?	23 + (3) + (1)	-	-	23
JW.67	23[53]	23 + (1) + (1)	-	-	(2) 21 + (1) + (1) (2)	RA.67	23[54]	22 + (2) (1)	-	-	22
SUB TOT	252	249 (11)	-	2	243[55]		236	223[56] (10)	-	5	218
TOTAL	811	808 (37)	38	58 + 2	708[57]		717	697 (43)	12	28 + (1)	657
Norwegian Relief Ships	-4	(-4)			-4						
	807	804	38	58 + (2)	704						
Less Ice-breakers	2	2			2						
	805	802	38	58 + (2)	702						

The merchant ships of JW.67 returned independently on various dates during June 1945

50. Auxiliaries shown as +
51. Other sources give 23. Total of 26 included 2 escort oilers and 1 rescue ship. Also 2 Norwegian relief ships
52. 2 Norwegian relief ships
53. 2 Norwegian relief ships
54. Discrepancy of 1
55. Excludes 4 Norwegian relief ships
56. Figures in Battle Summary 22 include RFAs
57. Total excludes 4 Norwegian relief ships

Table 3. Summary of Convoy Departures, Returns, Losses and Arrivals

SAILINGS TO RUSSIA

Phase	Convoys	Dates	Number of Convoys	Merchant Ships Sailed	Merchant Ships Returned/ Diverted	Merchant Ships Lost	Merchant Ships Arrived
One	Dervish – PQ.11	21 Aug 1941 – 22 Feb 1942	12	93	1	1	91
Two	PQ.12	1-12 Mar 1942	1	17	1	–	16
	PQ.13 – PQ.18	20 Mar 1942 – 21 Sep 1942	6	179	21	51	107
Three	JW.51A – JW.53	15 Dec 1942 – 27 Feb 1943	4	73	8	1	64
Four	JW.54A – JW.58	15 Nov 1943 – 4 Apr 1944	8	197	7	3	187
Five	JW.59 – JW.67	15 Aug 1944 – 20 May 1945	9	247	4[1]	2	241
TOTAL			40	806	42	58	706

SAILINGS FROM RUSSIA

Phase	Convoys	Dates	Number of Convoys	Merchant Ships Sailed	Merchant Ships Returned/ Diverted	Merchant Ships Lost	Merchant Ships Arrived
One	QP.1 – QP.8	28 Sep 1941 – 11 Mar 1942	8	82	3	1	78
Two	QP.9 – QP.15	21 Mar 1942 – 30 Nov 1942	7	143	5	15	123
Three	RA.51 – RA.53	30 Dec 1942 – 14 Mar 1943	3	52	–	5	47
Four	RA.54A – RA.59	1 Nov 1943 – 6 May 1944	8	197	4	2	191
Five	RA.59A – RA.67	28 Aug 1944 – 30 May 1945	9	223		5[2]	218
TOTAL			35	697	12	28	657

Notes
1. Norwegian relief ships, sailed to Kirkenes
2. Figures exclude two ships ex-convoy BZ-3. One sunk and one damaged en route to join RA.64

Table 4. American & Panamanian Merchant Ships in Convoys

Abner Nash			*Charles Dauray*	
Africander (Panama)	PQ.18		*Charles Gordon Curtis*	
Alamar	PQ.16		*Charles Henderson*	
Alanson B. Houghton			*Charles M. Schwab*	
Albert C. Ritchie			*Charles R. McCormick*	
Alcoa Banner			*Charles Scribner*	
Alcoa Cadet	Mined		*Chester Valley*	
	Murmansk		**Christopher Newport**	PQ.17
Alcoa Rambler			*City of Flint*	
Alcoa Ranger	PQ.17		**City of Joliet**	PQ.16
Alexander White			*City of Omaha*	
Amasa Delano			*Clark Howell*	
American Press			*Cocle* (Panama)	
American Robin			*Cold Harbor* (Panama)	
Andrew Carnegie			*Collis P. Huntington*	
Andrew George Curtin	JW.56A		*Cornelius Harnett*	
Andrew Turnbull			*Crosby S. Noyes*	
Andrew W. Preston			**Daniel Morgan**	PQ.17
Aneroid (Panama)			*Daniel Drake*	
Arthur L. Perry			*Daniel Willard*	
Artigas (Panama)			*David B. Johnson*	
Arunah S. Abell			*David Stone*	
August Belmont			*Deer Lodge*	
Ballot	Wrecked		*Delsud*	
	Murmansk		*Dexter W. Fellows*	
Barbara Frietchie			*Donald W. Bain*	
Bateau (Panama)	PQ.13		*Dunboyne*	
Bayou Chico			*Dynastic*	
Beauregard			*Edmund Fanning*	
Bellingham	QP.14		*Edward A. Savoy*	
Ben F. Dixon			*Edward E. Spafford*	
Benjamin H. Hill			**Edward H. Crockett**	RA.60
Benjamin H. Latrobe			*Edward L. Grant*	
Benjamin Harrison			*Edward N. Hurley*	
Benjamin Schlesinger			*Edward P. Alexander*	
Bering			*Edward Sparrow*	
Bernard N. Baker			*Edwin L. Drake*	
Byron Darnton			**Effingham**	PQ.13
Caesar Rodney			*El Almirante* (Panama)	
Calobre (Panama)			**El Capitan** (Panama)	PQ.17
Campfire			*El Coston* (Panama)	
Capira (Panama)			*El Estero* (Panama)	
Capulin (Panama)			*El Lago* (Panama)	
Cardinal Gibbons			**El Occidente** (Panama)	QP.10
Carlton	PQ.17		*El Oceano* (Panama)	
Cecil N. Bean			*El Oriente* (Panama)	
Charles A. McAllister			*Eleazar Lord*	
Charles Bulfinch			*Eldena*	

Cont.

Elijah Kellogg		*James Bowie*	
Eloy Alfaro		*James Gordon Bennett*	
Esek Hopkins		*James Kerney*	
Eugene Field		*James M. Gillis*	
Executive	RA.53	*James Smith*	
Exford		*James Woodrow*	
Expositor		*Jefferson Davis*	
Exterminator (Panama)		*Jefferson Myers*	
F. T. Frelinghuysen		*John A. Donald*	
Fairfield City	PQ.17	*John A. Quitman*	
Francis C. Harrington		*John B. Lennon*	
Francis Scott Key		*John Carver*	
Francis Vigo		*John Davenport*	
Frank Gilbreth		*John Fitch*	
Frederic A. Kummer		*John Gibbon*	
Frederick W. Taylor		*John H. B. Latrobe*	
Gallant Fox (Panama)		*John Ireland*	
Gateway City		*John J. Abel*	
George Gale		*John La Farge*	
George H. Pendleton		*John Langdon*	
George M. Cohan		*John Laurance*	
George Steers		*John McDonogh*	
George T. Angell		**John Penn**	PQ.18
George Weems		*John Randolph*	
Gilbert Stuart		*John Rutledge*	
Grace Abbott		*John Sharp Williams*	
Greylock	RA.52	*John Stevenson*	
Gulfwing		*John T. Holt*	
Harold L. Winslow		*John Vining*	
Hawkins Fudske		*John W. Powell*	
Heffron	QP.13	*John Witherspoon*	PQ.17
Hegira		*John Walker*	
Henry Adams		*John Wanamaker*	
Henry B. Brown		*John Woolman*	
Henry Bacon	RA.64	*Jose Marti*	
Henry Lomb		*Joseph E. Johnston* (returned ex JW.53	
Henry Villard		Did not sail again)	
Henry Wynkoop		*Joseph N. Nicollet*	
Hollywood		*Josephine Shaw Lowell*	
Honomu	PQ.17	*Joshua Thomas*	
Hoosier	PQ.17	*Joshua W. Alexander*	
Horace Bushnell	JW.65	*Joyce Kilmer*	
Horace Gray	BK.3 (RA.64)	*Julien Poydras*	
Hybert	QP.13	*Julius Olsen*	
Ironclad		*Keith Palmer*	
Israel Putnam		**Kentucky**	PQ.18
J. D. Yeager		*Lafayette*	
J. L. M. Curry	QP.13	*Lancaster*	
James A. Farrell		*Larranga*	

Cont.

Lawrence J. Brengle		Philip F. Thomas	
Lebaron Russell Briggs		Philip Livingston	
Leo J. Duster		Pierre S. Dupont	
Lewis Emery Jr.		**Puerto Rican**	RA.53
Linn Boyd		R. Ney McNeely	
Lord Delaware		Raceland (Panama)	PQ.13
Louis D. Brandeis		Ralph Waldo Emerson	
Macbeth (Panama)	PQ.18	Raymond B. Stevens	
Makawao (Honduras)		Reigh Count (Panama)	
Mana (Honduras)		Renald Fernald	
Marie M. Meloney		Richard Bassett	
Mary Luckenbach	PQ.18	**Richard Bland**	RA.53
Massmar	QP.13	Richard Henry Lee	
Mauna Kea		Richard H. Alvey	
Meanticut		Richard M. Johnson	
Michigan		Robert Eden	
Minotaur		Robert J. Collier	
Mobile City		Robert Lowry	
Mormacmar		Sahale	
Mormacrey		Samuel Chase	
Mormacrio		Samuel MacIntyre	
Mormacsul	PQ.16	Schoharie	
Morris Hillquit		Seattle Spirit	
Mount Evans (Panama)		Silas Weir Mitchell	
Nathan Towson		**Silver Sword**	QP.14
Nathaniel Alexander		St Olaf	
Nathaniel Greene		Stage Door Canteen	
Nelson W. Aldrich		Stanton H. King	
Nemaha		**Steel Worker**	Mined
Nicholas Biddle			Murmansk
Nicholas Gilman		Stephen Leacock	
Norlys (Panama)		Stevenson Taylor	
North King (Panama)		Stone Street (Panama)	
Oakley Wood		**Syros**	PQ.16
Oliver Ellsworth	PQ.18	Texas	
Olopana	PQ.17	**Thomas Donaldson**	JW.65
Oregonian	PQ.18	Thomas H. Sumner	
Oremar		Thomas Hartley	
Owen Wister		Thomas Kearns	
Pan Atlantic	PQ.17	**Thomas Scott**	RA.64
Pan Kraft	PQ.17	Thomas Sim Lee	
Park Benjamin		Thomas U. Walter	
Park Holland		Thorstein Veblen	
Patrick Henry		Topa Topa	
Paul H. Harwood		Townsend Harris	
Paul Hamilton Hayne		Troubador	
Paul Luckenbach		U.S.O.	
Penelope Barker	JW.56A	Vermont	
Peter Kerr	PQ.17	Virginia Dare	

Cont.

W. R. Grace	
Wacosta	PQ.18
Warren Delano	
Washington	PQ.17
West Cheswald	
West Gotomska	
West Nilus	
West Nohno	
White Clover (Panama)	
Will Rogers	
Willard Hall	
William Clark	OP FB
William D. Byron	
William H. Webb	
William H. Wilmer	
William Hooper	PQ.17
William L. Marcy	

William Matson	
William McKinley	
William Moultrie	
William Pepper	
William S. Thayer	RA.59
William Tyler Page	
William Wheelwright	
William Windom	
Wind Rush	
Winfred L. Smith	
Winston-Salem	
Woodbridge N. Ferris	
Yaka	
Yorkmar	
Zebulon B. Vance	

TOTAL 319

US Register	290
Panama Register	27
Honduras Register	2

Note: Ships shown in bold sank

Table 5. British Merchant Ships in Convoys

Adolph S. Ochs		Empire Fortune	
Aldersdale		Empire Galliard	
Atheltemplar		Empire Garrick	
Atlantic		Empire Gilbert	
Barrwhin		Empire Halley	
Beaconstreet		Empire Howard	
Black Ranger	RFA	Empire Kinsman	
Blairnevis		Empire Lawrence	
Blue Ranger	RFA	Empire Lionel	
Bolton Castle		Empire Magpie	
Botavon		Empire Mavis	
Briarwood		Empire Meteor	
British Corporal		Empire Morn	
British Governor		Empire Nigel	
British Merit		Empire Pickwick	
British Patience		Empire Ploughman	
British Pride		Empire Portia	
British Promise		Empire Prowess	
British Respect		Empire Purcell	
British Statesman		Empire Ranger	
British Valour		Empire Redshank	
British Workman		Empire Scott	
Cape Corso		Empire Selwyn	
Cape Race		Empire Sky	
Chulmleigh		Empire Snow	
Copeland	Rescue Ship	Empire Stalwart	
Daldorch		Empire Starlight	
Dan-Y-Bryn		Empire Stevenson	
Daphnella		Empire Tide	
Dartford		Empire Tourist	
Dolabella		Empire Tristram	
Dover Hill		Empress of Australia	Liner
Earlston		Esneh	
El Mirlo		Eulima	
Elona		Explorer	
Empire Archer		Fort Astoria	
Empire Baffin		Fort Bellingham	
Empire Bard		Fort Boise	
Empire Beaumont		Fort Brule	
Empire Buttress		Fort Columbia	
Empire Byron		Fort Crevecoeur	
Empire Carpenter		Fort Glenora	
Empire Celia		Fort Hall	
Empire Clarion		Fort Highfield	
Empire Cowper		Fort Island	
Empire Elgar		Fort Kullyspell	
Empire Emerald		Fort Massac	
Empire Flint		Fort McMurray	

Cont.

Fort Missanabie	Ocean Pride	
Fort Nakasley	Ocean Strength	
Fort Norfolk	Ocean Valour	
Fort Poplar	Ocean Vanity	
Fort Romaine	Ocean Verity	
Fort Slave	Ocean Viceroy	
Fort Thompson	Ocean Voice	
Fort Vercheres	Oligarch	RFA
Fort Yukon	Orient City	
Gemstone	Pontfield	
Goolistan	Queen City	
Gray Ranger RFA	Rathlin	Rescue Ship
Harmatris	River Afton	
Harmonic	Samannanw	
Harpalion	Samaritan	
Hartlebury	Samcalia	
Hopemount	Samconstant	
Induna	Samgara	
Junecrest	Samidway	
Jutland	Samloyal	
Kingswood	Samlyth	
Lacklan	Samsuva	
Lancaster Castle	Samtredy	
Lancastrian Prince	San Adolfo	RFA
Lapland	San Ambrosio	RFA
Laurelwood	San Cipriano	RFA
Llandaff	San Cirilo	RFA
Llanstephan Castle	San Venancio	RFA
Longwood	Scottish American	RFA
Lorca	Scythia	Liner
Lowther Castle	Southgate	
Lucerna	St Clears	
Luculus	Syrian Prince	Rescue Ship
Marylyn	Temple Arch	
Nacella	Thistledale	
Navarino	Trehata	
Neritina	Trekieve	
New Westminster City	Trevorian	
Ocean Faith	Wanstead	
Ocean Freedom	Waziristan	
Ocean Gypsy	Zaafaran	Rescue Ship
Ocean Messenger	Zamalek	Rescue Ship

Table 6.　Russian Merchant Ships in Convoys and Independent Sailings To and From North Russia

Ship	Losses	Ship	Losses
CONVOY SAILINGS TO/FROM RUSSIA		**OP FB West**	
Alma Ata			
Andre Marti		*Donbass*	
Archangelsk		*Dvina*	
Arcos		*Konsomoletz Arctiki*	
Ashkhabad		*Mironich*	
Azerbaidjan		*Yelnya*	
Belomorcanal			
Belorussia		**TOTAL 5**	
Budenni			
Chernyshevski		**RUSSIAN INDEPENDENT SAILINGS**	
Dekabrist	sunk		
Dneprostroi		*Aldan*	
Donbass	sunk	*Betloga*	
Elna 11		*Kara*	
Friedrich Engels		*Krasnoe Partizan*	sunk
Ijora	sunk	*Krasnoe Znamya*	
Kiev	sunk	*Leonid Krasin*	
Komiles		*Msta*	
Kotlin		*Nusbass*	
Kuzbass		*Ob*	
Kuznets Lesov	sunk	*Osmussaar*	
Mossovet		*Sanko*	
Revolutsioner		*Sheksna*	
Rodina	sunk	*Shilka*	
Sevzaples		*Ufa*	sunk
Shelon		*Uritski*	
Stalingrad	sunk	*Vanzetti*	
Stary Bolshevik			
Stepan Khalturin		**TOTAL 16**	
Sukhona	sunk		
Tiblisi		Independent	16
Tsiolkovsky	sunk	OP FB West	5
Okhata			
Petrovski		**TOTAL**	**21**
Volga			
TOTAL 35			

Note: No Russian ships sailed in convoys after RA.51

Table 7. Other Allied Merchant Ships in Convoys
To and From North Russia

Nationality	Name	Loss
Belgian	*Ville d'Anvers*	
Dutch	*Alchiba*	
	Pieter de Hoogh	
	Paulus Potter	Sunk PQ.17
	Aert van der Neer	
	Mijdrecht	
Honduran	*Mana*	
	Makawao	
Norwegian	*Egerø*	
	Herbrand	
	Idefjord	
	Ivaran	
	Kong Haakon VII	
	Kronprinsen	
	Marathon	
	Noreg	
	Norfjell	
	Norlys	
	Roald Amundsen	
	Skiensfjord	
	Mirlo	
Polish	*Tobruk*	

Table 8. American and Panamanian Merchant Ship Losses

Vessel	Nature of Loss	Convoy	Vessel	Nature of Loss	Convoy
Alamar	Sunk	PQ.16	*John Witherspoon*	Sunk	PQ.17
Alcoa Cadet	Mined in Murmansk		*Macbeth*	Sunk	PQ.18
Alcoa Ranger	Sunk	PQ.17	*Mary Luckenbach*	Sunk	PQ.18
Africander	Sunk	PQ.18	*Massmar*	Mined	QP.13
Andrew G. Curtin	Sunk	JW.56A	*Mormacsul*	Sunk	PQ.16
Ballot	Wrecked Murmansk		*Oliver Ellsworth*	Sunk	PQ.18
Bateau	Sunk	PQ.13	*Olopana*	Sunk	PQ.18
Bellingham	Sunk	QP.14	*Oregonian*	Sunk	PQ.17
Carlton	Sunk	PQ.17	*Pan Atlantic*	Sunk	PQ.17
Christopher Newport	Sunk	PQ.17	*Pan Kraft*	Sunk	PQ.18
City of Joliet	Sunk	PQ.16	*Penelope Barker*	Sunk	PQ.17
Daniel Morgan	Sunk	PQ.17	*Peter Kerr*	Sunk	PQ.17
Edward H. Crockett	Sunk	RA.60	*Puerto Rican*	Sunk	JW.56A
Effingham	Sunk	PQ.13	*Raceland*	Sunk	PQ.17
Executive	Sunk	RA.53	*Richard Bland*	Sunk	RA.53
El Occidente	Sunk	QP.10	*Silver Sword*	Sunk	PQ.13
Fairfield City	Sunk	PQ.17	*John Randolph*	Sunk	RA.53
Graylock	Sunk	RA.52	*John Witherspoon*	Sunk	QP.14
Heffron	Mined	QP.13	*Kentucky*	Wrecked	PQ.18
Henry Bacon	Sunk	RA.64	*Steel Worker*	Wrecked	QP.13
Honomu	Sunk	PQ.17	*Syros*	Sunk	PQ.17
Hoosier	Sunk	PQ.17	*Thomas Donaldson*	Sunk	PQ.18
Horace Bushnell	Sunk	JW.65	*Thomas Scott*	Mined in Murmansk	
Horace Gray	Sunk	BK/RA.64	*Wacosta*	Sunk	PQ.16
Hybert	Mined	QP.13	*Washington*	Sunk	JW.65
J. L. M. Curry	Foundered	RA.53	*William Clark*	Sunk	OP FB
John Penn	Sunk	PQ.18	*William Hooper*	Sunk	PQ.17
John Randolph	Wrecked	QP.13	*William S. Thayer*	Sunk	RA.59

Table 9. British Merchant Ship Losses

Vessel	Nature of Loss	Convoy
RFA *Aldersdale* (Aux)	Sunk	PQ.17
Atheltemplar	Sunk	PQ.18
Bolton Castle	Sunk	PQ.17
Botavon	Sunk	PQ.15
Cape Corso	Sunk	PQ.15
Chulmleigh	Sunk	OP FB
Earlston	Sunk	PQ.17
Empire Beaumont	Sunk	PQ.18
Empire Byron	Sunk	PQ.17
Empire Cowper	Sunk	QP.10
Empire Gilbert	Sunk	OP FB
Empire Howard	Sunk	PQ.14
Empire Lawrence	Sunk	PQ.16
Empire Purcell	Sunk	PQ.16
Empire Ranger	Sunk	PQ.13
Empire Sky	Sunk	OP FB
Empire Starlight	Bombed Murmansk. Later Salvaged	Ex PQ.13
Empire Stevenson	Sunk	PQ.18
Empire Tourist	Sunk	RA.57
Fort Bellingham	Sunk	JW.56A
Goolistan	Sunk	QP.15
RFA *Gray Ranger* (Aux)	Sunk	QP.14
Harpalion	Sunk	QP.10
Hartlebury	Sunk	PQ.17
Induna	Sunk	PQ.13
Jutland	Sunk	PQ.15
Lancaster Castle	Bombed & sunk Murmansk	Ex PQ.12
Lowther Castle	Sunk	PQ.16
Navarino	Sunk	PQ.17
New Westminster City	Bombed & sunk Murmansk	Ex PQ.13
Ocean Freedom	Bombed & sunk Murmansk	Ex JW.53
Ocean Voice	Sunk	QP.14
River Afton	Sunk	PQ.17
Samsuva	Sunk	RA.60
Waziristan	Sunk	PQ.7A
Zaafaran (Aux)	Sunk	PQ.17

Note: TOTAL 36, less 4 lost North Russia, less 3 Independents, less 3 Naval Auxiliaries = 26 nett losses

Table 10. Other Allied Merchant Ship Losses

RUSSIAN

Vessel	Nature of Loss	Convoy
Dekabrist	Sunk	OP FB
Donbass	Sunk	Independent
Ijora	Sunk	QP.8
Kiev	Sunk	QP.10
Krasny Partizan	Sunk	Independent
Kuznetz Lesov	Sunk	QP.15
Rodina	Mined	QP.13
Stalingrad	Sunk	PQ.18
Sukhona	Sunk	PQ.18
Tsiolkovsky	Sunk	QP.11
UFA	Sunk	Independent

DUTCH

Paulus Potter	Sunk	PQ.17

PQ/JW

	DATES	CONVOY	AMERICAN[1]	BRITISH	DUTCH	RUSSIAN	NORWEGIAN	TOTAL
PHASE ONE	August 1941 – February 1942	PQ.7A	–	1	–	–	–	1
PHASE TWO		PQ.13	3	2	–	–	–	5
		PQ.14	–	1	–	–	–	1
	March – September 1942	PQ.15	–	3	–	–	–	3
		PQ.16	4	3	–	–	–	7
		PQ.17	15	6[2]	1	–	–	22
		PQ.18	8	3	–	2	–	13
	Sub Total		30	18	1	2	–	51
PHASE THREE	December 1942 – March 1943	JW.51A to JW.53	1	–	–	–	–	1
PHASE FOUR	November 1943 – March 1944	JW.56A	2	1	–	–	–	3
PHASE FIVE	August 1944 – May 1945	JW.65	2		–	–	–	2
	TOTAL		35	20[3]	1	2		58

QP/RA

	DATES	CONVOY	AMERICAN[1]	BRITISH	DUTCH	RUSSIAN	NORWEGIAN	TOTAL
PHASE ONE	Aug 1941 – February 1942	QP.8	–	–	–	1	–	1
PHASE TWO		QP.10	1	2	–	1	–	4
		QP.11	–	–	–	1	–	1
	March – November 1942	QP.13	4[4]	–	–	1	–	5
		QP.14	2	1	–	–	–	3
		QP.15	–	1	–	1	–	2
PHASE THREE	December 1942 – April 1943	RA.52	1	–	–	–	–	1
		RA.53	4[5]	–	–	–	–	4
PHASE FOUR	November 1943 – April 1944	RA.57		1	–	–	–	1
		RA.59	1	–	–	–	–	1
PHASE FIVE	August 1944 – May 1945	RA.60	1	1	–	–	–	2
		RA.64	3	–	–	–	–	3
	TOTAL		17	6		5		28

Notes

1. Including Panamanian
2. PQ.17 excludes *Aldersdale* and *Zaafaran*. Contrary to statements in Battle Summary 22 *Aldersdale* undertook refuelling at sea operations between 1 and 4 July
3. Excludes Naval auxiliaries = RFA tankers and rescue ships
4. Plus *John Randolph* broke in two, only bow section salvaged. *Exterminator* not sunk, salvaged
5. One of these, *J. L. M. Curry* foundered

Table 12. Total Merchant Ship Losses by Convoy Cycle and Nationality

MERCHANT SHIP LOSSES BY CONVOY CYCLE

PQ/JW

	NUMBER OF CONVOYS	Sailed	Returned	NUMBER OF SHIPS Lost	Diverted	Arrived
PHASE ONE[1]	11	93	1	1		91
PHASE TWO (Part One)	2	17	1	–		16
PHASE TWO[2]	6	179	21	51		107
PHASE THREE[3]	4	73	8	1		64
PHASE FOUR[4]	8	197	7	3		187
PHASE FIVE[5]	9	247	–	2	4	241[6]
TOTALS	40	806	38	58	4	706

QP/RA

	NUMBER OF CONVOYS	Sailed	Returned	NUMBER OF SHIPS Lost	Diverted	Arrived
PHASE ONE	8	82	3	1	–	78
PHASE TWO	7	143	5	15		123
PHASE THREE	3	52		5		47
PHASE FOUR	7	197	4	2		191
PHASE FIVE	10	223		5		218
TOTALS	35	697	12	28		657

Notes
1. August 1941 to February 1942
2. March to November 1942
3. December 1942 to March 1943
4. November 1943 – May 1944
5. August 1944 – May 1945
6. Less 4 Norwegian relief ships sailed with convoy but detached to Kirkenes, Norway

LOSSES OF MERCHANT SHIPS BY NATIONALITY

NATIONALITY	Number of Ships	Exclusions	Number on Passage	Sunk	Foundered	Arrived	Lost in North Russia	OP FB	TOTAL LOST
American	290	1[7]	289	46	2	243	3	1	52[8]
Belgian	1		1	-		1			
British	160	2	158	26		132	4	3	33
Dutch	5		5	1		4			1
Honduran	2		2	-		2			
Norwegian	11	2[9]	9			9			
Panamanian	27		27	6		21			6
Polish	1		1	-		1			
Russian	58[10]	23	35	7		28		1	8
TOTAL	555	28	527	86	2	441	7	5	100
Naval Auxiliaries				3					3
TOTAL LOST				99	2		7	5	103

7. *Joseph E. Johnston* returned ex JW.53. Did not sail again
8. *John Randolph* and *J. L. M. Curry*
9. Norwegian relief ships left convoys for Kirkenes, Norway
10. 23 of these sailed independently and did not participate in convoys

Table 13. Cause of Merchant Ship Losses by Convoy

PQ/JW CONVOYS

CONVOY	A/C TORPEDO	A/C BOMB	SURFACE SHIP	U-BOAT	JOINT KILL	OTHER	TOTAL
PQ.7A				1			1
PQ.13		2	1	2			5
PQ.14				1			1
PQ.15	3						3
PQ.16		6		1			7
PQ.17	1	5		5	11		22
PQ.18	10			3			13
JW.51B						1	1
JW.56A				3			3
JW.65				2			2
TOTALS	14	13	1	18	11	1	58

Cont.

QP/RA CONVOYS

CONVOY	A/C TORPEDO	A/C BOMB	SURFACE SHIP	U-BOAT	JOINT KILL	OTHER	TOTAL
QP.8			1				1
QP.10		2		2			4
QP.11			1				1
QP.13					5		5
QP.14				3			3
QP.15				2			2
RA.52				1			1
RA.53				3		1	4
RA.57				1			1
RA.59				1			1
RA.60				2			2
RA.64	1			1			2
BK-3				1			1
TOTAL	1	2	2	17	5	1	28

Table 14. Merchant Ships Lost in North Russia or
Not Included in Return Convoys

MERCHANT SHIPS LOST IN NORTH RUSSIAN PORTS

SHIP	NATIONALITY	LOCATION	DATE OF LOSS	NATURE OF LOSS	EX CONVOY
Ballot	Panamanian	Murmansk	3 January 1942	Wrecked	PQ.15
Empire Starlight	British	Murmansk	3 April 1942	Bombed and sunk	PQ.13
New Westminster City	British	Murmansk	3 April 1942	Bombed and sunk	PQ.13
Lancaster Castle	British	Murmansk	14 April 1942	Bombed and sunk	PQ.12
Steel Worker	American	Murmansk	3 June 1942	Mined and sunk	PQ.16
Alcoa Cadet	American	Murmansk	21 June 1942	Mined and sunk	PQ.15
Ocean Freedom	British	Murmansk	13 March 1943	Bombed and sunk	JW.53

SHIPS RETURNED AFTER CESSATION OF CONVOY CYCLE

JULY 1945

DATE	VESSEL	PORT OF DEPARTURE
02/07/45	*John Collier*	Murmansk
02/07/45	*British Promise*	Archangel
	Empire Emerald	Archangel
04/07/45	*Fort Highfield*	Archangel
	Cardinal Gibbons	Murmansk
	Charles Weems	Murmansk
	Samuel McIntyre	Murmansk
05/07/45	*Edward N. Hurley*	Murmansk
06/07/45	*Caesar Rodney*	Murmansk
	Henry Wynkoop	Murmansk
	Julian Poydras	Murmansk
07/07/45	*John Ireland*	Murmansk
	Adolph S. Ochs	Archangel
	Barbara Frietchie	Archangel
	Bernard N. Baker	Archangel
08/07/45	*George H. Pendleton*	Archangel
	Joshua W. Alexander	Archangel
	Philip F. Thomas	Archangel
09/07/45	*Alanson B. Houghton*	Archangel
01/08/45	*Empire Buttress* ex JW.59	
N/K	*Lapland* ex JW.61	

NORWEGIAN SHIPS WHICH DID NOT RETURN
FROM NORTH RUSSIA/NORWAY

Idefjord	ex JW.65
Ivaran	ex JW.67
Kong Haakon	ex JW.66
Norfjell	ex JW.63 – Damaged BK-3
Roald Amundsen	ex JW.67

MERCHANT SHIPS RETAINED IN RUSSIA

John Landon	ex JW.57 renamed *Tiblisi*
Charles Gordon Curtis	ex JW.58 renamed *Sergei Kirov*. Transferred
Empire Carpenter	ex JW.57 renamed *Dickson*. Transferred 26/4/44
Empire Nigel	ex JW.57 renamed *Archangelsk*. Loaned 1944, returned 1946

Table 15. Royal Navy, Naval Auxiliary & Allied Naval Losses

ROYAL NAVY

SHIP TYPE	NAME	DATE OF LOSS	NATURE OF LOSS	CONVOY
Carrier	*Nabob*	22.08.44	Badly damaged by torpedo. Salvaged	JW.65 Cover Force
Cruiser	*Trinidad*	29.03.42	Badly damaged by torpedo. Salvaged	
Cruiser	*Trinidad*	15.05.42	Badly damaged by dive bombing. Torpedoed and scuttled by destroyer *Matchless*	PQ.13
Cruiser	*Edinburgh*	30.04.42 02.05.42	Torpedoed by U-boat. Abandoned. Scuttled by destroyer *Foresight*	QP.11
Cruiser	*Norfolk*	26.12.43	Damaged by shellfire	JW.55B
Destroyer	*Achates*	31.12.42	Shelled and sunk	JW.51B
Destroyer	*Hardy*	31.01.44	Torpedoed by U-boat. Badly damaged. Scuttled	JW.56B
Destroyer	*Mahratta*	25.02.44	Torpedoed by U-boat and sunk	JW.57
Destroyer	*Matabele*	17.01.42	Torpedoed by U-boat and sunk	PQ.8
Destroyer	*Punjabi*	01.05.42	Rammed and sunk in collision by battleship *King George V*	PQ.15
Destroyer	*Somali*	20.09.42 24.09.02	Torpedoed by U-boat. Broke in two under tow and sank	QP.14
Destroyer	*Cassandra*	11.12.44	Torpedoed by *U-365*. Damaged	RA.62
Destroyer	*Onslow*	31.12.42	Shelled and damaged	JW.51B
Destroyer	*Oribi*		Crew members washed overboard	
Frigate	*Goodall*	29.4.45	Trpedoed by U-boat off Kola Inlet. Badly damaged. Scuttled	RA.66
Frigate	*Bickerton*	22.8.44	Torpedoed. Disabled. Sunk by destroyer *Vigilant*	JW.65 Cover Force

Cont.

SHIP TYPE	NAME	DATE OF LOSS	NATURE OF LOSS	CONVOY
Frigate	*Mounsey*	31.10.44	Torpedoed by U-295. Damaged. Towed to Kola Inlet	RA.61
Corvette	*Denbigh Castle*	13.02.45	Mined or torpedoed. Grounded. Total loss.	JW.64
Corvette	*Bluebell*	17.02.45	Torpedoed by U-boat. Sunk	RA.64
Sloop	*Kite*	21.08.44	Torpedoed by U-boat. Sunk	JW.59
Sloop	*Lapwing*	20.03.44	Torpedoed by U-boat. Sunk	JW.65
Sloop	*Lark*	17.02.45	Torpedoed by U-boat. Badly damaged. Towed to Kola Inlet	RA.64
Minesweeper	*Bramble*	31.12.42	Shelled German destroyers and sunk	JW.51B
Minesweeper	*Gossamer*	24.06.42	Bombed and sunk by a direct bomb hit during air attack while at anchor in the Kola Inlet. 3 officers killed, 20 ratings missing, 1 rating died of wounds following day	
Minesweeper	*Leda*	20.09.42	Torpedoed by U-boat. Sunk	QP.14
Minesweeper	*Niger*	05.07.42	Strayed into minefield off Iceland. Mined and sunk	QP.13
Armed Whaler	*Shera*	09.03.42	Foundered	PQ.12
Armed Whaler	*Sulla*	25.03.42	Lost	PQ.13
NAVAL AUXILIARIES				
RFA Tanker	*Aldersdale*	07.07.42	05.07.42. Bombed by aircraft 07.07.42. Shelled and torpedoed by U-boat. Sunk	PQ.17
Rescue Ship	*Zaafaran*	05.07.42	Bombed by aircraft and sunk	PQ.17
RFA Tanker	*Gray Ranger*	22.09.42	Torpedoed by U-boat and sunk.	QP.14

Cont.

OTHER ALLIED NAVAL LOSSES

SHIP TYPE	NAME OF VESSEL	DATE OF LOSS	NATURE OF LOSS	REMARKS
Submarine	*Jastrzab* (Ex P-551 Polish)	02.05.42	Accidentally sunk by *Seagull* and *St Albans*. Scuttled under gunfire by *Seagull*	PQ.15
Destroyer	*Sokrushitelny* Russian	22.11.42	Foundered: sank in storm	QP.15
Corvette	*Tunsberg Castle* Norwegian (Ex *Shrewsbury Castle*)	12.12.44	Mined. Sunk	RA.62

Table 16. German Naval Losses

SURFACE SHIPS

SHIP TYPE	NAME	DATE OF LOSS	NATURE OF LOSS	REMARKS
Battle Cruiser	*Scharnhorst*	31.12.43	Sunk in Action	JW.55B
Destroyer	*Z-7 Hermann Schoemann*	02.05.42	Damaged in action and scuttled	QP.11
Destroyer	*Z-16 Friedrich Eckholdt*	31.12.42	Shelled and sunk by HMS *Sheffield*	JW.51B
Destroyer	*Z-26*	29.03.42	Shelled and sunk in action by HMS *Trinidad* and HMS *Eclipse*	PQ.13

SUBMARINES

U-BOAT	DATE	NATURE OF LOSS	CONVOY	SUNK BY
U-88	14.09.42.	Depth Charge	PQ.18	*Onslow*
U-253	28.09.42	Depth Charge	QP.14	Catalina A/C
U-277	01.05.44	Depth Charge	RA.59	Swordfish
U-286	29.04.45	Gunfire	RA 66	*Loch Insh, Anguilla, Cotton*
U-288	03.04.44	Depth Charge	JW.58	A/C from *Tracker* and *Active*
U-307	29.04.45	Gunfire	RA.66	*Loch Insh*
U-314	30.01.44	Depth Charge	JW.56B	*Whitehall* and *Meteor*
U-344	23.08.44	Depth Charge	JW 59	*Keppel, Peacock, Mermaid, Loch Dunvegan*
U-347	17.07.44	Depth Charge		*Catalina a/c*
U-354	22.08.44	Depth Charge	JW.59	Swordfish
U-355	01.04.44	Depth Charge	JW.58	*Beagle* and *Avenger* a/c
U-360	02.04.44	Hedgehog	JW.58	*Keppel*
U-361	17.07.44	Depth Charge		*Liberator* A/C
U-365	13.12.44	Depth Charge	RA.62	Swordfish
U-366	05.03.44	Rocket & Gunfire	RA.57	Swordfish
U-387	09.12.44	Depth Charge	RA.62	*Bamborough Castle*
U-394	02.09.44	Depth Charge & Rocket	RA.59A	Swordfish, *Keppel, Mermaid, Peacock*
U-425	17.02.45	Squid A/S Projectile	*Lark, Alnwick Castle*	

Cont.

U-BOAT	DATE	NATURE OF LOSS	CONVOY	SUNK BY
U-457	16.09.42	Depth Charge	PQ.18	*Impulsive*
U-472	04.03.44	Rocket & gunfire	RA.57	Swordfish and *Onslaught*
U-585	29.03.42	Depth Charge	Conflicting accounts as to whether sunk by HMS *Fury* (PQ.13) or a floating mine.[1] The latter is now regarded as correct	
U-589	12.09.42	Depth Charge	PQ.18	*Faulknor*
U-601	25.02.44	Depth Charge	JW.57	Catalina
U-644	07.04.43.	Torpedoed		HM S/M *Tuna*
U-655	24.03.42	Rammed	QP.9	*Sharpshooter*
U-674	02.05.44	Depth Charge	RA.59	Swordfish
U-713	24.02.44	Depth Charge	JW.57	*Keppel*
U-742	18.07.44	Depth Charge		Catalina
U-921	30.09.44	Depth Charge		Swordfish
U-959	02.05.44.	Depth Charge	RA.59	Swordfish
U-961	29.03.44	Depth Charge	JW.58	*Starling*
U-973	06.03.44	Rocket & Gunfire	RA.57	Swordfish

TOTAL NUMBER CONFIRMED LOST: 31 (Excludes *U-585*)

Note
1. Naval-History.net and Admiralty War Diary entries for HMS *Fury* record unsuccessful attack made on *U-378* on the 29th and recorded as a sinking. (Note: Post war analysis showed *U-378* escaped and *U-585* was mined on the 30th)

Table 17. Operation FB Independent Sailings

ICELAND TO NORTH RUSSIA

EASTBOUND FROM ICELAND	SAILED	ARRIVED, SUNK, OR RETURNED
Richard H. Alvey US	29 October	Arrived 7 November
Empire Galliard Br	29 October	Arrived 7 November
John Walker US	30 October	Arrived 8 November
Empire Gilbert Br	30 October	Sunk by U-boat 2 November
John H. B. Latrobe US	31 October	Returned to Reykjavik 13 November
Chulmleigh Br	31 October	Wrecked near South Cape, Spitzbergen 6 November
Hugh Williamson US	1 November	Arrived 11 November
Empire Sky Br	1 November	Sunk by U-boat 5 November
Empire Scott Br	2 November	Arrived 18 November
William Clark US	2 November	Sunk by U-boat 4 November
Daldorch Br	3 November	Recalled to Reykjavik 6 November
Briarwood Br	4 November	Recalled to Reykjavik 6 November
Additional sailing of Soviet Union Ship		
Dekabrist	30 October	Torpedoed and sunk by Ju-88 4 November

Table 18. Russian Independent Sailings

NORTH RUSSIA TO ICELAND

Following Operation FB the Russians carried out a further separate series of independent sailings using their own ships. These overlapped with the resumption of the next convoy cycle in December.

PHASE 1: WESTBOUND FROM BYCLUSKYA BAY[1]

SHIP	SAILED	ARRIVED AKUREYRI OR SUNK
Mossovet	29 October	7 November
Azerbaidjan	31 October	9 November
Chernyshevski	2 November	11 November
Donbass	4 November	Sunk 5 November by German destroyer Z-27

PHASE 2: WESTBOUND FROM ARCHANGEL

SHIP	SAILED	ARRIVED AKUREYRI
Konsomoletz	14 November	24 November
Dvina	24 November	5 December
Mironich	25 November	5 December
Yelnya	25 November	5 December
Shilka	12 December	25 December
Okhta	13 December	26 December
Vetluga	14 December	26 December
Kuzbass?	14 December	26 December
Ob	15 December	26 December

WESTBOUND FROM IOKANKA[2]

SHIP	SAILED	ARRIVED AKUREYRI
Msta	22 December	6 January
Aldan	23 December	6 January
Uritski	23 December	6 January
Soroka	24 December	6 January
Kara	24 December	6 January
Vanzetti	29 December	18 January

WESTBOUND FROM KOLA INLET

SHIP	SAILED	ARRIVED AKUREYRI
Krasnoe Znamya	30 December	9 January
Osmussaar	30 December	9 January
Sheksna	31 December	12 January
Leonid Krasin	20 January	31 January
Ufa	23 January	Sunk 29 January by U-255
Krasny Partizan	24 January	Sunk 26 January by U-255

Notes
1. Bycluskya Bay, Novaya Zemlya – Admiralty Records (also referred to as Beyslushaya Bay), and Byelushya Bay, Novaya Zemlya – German records, and Belushya Guba – or Beluga Whale Bay – Russian.
2. Also known as Iokanga, located on the northeastern shore of Kola Peninsula.

Notes

Chapter 1
1. For a report on the outcome of the Moscow Conference see W.P. (41) 238. October 8, 1941 [CAB/66/19/11].
2. Hansard: HC Deb 17 December 1946, Vol. 431 CC 1777–81.

Chapter 2
1. Hague says the convoy departed from Liverpool on 13 October – in fact only one ship the *Kheti* sailed. Other ships sailed from Liverpool and the Clyde on other dates.
2. Note: *Forgotten Sacrifice* (2016) by American author Michael G. Walling claims the convoy was attacked and dive-bombed on 22 November by Stukas [probably meant Ju.88s] when in the vicinity of Jan Mayen Island. This is one of many inaccuracies in the book as the convoy had arrived in Murmansk on 22 November. Unfortunately, the claim has been re-referenced in other sources.
3. Some sources claim PQ.4 was attacked unsuccessfully by a small group of Ju.88 bombers south of Jan Mayen Island and that single planes continued to attack the convoy until it reached the White Sea, but no ships were hit and no damage done. There is however no authoritative evidence to support the claim.
4. *The Road to Russia: Arctic Convoys 1942*, Edwards.

Chapter 4
1. *Eldena*'s group eventually comprised *Empire Cowper, New Westminster City, Scottish American* (Acting Commodore), *Eldena, El Estero, Mormacmar, Tobruk, Gallant Fox*, Harpalion. Entered late on 30th with local escort *Oribi, Paynter*, and *Sumba*.
2. The Convoy Report was submitted by the Vice Commodore, as the Convoy Commodore, Captain D. C. Rees RNR, was lost in the sinking of the *Empire Howard*.
3. This condition is now known as 'post-immersion collapse', when hypothermia causes arterial blood pressure to drop, and the experience of the *Empire Howard* casualties informed several subsequent studies of survival at sea.
4. Task Group 39, later renamed Task Group 99, provided cover for PQ.15, PQ.16, QP.12, PQ.17, and QP.13.
5. Official Admiralty reports make reference to only two air attacks on PQ.15, whereas the Convoy Commodore's report and those of the COs of a number of warships and Masters of merchant ships include details of three.
6. German records state: 'On 2 May nine torpedo-bombers on their first mission in the Arctic attacked PQ.15 and reported three sinkings.'
7. Bravo Time. The Bravo Time Zone is often used in aviation and the military as another name for Coordinated Universal Time +2. Bravo Time Zone is also commonly used at sea between longitudes 22.5° East and 37.5° East.

8. Based on official CWGC and RN records; some sources claim between 19 and 25 killed.

9. Michael Walling in *Forgotten Sacrifice* gives the timing of this as 19.50.

10. 4476. Honours and Awards—Polish Navy (H. & A. 515/42.—17.9.1942.) 'The King has been graciously pleased to approve the Honorary Appointment as Companion of the Distinguished Service Order of Commander Henryk Eibel, Polish Navy, for his gallant services in command of O.R.P. 'Garland' in the escort of convoys to Russia.'

11. When ignited in a confined space Cordite produces sufficient hot gases under pressure to propel a shell from a gun barrel. It is classified as highly flammable but not a high explosive.

12. Two extra tankers were included, as the destroyers of the FDE would be making the double passage without entering harbour and would need to refuel at sea.

13. Report of Senior Officer MS.6.

14. US Department of Transportation – Maritime Administration.

15. http://www.halcyon-class.co.uk/sharpshooter/sharpshooter_1942.htm. Accessed 2 January 2022.

16. SBNO Report September 1942.

17. Force Q sailed with PQ.18, remained with the convoy until 17 September, then transferred to QP.14 with RA (D). *Grey Ranger* was torpedoed and sunk on 22 September. *Black Ranger* arrived back at Scapa on 26 September after being detached from the convoy the same day.

Chapter 5

1. 19.57/A

2. https://www.thegazette.co.uk/London/issue/36237/supplement/4900/data.pdf

3. The five vessels referred to here are British ships only, not including the recalled *Daldorch* and *Briarwood*.

Chapter 6

1. The Convoy codes had been changed from PQ to JW, and QP to RA for security reasons, but the German Navy continued to use the old titles never realizing they had been replaced.

2. Five British, nine American and one Panamanian which carried 2,046 vehicles, 202 tanks, 87 crated fighter planes, 33 crated bombers, 11,600 tons of fuel oil, 12,650 tons of aviation spirit, and 54,000 tons of other equipment and supplies.

3. Official records state 10 merchant ships arrived at Murmansk and 5 at Archangel. Eleven reached the Kola Inlet but one was wrecked, for a total of 10. Only 3 arrived at Archangel. Of the original 15 ships in the convoy, 13 arrived safely, one turned back (arrived in the Clyde on 6 January) and one was wrecked.

4. After her repair in the UK *Dasher* was conducting flying exercises in the Clyde when she blew up and sank, on 27 March 1943.

5. The Master kept Confidential Books (CBs) and security classified papers such as convoy codes in his safe while his vessel was in port. At sea, such material was to be kept in a weighted canvas bag so that in an emergency it could be thrown over the side to prevent the contents falling into the hands of the enemy.

Chapter 7

1. The figures for the numbers of merchant ships which arrived in Archangel and Murmansk respectively are confused. Different sources quote varying numbers with inconsistencies even within a single source. What can be said is that all 13 merchant ships, the fleet oiler and rescue ship, arrived safely.
2. The Federapparat or Flächenabsuchender Torpedo (FAT) had a spring device that meant its course varied – it ran up and down on parallel lines of 800 or 1,600 metres' length.
3. A device that launched up to 24 small high-explosive bombs to a distance of 250 yards (228 metres) and which exploded on contact as they sank through the water.

Chapter 8

1. Schofield gives 28 August.
2. Naval History Net says 29 ships, Kemp says 30. Hague says sailed from Loch Ewe, Admiralty War Diaries, Destroyer Home Command gives Liverpool.
3. Operated from 21 Nov 1944 to 8 Jan 1945: *U-286, U-293, U-295, U-299, U-310, U-315, U-318, U-363, U-365, U-387, U-636, U-668, U-956, U-965, U-992, U-995, U-997, U-1163*.
4. II./KG 26 transferred from Trondheim to Bardufoss on 15 January 1945 to take up the duties of I./KG 26, which was being disbanded. All 30 Ju.88s belonging to I./KG 26 Gruppe were incorporated into II./KG 26 now assigned to standby for torpedo attacks on convoys in the Norwegian Sea and Arctic.
5. *Haida* sailed from Clyde on 11 April with seven sub chasers. Arrived Faroes 16 April, sailed 19 April. *Iroquois* sailed from Rosyth 12 April with remaining sub chasers. Arrived Faroes 14 April, left 19 April.

Chapter 9

1. https://www.thegazette.co.uk/London/issue/39041/supplement/5139/data.pdf
2. Excludes two icebreakers on delivery from Canada which sailed with a convoy.
3. From the *London Gazette*: 'The total casualties in Merchant ships on the Russian route were 829 officers and men. The Royal Navy, too, paid a heavy price, for two cruisers, six destroyers, three sloops, two frigates, three corvettes and three minesweepers were sunk with the loss of 1,840 officers and men.' Peter Kemp also quotes these figures as accurate in *Convoy*!

Bibliography

Blair, Clay *Hitler's U-boat War: The Hunted, 1942–45* Orion, 1999

British Admiralty *The Fuehrer Conferences on Naval Affairs* Greenhill Books, 1990

Browning Jr, Robert M. *United States Merchant Marine Casualties of World War II* McFarland, 2011

Burn, Alan *The Fighting Commodores: The Convoy Commanders in the Second World War* Naval Institute Press, 1999

Carruthers, Bob *Hitler's Wartime Orders: The Complete Führer Directives, 1939–1945* Pen & Sword, 2018

Churchill, Winston *The Second World War.* Vols I to IV. Houghton Mifflin, 1948–50

Cressman, Robert J. *The Official Chronology of the U.S. Navy in World War II* Naval Institute Press, 2000

Dönitz, Admiral Karl *The Conduct of the War at Sea, An Essay* [1946] Lucknow Books, 2014

Edwards, Bernard *The Road to Russia: Arctic Convoys 1942* Pen & Sword, 2002

Hague, Arnold *The Allied Convoy System, 1939–1945. Its Organization, Defence and Operation* The Naval Institute, 2000

Hague, Arnold and Bob Ruegg *Convoys to Russia; Allied Convoys and Naval Surface Operations in Arctic Waters 1941–1945* World Ship Society, 1993

Hughes, Robert *Flagship to Murmansk* Futura, 1975

Hutson, Harry C. *Arctic Interlude: Independent to North Russia* CSIPP, 2012

Irving, David *The Destruction of Convoy PQ 17* Corgi Books, 1970

Kemp, Paul *Convoy! Drama in Arctic Waters* Weidenfeld, 1983

Kimball, Warren F. *Churchill and Roosevelt. The Complete Correspondence* Vols I–III. Princeton University Press, 1984

Kuznetsov (Admiral) *Memoirs of Wartime Minister of the Navy* Progress, 1990

Llewellyn-Jones, M. (Ed.) *The Royal Navy and the Arctic Convoys: A Naval Staff History* Routledge 2006

Richards, R. and Saunders, H. *Royal Air Force 1939–1945. Volume II: The Fight Avails* (Chapter 5). History of the Second World War, HMSO 1954

Roskill, S. W. *The War At Sea, 1939–45*: I The Defensive. II. The Period of Balance. III. The Offensive Part 1, 1st June 1943 – 31 May 1944 (1960) III. The Offensive Part 2 . 1 June 1944 – 15 May 1945 (1961), History of the Second World War, HMSO 1954

Ryan, J. F. The Royal Navy and Soviet Seapower, 1930–1950: Intelligence, Naval Cooperation and Antagonism, Ph.D Thesis, 1996

Schofield, B. B. *The Arctic Convoys*, TBS (|The Book Service Ltd) 1977

Smith, Peter C. *Arctic Victory: The Story of PQ 18* Crecy Publishing 1994

Sokol, A. E. 'German Attacks on the Murmansk Run' *US Naval Institute Proceedings*, Vol 71/28/258, December 1952

Syrett, David 'The Last Murmansk Convoys, 11 March– 30 May 1945' at https://www.cnrs-scrn.org/northern_mariner/vol04/nm_4_1_55-63.pdf

Walling, Michael G. *Forgotten Sacrifice: The Arctic Convoys of World War II* Osprey Publishing 2012

Ziemke, Earl F. *The German Northern Theatre of Operations 1940–1945*, Army pamphlet 20-271, 1959

Other sources and websites:

Captain U-boats Norway, War Diary, 18 January 1943–14 October 1944. https://archive.org/stream/wardiaryofcaptai00germ/wardiaryofcaptai00germ_djvu.txt

Correspondence between the Chairman of the Council of Ministers of the USSR and the Presidents of the USA and the Prime Ministers of Great Britain during the Great Patriotic War of 1941–1945. Available at https://www.marxists.org/reference/archive/stalin/works/correspondence/01/index.htm

C.B. 4501 History Of U-Boat Policy 1939-1945 available at http://www.uboatarchive.net/British%20Reports/U-boatPolicy.htm

Führer Directives 1939–1945 online at https://der-fuehrer.org/reden/english/wardirectives/01.html

Halcyon Minesweepers in Russia. www.Halcyon-Class.co.uk

Hansard records: hansard.parliament.uk

Historical RFA: historicalrfa.org

History of the US Naval Armed Guard Afloat at https://www.ibiblio.org/hyperwar/USN/Admin-Hist/173-ArmedGuards/index.html

London Gazette 13 October 1950 Convoys to North Russia. At https://www.thegazette.co.uk/London/issue/39041/supplement/5139/data.pdf Accessed January 2022

Naval Armed Guard Service in World War Two: Russian Convoys. USN Naval History and Heritage Command at https://www.history.navy.mil/research/library/online-reading-room/title-list-alphabetically/n/naval-armed-guard-service-in-world-war-ii/russian-convoys.html

Royal Navy *Battle Summary No. 22*

The United States Merchant Marine at War – Report of the War Shipping Administrator to the President. Washington, January 15, 1946. usmm.org

US Naval Administration in WW2 – History of Convoy and Routing at https://www.ibiblio.org/hyperwar/USN/Admin-Hist/011-Convoy/index.html

US Office of the Historian Milestones: 1937–1945 U.S.-Soviet Alliance, 1941–1945 at https://history.state.gov/milestones/1937-1945/us-soviet

US Ships Sunk or Damaged in Murmansk Run, Normandy, Northeast Atlantic, Northern European ports at http://www.usmm.org/europe.html

War Diaries of German Naval Staff (Operations Division) available at https://usnwcarchives.org/repositories/2/archival_objects/34404

www.convoyweb.org.uk

www.naval-history.net

www.u-boat.net

www.uboatarchive.net

www.warsailors.com

www.worldnavalships.com

Index